UNDERSTANDING UNCONSTITUTIONALITY

How a Country Lost its Way

An Essay in Three Parts

Part 1 – Some Misconceptions About Constitutional Invalidation

Part 2 – Fidelity to the Law: The Good, the Bad, and the Ugly

Part 3 –Trying to Right the Ship

Arthur Peltomaa

Teja Press

ISBN: 978-1-9994640-0-4

LIBRARY AND ARCHIVES CANADA CATLOGUING IN
PUBLICATION

Teja Press

AN OVERVIEW

Courts are often said to "strike down" laws that conflict with the Constitution. An image is evoked of black-robed judges hurling bolts of lightning in Zeus-like manner, thereby destroying the legal efficacy of unconstitutional laws and expunging them from the statute books. This conception of the invalidation process is, however, erroneous and misleading. A law does not become unconstitutional because a court makes a declaration to that effect. An unconstitutional law is invalid and of no legal force or effect from the moment of its enactment. The court's declaration does nothing more than recognize what has always been the law's legal status. It follows that a court cannot, by refraining from striking down a law or by purporting to delay the effective date of its strike-down order, allow an unconstitutional enactment to operate as valid law even temporarily.

This is not how things work in Canada, however. As strange as it may seem, Canadian courts routinely make orders which allow governments to act unlawfully following findings of unconstitutionality. Labelled euphemistically as suspended or delayed declarations of invalidity, they purport to give temporary force and effect to laws which violate the Constitution. Ironically, the rule of law is often invoked to help justify the making of such orders. The courts act pragmatically under guise of a self-invented power to deem the law to be different than it actually is. This has resulted, among other things, in the prosecution and conviction of persons under unconstitutional laws, orders allowing governments to exact illegal taxes, unlawful participation of police officers at bail hearings, and denials of a constitutional right to medically-assisted death.

The judges offer no legally coherent explanation or justification for their claims to these extraordinary powers. Invariably, they point to the Supreme Court's much-celebrated – though widely misunderstand – decision in *Manitoba Language Rights*, a 1985 case in which it was decided that substantially all of Manitoba's statutes which had been invalidly enacted in English only since 1890 should be deemed temporarily valid and enforceable pending translation and re-enactment in French. This was to prevent a legal void in the province. Having identified a state of emergency, the Court, in the spirit of German political theorist Carl Schmitt, effectively declared itself sovereign to deal with it. This it did by deeming the unlawful to be lawful. By arrogating to itself the authority to manage the apprehended crisis, the Court pre-empted the executive and legislative branches from exercising their recognized powers and prerogatives over public emergencies. The jurisprudential legacy of the *Manitoba Language Rights* decision has been an erosion of Canadian judicial fidelity to the rule of law. It is as though the Canadian judicial fleet has become unanchored from core principles of the law and allowed to drift off in search of a more discretion-based and pragmatic approach to constitutional decision-making.

Judges in other common law jurisdictions have generally refused to follow the lead of Canadian courts in asserting a power to turn unlawful water into lawful wine. They have remained faithful to the rule of law. Canadian courts, on the other hand, seem to have found refuge in a Lewis Carroll-like place of constitutional enchantment: where language can be added to or subtracted from legislative text; where words in the Constitution do not necessarily mean what they say; where life can mysteriously be breathed into constitutionally comatose enactments; and where laws can be regarded, like Schrodinger's cat, as both valid and invalid at the same time. This has resulted, among other things, in

Canadian judges believing that they have the power to reconstruct or repair constitutionally-flawed enactments in order to bring them into line with the Constitution. As will be shown, that is exclusively the job of the legislative branch. Contrary to popular belief, there is no such thing as a remedy of constitutional invalidation, and courts have no power to add to, subtract from, vary, or amend constitutionally infirm statutes.

Another consequence of Canadian judges believing that they have the power to deem the law temporarily to be what it is not, is that they have decided that they must also have discretion as to the very existence of constitutional rights. More than a century ago Lord Shaw famously warned that: "To remit the maintenance of constitutional right to the region of judicial discretion is to shift the foundations of freedom from the rock to the sand." The road to authoritarianism begins when the rock of the law is allowed to be eroded by the sand of discretion. Rights are rights are rights. Conceding to courts any discretion as to the existence of constitutional rights is to allow the rule of law to be supplanted by the rule of judges. Former Canadian Chief Justice Antonio Lamer described the preamble to Canada's Constitution in eloquent and inspired prose in a 1997 decision: "[It] serves as the grand entrance hall to the castle of the Constitution." A castle built on foundations of sand, however, will eventually crumble to the ground.

A principle-based order and structure needs to be established in this embarrassingly muddled area of the law. The pragmatic utility of suspended declarations and similar devices does not permit courts to ignore the dictates of the Constitution. Pragmatism – like public policy – if not confined to the parameters of the law, can become a very unruly horse. As it was explained by an English judge almost two hundred years ago: "[O]nce you get astride it you never know where it will carry you.

A great deal of work lies ahead. Canada's legal academy needs especially to step up to the plate. The principles of constitutional supremacy and the rule of law are too important to leave solely in the hands of judges.

TABLE OF CASES

CANADA

UNITED STATES

(xxi)

HONG KONG

SOUTH AFRICA

CYPRUS

PAKISTAN

TABLE OF CONTENTS

PART 1 – SOME MISCONCEPTIONS ABOUT CONSTITUTIONAL INVALIDATION

PART 2 –FIDELITY TO THE LAW: THE GOOD, THE BAD, AND THE UGLY

PART 3 – TRYING TO RIGHT THE SHIP

(xxv)

PART 1 – SOME MISCONCEPTIONS ABOUT CONSTITUTIONAL INVALIDATION

SUMMARY

A common misconception is that unconstitutional legislation is struck down or invalidated by judicial order. This misconception has nourished the erroneous belief that courts can suspend or delay the effects of findings of invalidity. More than that, it has led to a belief that courts can breathe life into constitutionally comatose laws. Ironically, the rule of law is often invoked to justify such orders. In fact, courts have no such powers and their purported exercise of them is unlawful. Moreover, the orthodox Canadian legal view that s. 52(1) of the *Constitution Act, 1982,* empowers courts to make orders which effectively reconstruct or repair constitutionally infirm statutes is wrong. In fact, s. 52(1) is an interpretation provision which confers no remedial powers on courts.

1. Introduction

Courts in Canada routinely make orders which purport to allow unlawful conduct by governmental actors on a temporary basis following determinations of unconstitutionality. They do so pragmatically under guise of a self-invented power to deem the law to be different than it actually is.

Judges in other common law jurisdictions have sometimes flirted with the Canadian approach, but for the most part they have rejected it.

Canadian courts offer no legally coherent foundation for their exercise of these extraordinary powers. It is as though the Canadian judicial fleet has become unanchored from core principles of the law and allowed to drift off in search of a more discretion-based and pragmatic approach to constitutional adjudication. As a result, the current state of Canadian law relating to the consequences and effects of findings of unconstitutionality is a veritable quagmire of incoherence, ambiguity, and contradiction.

This essay argues that it is illegal for courts to purport to confer temporary validity on invalid laws unless there is express constitutional authorization for such orders. Provision for such orders is found in certain countries, but notably not in Canada, nor in most other common law jurisdictions.

It is further argued, again contrary to Supreme Court of Canada authority, that courts have no power to add to, subtract from, vary, or amend constitutionally infirm statutes. There is no such thing as a remedy of statutory invalidation. The judicial branch cannot reconstruct or repair a constitutionally-flawed enactment in order to bring it into compliance with the Constitution. That is exclusively the job of the legislative branch.

2. Constitutional Invalidation – Metaphors, Euphemisms, and Reality

When courts are asked to rule upon challenges to the constitutional validity of laws, they must determine whether the impugned law is inconsistent with the Constitution, and, if so, what consequences should flow from that determination. Conventional thought and practice have it that a court will strike down or invalidate a statutory provision which it finds inconsistent with the Constitution. Sometimes, the provision is struck down in its entirety. At other times, limiting doctrines such as severance, reading-in, or reading-down, may be applied to preserve constitutionally permitted applications of the provision. Although courts describe the process in terms of judicial invalidation or, more dramatically, striking down of unconstitutional laws, it is not actually the court that strikes down or invalidates the law; rather, this occurs as a result of the operation of the Constitution itself. The court needs only to identify inconsistency between a statute and the Constitution. At that juncture, the Constitution, as the supreme law, must be given overriding effect, and the statute, as the subordinate law, must be disregarded by the court and given no force or effect. The court exercises no discretion, and grants no remedy. It simply figures out what the law is and applies that law to the facts of the case.

Thus, the concept of the court striking down or invalidating the law is simply a metaphor for the actual process, which involves the Constitution operating in an automatic and self-executing manner, and requiring the court to resolve conflicts between the Constitution and other laws in favour of the Constitution. In other words, "Invalidation … is a remedy only figuratively, not literally. The Constitution, not any judicial decree, produces invalidity."[1]

---

[1] J. Harrison, "Severability, Remedies, and Constitutional Adjudication" (2014) 83 *Geo. Wash. L. Rev.* 56 at p. 56

It has been written that a "metaphor is at best a dash of poetry adorning lawerly analysis, and at worst an unjustifiable distraction from what is actually at stake in a legal contest."[2] While figurative expressions can help explain complicated processes in simple and memorable terms, they can also be misleading and potentially dangerous if taken literally.[3] That seems to have happened with the judicial striking down or invalidation metaphor. Judges, practitioners, and constitutional scholars have apparently come to believe that the court's declaration of constitutional invalidity *causes* an impugned statute to lose its legal vitality. As will be shown below, this belief is wrong; but it comes with a seemingly impressive pedigree, given that in 2016 the Supreme Court of Canada opined that "a law [that] does not conform to the Constitution .... remains in full force or effect, absent a formal declaration of invalidity by a court of inherent jurisdiction."[4] That is to be contrasted with a contrary pronouncement by a unanimous Supreme Court in a 2003 case:

> The invalidity of a legislative provision inconsistent with the *Charter* does not arise from the fact of its being declared unconstitutional by a court, but from the

---

[2] R.L. Tsai, "Fire, Metaphor, and Constitutional Myth-Making" (2004) 93 *Geo. L.J.* 181 at p. 182

[3] Concern about the capacity of metaphors to distort legal thought led Benjamin Cardoza to issue this warning: "Metaphors in law are to be narrowly watched, for starting as devices to liberate thought, they end often by enslaving it." (*Berkey v. Third Ave. Ry. Co..* 155 N.E. 58 at 61 (N.Y. 1926)), quoted in M. R. Smith, "Levels of Metaphor in Persuasive Legal Writing" (2007) 58 *Mercer L. Rev.* 919 at p. 923. Lord Mansfield observed in the eighteenth century that "nothing in law is so apt to mislead as a metaphor." (Quoted in T. Ross, "Metaphors and Paradox" (1989) 23 *Ga. L. Rev.* 1053 at p. 1057, footnote 9) Metaphors tend to run away with us, noted the philosopher Monroe Beardsley: "It is not only meanings that sometimes tend to run away with us in metaphor. It is thinking itself. A metaphor can be extremely helpful to thought, when it suggests an anology that opens up new lines of inquiry; but if the image is strong and colorful, it can fasten itself upon us and control our thinking too rigidly." M.C. Beardsley, *Thinking Straight*, (New York: Prentice-Hall, 1950) at p. 245, quoted in H. Bosmajian, *Metaphor and Reason in Judicial Opinions*, (Carbondale and Edwardsville: So. Ill. Univ. Press, 1992) at pp. 38-39

[4] *R. v. Lloyd*, [2016] 1 S.C.R. 130 at para. 19

operation of s. 52(1) [the supremacy clause in Canada's Constitution].[5]

It also departs from this statement by another unanimous Supreme Court in 2008:

> When a litigant claims that a law violates the *Charter*, and the court rules or "declares" that it does, the effect of s. 52(1) is to render the law null and void. It is common to describe this as the court "striking down" the law. In fact, when a court "strikes down" a law, the law has failed by operation of s. 52 of the *Constitution Act, 1982*.[6]

How and why the Supreme Court of Canada's thinking on the process of constitutional invalidation apparently reversed course between 2008 and 2016 is somewhat of a mystery. It offers no explanation for this shift. One plausible explanation is that the Court was forced to come to grips with the logical implications of its jurisprudence surrounding the making of suspended declarations of constitutional invalidity. The efficacy of suspending a declaration of invalidity (ostensibly to allow the legislature time to enact a constitutionally-compliant replacement law), requires that the declaration itself carries some legally meaningful effect. If the declaration merely describes the law, and changes nothing, a suspension of that declaration would likewise accomplish nothing.[7]

Such was the problem facing the Supreme Court of Canada as it set about inventing the so-called suspended declaration of invalidity. The weight of authority – not just in Canada, but throughout the common law world – was that constitutionally invalid statutes are invalidated not by court order, but by the

---

[5] *Nova Scotia (Workers' Compensation Board) v. Martin*, [2003] 2 S.C.R. 504 at para. 28
[6] *R. v. Ferguson*, [2008] 1 S.C.R. 96 at para. 35
[7] Unless, as will be explained later, the court is using the term "suspended declaration" as a euphemism for the decidedly legislative act of deeming an invalid law to be valid.

operation of the Constitution itself. Thus, when a court makes a declaration of invalidity, it merely describes the law. A statute is no less and no more valid or invalid as a result of the court's declaration. As the declaration itself changes nothing, it follows that a suspension of that declaration also changes nothing. This simple syllogism seems to have caused the Court to abandon a well-established body of law regarding the nature and effects of a declaration of invalidity. Thus, as noted above, it has recently pronounced, without explanation or citation of authority, that an unconstitutional statute is, in effect, voidable, as it "remains in full force and effect, absent a formal declaration of invalidity by a court of inherent jurisdiction."[8]

A rigorous analysis of the issue lays bare the illogic of the belief that a court, merely by suspending its declaration of invalidity, can allow an unconstitutional law to operate with legal force and effect. When the truth is revealed, proponents of this judicial contrivance are forced to come to grips with the true nature of the process at play. They are forced to explain the source of a judicial power to create – not to preserve, but to create – law that purports to have legal force and effect notwithstanding its inconsistency with the Constitution. A situation involving the non-existence of valid and enforceable law is transformed by judicial fiat into a situation involving the existence of valid and enforceable law. No legally coherent explanation has ever been offered to support this supposed judicial law-making power. It continues to be described in euphemistic terms, as a power of suspension (a judicial-sounding term), rather than according to its true nature – a power of creation (a decidedly legislative concept). It is now time to examine seriously the question of whether courts have the power to put into legally effective operation laws that are inconsistent with the Constitution.

Describing the device as a suspended declaration of invalidity tends to disguise and obfuscate the reality of what the courts are

---

[8] *R. v. Lloyd,* [2016] 1 S.C.R. 130 at para. 19

doing. That, of course, is the purpose of a euphemism.[9] Calling it a suspended or delayed declaration suggests that the courts are acting with restraint – that they merely are allowing a pre-existing legal state of affairs to continue while the legislature decides what to do about the constitutionally infirm law. Thus, the use of the word "allows" in this Supreme Court description of the suspended declaration device suggests the continuation of an existing state of affairs:

> By suspending the declaration of invalidity, the Court *allows* the constitutional infirmity *to continue* temporarily so that the legislature can fix the problem.[10] (emphasis added)

That sounds very reasonable and judicial. It fits nicely with the popular narrative of an ongoing constitutional dialogue between courts and legislatures. But it is not the truth. In fact, courts cannot and do not *suspend* declarations of invalidity (in the sense of suspending or delaying changes in substantive legal effects). They merely say they do. The reality is that the courts decree that the law temporarily will be different than it actually is, and that such judicially-decreed law will be of force and effect notwithstanding its inconsistency with the Constitution.

The greater problem may not be that courts are doing this, but rather that they are not openly and honestly acknowledging what they are doing, nor attempting to provide a *law-based* explanation for the exercise of these extraordinary law-making powers.[11] To date, pragmatic explanations have been offered – some of them quite good. Suspended declarations often provide workable solutions to difficult problems. They can help fill legal voids.

---

[9] It has been explained that: "In euphemizing, an inoffensive or pleasant term is substituted for a more explicit, offensive one, thereby veneering the reality. It may be called a linguistic fig leaf." R. Slovenko, "Euphemisms" (2005) 33 *J. Psychiatry & Law* 533 at p. 533

[10] *Canada (Attorney General) v. Hislop,* [2007] 1 S.C.R. 429 at para. 91

[11] As will be argued in Part 3 of this essay, "Trying to Right the Ship" at pp. 204-205, judicial candor matters. For a cynical assessment, see M. Shapiro, "Judges as Liars" (1994) 17 *Harv. J.L. & Pub. Policy* 155

However, pragmatism, if not confined to the parameters of the law, can become much more than an unruly horse.[12] It can overpower the rule of law. This is not necessarily done deliberately, and it does not happen suddenly. It is an erosive process. Drip, drip, drip – bit by bit – courts succumb to the allure of doing what appears to work, and what seems to be just and right in the particular circumstances, while showing increasingly less regard for the law and its underlying principles.

No doubt, some positive things can be said about suspended declarations' ability to mitigate the disruptive effects of findings of unconstitutionality, although they often have the troubling downside of denying remedies to deserving claimants.[13] However, entirely absent from judicial consideration of the issues, and largely absent from scholarly debate about them – and this is both surprising and concerning – is a much more fundamental point. Whether good or bad from a policy perspective, are suspended declarations of invalidity even legal? Put aside for the moment consideration of whether under a perfect legal and constitutional structure, courts would have this power. Does Canada's Constitution – its actual Constitution, not an idealized or imagined one – permit courts to accord legal force

---

[12] Public policy was described by Burrough J. as an "unruly horse" in a 1824 case: "Public policy is a very unruly horse, and when once you get astride it you never know where it will carry you." *Richardson v. Mellish* (1824), 2 Bing. 229 at p. 252

[13] "Suspended declarations of invalidity are deeply controversial, because they allow an unconstitutional state of affairs to persist, thereby posing a threat to the very idea of constitutional supremacy." S. Choudhry and K. Roach, "Putting the Past Behind Us? Prospective Judicial and Legislative Constitutional Remedies," (2003) 21 *S.C.L.R. (2d)* 205 at p. 230. That much is true, but Choudhry and Roach fail to explain that the suspended declaration actually allows the unconstitutional state of affairs *to exist* and not merely *to persist*. The suspension supposedly breathes life into an otherwise constitutionally comatose law. The status quo is a law that is of no force or effect. That situation is not simply allowed to persist. Rather, a law with temporary force and effect is brought into existence. The legal status quo is changed by judicial fiat.

and effect, even temporarily, to laws which the supremacy clause states are of no force or effect?

Furthermore, if suspended declarations are not permitted by the Constitution, what are the implications for the rule of law if courts are allowed to make up their own preferred constitutional rules in place of those actually contained in the Constitution? It is submitted that deviations by courts from legal principles and norms, even if in pursuit of noble ends, tend to corrode judicial fidelity to the rule of law. Evidence of this phenomenon can be found in the Canadian experience. It should serve as a caution to judges in other jurisdictions who may be invited to follow the Canadian approach to constitutional invalidation.

3. Suspended Declarations of Constitutional Invalidity in Canada – A Brief Summary

When a law is determined to be unconstitutional, problems inevitably arise, especially if the law has been on the books for a lengthy time-period, as citizens will have relied upon it in ordering their conduct and affairs. On the basis that an unconstitutional law is of no force or effect and never has been, does everything have to be unravelled? Fortunately, the common law has developed a number of saving doctrines which substantially mitigate the full retrospective impact of determinations of unconstitutionality. These include the *de facto* officer and limited immunity doctrines, the law of mistake, *res judicata*, and laches and prescription.

Thus, for already concluded cases and transactions, a determination that they were conducted or concluded under constitutionally invalid laws will generally not open them up to challenge or reconsideration. However, more recently concluded cases and transactions, which are not yet barred by limitation periods or have not yet found their way to final and binding judgment, are different. They will generally be subject to scrutiny according to the law as now identified by the court – that the relevant legislation is inconsistent with the Constitution and thus of no force or effect – even if the parties believed the legislation to be valid and enforceable at the time of the relevant conduct. Constitutional adjudication is therefore an inherently messy business which can result in unfairness to parties who act on the assumption that the law as written is valid and enforceable.

Beginning in the early 1990's, Canadian courts began a practice of mitigating the effects of their determinations of unconstitutionality by purporting to suspend their declarations of invalidity. The objective was essentially to freeze things for a temporary period while the legislators decided what, if anything, to do in response to the court's determination that the subject law conflicts with the Constitution. If the legislators opted to do nothing, the declaration of invalidity would come into effect at the end of the suspension period with full retroactive force. If the legislators enacted new, constitutionally-compliant legislation, it would be applied prospectively to future conduct, and, depending on its terms, perhaps also retroactively to conduct which had occurred in the past (although retroactive application of curative legislation is rare).

While described as a suspended declaration of invalidity, this is an inaccurate and misleading description of what is really happening. Laws which are inconsistent with the Constitution, are, and always have been, of no force or effect, and no declaration of a court is necessary to bring about that result. The court finds that the law is invalid, *but it does not make it so*. The Constitution does that. Therefore, as will be more fully explained below, when Canadian courts say that they are suspending a declaration of invalidity, they are either speaking nonsense, or they are speaking euphemistically about something quite different. Their actual objective is to deem the constitutionally invalid law to be valid. What s. 52(1) of the *Constitution Act, 1982* (the "Constitution") says "is … of *no* force or effect", the court to the contrary says "is … of *full* force and effect." How courts get the power to do this has never really been explained, other than by reliance on the Supreme Court's 1985 decision in *Manitoba Language Rights.*[14]

Manitoba Language Rights involved a decision by the Supreme Court that the entirety of Manitoba's legislation enacted over the previous ninety-five years in English only was constitutionally invalid and of no force or effect. To avoid public chaos and to preserve the rule of law, the Court deemed these invalid laws to be temporarily valid and effective in order to give the Manitoba Legislature time to re-enact its legislation in both French and English. As will be shown in Part 2 of this essay, *Manitoba Language Rights* provides no basis for a general judicial power to suspend or override the Constitution. At most, it may recognize a narrow range for extra-legal conduct in circumstances of extreme crisis.[15]

The Supreme Court of Canada initially provided some guidelines in the 1992 *Schachter* case for circumstances where these so-called suspended declarations of invalidity might properly be granted; namely, where immediate invalidation would: (1) endanger public safety; (2) threaten the rule of law; or (3) deprive a deserving person of a benefit under a constitutionally underinclusive statute.[16] There was no analysis of the underlying legal theory and principles relevant to whether a court has the

---

[14] *Re Manitoba Language Rights,* [1985] 1 S.C.R. 721. An in-depth analysis of *Manitoba Language Rights* will follow in Part 2 of this essay, "Fidelity to the Law: The Good, the Bad, and the Ugly".

[15] Ironically, the Supreme Court in *Manitoba Language Rights* went to great lengths to try to justify its decision as necessary to preserve the rule of law, although the very notion of emergency powers has been said to contradict the rule of law:

> The notion of emergency powers contradicts the Rule of Law because it posits that, in times of national crisis, the state may act outside constitutional norms. The idea is that whenever the existence of the state is imperilled, it may take extraordinary steps in order to save itself.

R. Martin, "Notes on Emergency Powers in Canada" (2005) 54 *U.N.B.L.J.* 161 at p. 162

[16] *Schachter v. Canada,* [1992] 2 S.C.R. 679 at pp. 715, 716, 719

power to put temporarily in place and give effect to laws which are inconsistent with the Constitution (and, as such, "of no force or effect" according to the Constitution). It appears that the Court saw it as a good thing that it should have these powers in certain situations, and so it purported to make it the law. It acted pragmatically. With *Manitoba Language Rights* serving as the thin edge, a thick wedge was thereby driven into the concepts of constitutional supremacy and the rule of law.

The Court in *Schachter* specifically stated that the question of whether to suspend a declaration of invalidity should not turn on considerations of the respective institutional roles of courts and legislatures. However, the courts eventually came to view the granting of suspended declarations as an important show of judicial deference to the legislative branch. Thus, suspended declarations have become an integral part of a metaphorical process of constitutional dialogue between courts and legislators.[17] This involves the court first identifying instances of unconstitutionality, and then suspending its declaration of invalidity; thereby effectively remanding the matter to the legislature for remedial response.[18]

Although the Court in *Schachter* counselled restraint because the use of delayed declarations is "a serious matter [which] allows a state of affairs which has been found to violate standards

---

[17] They have been described as "a powerful dialogic device that allows a court to remand complex issues to legislative institutions." S. Choudhry and K. Roach, "Putting the Past Behind Us? Prospective Judicial and Legislative Constitutional Remedies" (2003) *21 S.C.I.R.* (2d) 205 at p. 232. See also: P.W. Hogg and A.A. Bushell, "The *Charter* Dialogue Between Courts and Legislatures (Or Perhaps the *Charter of Rights* Isn't Such a Bad Thing After All") (1997) 35 *Osgoode Hall L.J.* 75; P.W. Hogg, A.A. Bushell Thornton and W.K. Wright, "*Charter* Dialogue Revisited – Or 'Much Ado About Metaphors"* (2007) 45 *Osgoode Hall Law J.* 1 at pp. 14-18

[18] "As a result, the delayed declaration of invalidity has become an instrument of 'remedial dialogue' between courts and legislatures and society." K. Roach, "Remedial Consensus and Dialogue under the *Charter*: General Declarations and Delayed Declarations of Invalidity" (2002) 35 *U.B.C. Law Rev.* 211 at p. 220

embodied in the *Charter* to persist for a time despite the violation,"[19] the courts have become increasingly willing to grant delayed declarations to the point that their use has been described as routine.[20] "It now appears that almost any inconvenience associated with an immediate declaration might lead the Court to temporarily suspend the operation of the Charter."[21] As of March, 2016 the Supreme Court had reportedly suspended declarations of invalidity in twenty-one cases.[22]

A short list of circumstances where courts have granted suspended declarations includes: to permit the government to collect unlawful taxes;[23] to prevent people suffering painful terminal illnesses from exercising their constitutional right to medically-assisted death;[24] to allow public hospitals to deny deaf patients constitutionally-required sign language assistance;[25] to permit the prosecution of persons under an unconstitutional by-law prohibiting the posting of commercial signs in a residential area;[26] to permit the unlawful continued detention of persons acquitted of crimes on grounds of insanity;[27] to deny Indigenous Canadians the right to vote in Band elections;[28] to permit the prosecution and conviction of persons under constitutionally

---

[19] *Schachter v. Canada*, [1992] 2 S.C.R. 679 at p. 716

[20] D. Guttman, "*Hislop v. Canada* – A Retroactive Look" (2008), 42 *S.C.L.R. (2d)* 547 at p. 552; K. Roach, "Remedial Consensus and Dialogue under the *Charter*: General Declarations and Delayed Declarations of Invalidity," (2002) 35 *U.B.C. Law Rev.* 211 at p. 218; B. Ryder, "Suspending the Charter" (2003) 21 *S.C.L.R. (2d)* 267 at p. 272; K. Roach, *The Supreme Court on Trial: Judicial Activism or Democratic Dialogue*, (Toronto: Irwin Law, rev'd ed. 2016) at p. 226

[21] B. Ryder, "Suspending the Charter" (2003), 21 *S.C.L.R. (2d)* 267 at p. 271

[22] G.J. Reynolds, "Reconsidering Copyright's Constitutionality" (2016) 53 *Osgoode Hall L.J.* 898 at pp. 941-942

[23] *Re Eurig Estate*, [1998] 2 S.C.R. 565

[24] *Carter v. Canada (Attorney General)*, [2015] 1 S.C.R. 331

[25] *Eldridge v. British Columbia,* [1997] 3 S.C.R. 624

[26] *R. v. Guignard*, [2002] 1 S.C.R. 472; *Vann Media Group Inc. v. Oakville (Town)*, 2008 ONCA 752 (CanLII)

[27] *R. v. Swain*, [1991] 1 S.C.R. 933

[28] *Corbiere v. Canada,* [1999] 2 S.C.R. 203

invalid laws pertaining to the sexual services industry;[29] and, to permit police officers to unlawfully participate in criminal court bail hearings.[30]

An earlier point deserves repetition. It is not the purpose of this essay to examine whether the use of suspended declarations in certain situations could be justified in a world where courts were unconstrained by the law. As a matter solely of public policy, the *Schachter* criteria: protection of public safety; preservation of the rule of law; and continuation of benefits under underinclusive statutes, are difficult to quarrel with. However, while public policy may help to inform legal decision-making, it cannot be given ownership of the judicial pen. Ultimately, suspended declarations must be shown to have a basis in the law.[31]

The academic review and commentary on suspended declarations is voluminous.[32] Somewhat unkindly, though not unfairly, one

---

[29] *Canada (Attorney General) v. Bedford,* [2013] 3 S.C.R. 1101

[30] *Hearing Office Bail Hearings (Re)*, 2017 ABQB 74 (CanLII)

[31] According to Professor Roach, courts have sought to justify their exercise of this power on the basis of the constitutional principle of the rule of law and the courts' "inherent powers." K. Roach, *Constitutional Remedies in Canada*, 2nd ed., (Toronto: Thomson Reuters, 2016) at para. 3.210. How the rule of law can justify the imposition of non-law has never been adequately explained. It has also never been explained how courts can possess "inherent powers" to deem what is unlawful to be lawful.

[32] A partial list of leading articles includes these: K. Roach, "Remedial Consensus and Dialogue under the *Charter*: General Declarations and Delayed Declarations of Invalidity" (2002) 35 *U.B.C. Law Rev.* 211; S. Choudhry and K. Roach, "Putting the Past Behind Us? Prospective Judicial and Legislative Constitutional Remedies" (2003) 21 *S.C.L.R. (2d)* 205; B. Ryder, "Suspending the Charter" (2003) 21 *S.C.L.R. (2d)* 267; K. Roach, "Principled Remedial Discretion Under the Charter" (2004) 25 *S.C.L.R. (2d)* 101; J. Lovell, "From Now On: Temporal Issues in Constitutional Adjudication" (2005) 18 *Nat'l J. Const. L.* 17; G. R. Hoole, "Proportionality as a Remedial Principle: A Framework for Suspended Declarations of Invalidity in Canadian Constitutional Law" (2011) 49 *Alta. L. Rev.* 107; K. Roach, "Enforcement of the Charter – Subsections 24(1) and 52(1)," (2013) 62 *S.C.L.R. (2d)* 473; R. Leckey, "The Harms of Remedial Discretion" (2016) 14 *Int'l J. Const. L.* 584; R. Leckey, "Realizing Rights Here and Now" (available online, forthcoming in the *Australian Journal of Human Rights*); C. Mouland, "Remedying the

author has suggested that the judicial use of suspended declarations and similar remedial orders is not likely to decline in the future given the encouragement being provided by the judges' "cheerleaders on the sidelines."[33] There appears to be an element of national self-admiration embedded in the descriptions of this dubious judicial device as important,[34] novel,[35] interesting,[36] ingenious,[37] remarkable,[38] powerful,[39] and innovative.[40] There has been little attention paid, however, to the fundamental question of whether there is any proper legal basis for courts to override the Constitution in this manner.[41]

In a nutshell, here is the question:

Remedy: Bedford's Suspended Declaration of Invalidity" ((2018) *Man. L. J.*, forthcoming)

[33] R. Leckey, "The Harms of Remedial Discretion" (2016) 14 *Int'l J. Const. L.* 584 at p. 603

[34] K. Roach, "Dialogic Judicial Review and its Critics" (2004) 23 *S.C.L.R. (2d)* 49 at p. 64

[35] K. Roach and G. Bunlender, "Mandatory Relief and Supervisory Jurisdiction: When is it Appropriate, Just and Equitable?" (2005) 122 *S. African L.J.* 325 at p. 339

[36] K. Roach, "The Judicial, Legislative and Executive Roles in Enforcing the Constitution: Three Manitoba Stories," in R. Albert and D.R. Cameron, eds, *Canada in the World: Comparative Perspectives on the Canadian Constitution* (Cambridge: Cambridge Univ. Press, 2018) 264 at p. 290

[37] P.W. Hogg, P.J. Monahan, and W.K. Wright, *Liability of the Crown,* 4th ed., (Toronto: Carswell, 2011) at p. 44

[38] M. Liston, *Honest Counsel: Institutional Dialogue and the Canadian Rule of Law,* PhD. Thesis, University of Toronto, 2007, at p. 172

[39] S. Choudhry and K. Roach, "Putting the Past Behind Us? Prospective Judicial and Legislative Constitutional Remedies" (2003) 21 *S.C.L.R. (2d)* 205 at p. 232

[40] K. Roach, "Dialogic Judicial Review and its Critics" (2004) 23 *S.C.L.R. (2d)* 49 at p. 64

[41] Professor Ryder demonstrates an understanding that suspended declarations involve an override of the Constitution in the title of his article: "Suspending the Charter" (2003) 21 *S.C.L.R. (2d)* 267. He is generally critical of suspended declarations, but he stops short of tackling the fundamental question of whether such orders are unconstitutional.

> *Do courts ever have lawful authority to put in place and enforce laws which are contrary to the Constitution and which the Constitution declares to be of no force or effect?*

According to the Supreme Court of Canada, the answer is "Yes." It will be argued in this essay that the correct answer is "No."

4. A Note on Prospective Overruling

The suspended declaration's first cousin is the doctrine of prospective overruling, which allows courts to manipulate the temporal effects of their decisions. According to this controversial doctrine, a court may order that the law as determined in a particular case shall apply only to future cases and not to cases based on facts which occurred prior to the court's decision. The rationale for prospective overruling is that when a court's decision departs from previously decided cases, or for the first time declares a statute or rule to be invalid, it is unfair to subject parties to the "new" legal rule without providing them with some advance warning that the law is actually different than was previously believed.

There are various types of prospective overruling. In its pure form, the court does not apply the "new" legal rule even to the case at bar in which it is first enunciated.[42] Unlike pure prospective overruling, selective prospective overruling allows the "new" rule to be applied to the case at bar, and perhaps also to other cases which were in the system (not yet finally adjudicated) as of the date of the decision enunciating the "new" legal rule. Then there is prospective prospective overruling which

---

[42] This means that whatever the court says about the "new" rule will, by definition, be *obiter dictum* since it has no effect on the outcome of the case at hand. See, *R. v. Governor of Brockhill Prison, ex parte Evans (No. 2)*, [2000] 4 All ER 15 at p. 39 (H.L.); R. Von Moschzisker, "Stare Decisis in Courts of Last Resort" (1924) 37 *Harvard L. Rev.* 409 at p. 426; N.O. Littlefield, "Stare Decisis, Prospective Overruling and Judicial Legislation in the Context of Sovereign Immunity" (1964) 9 *St. Louis Univ. L.J.* 56 at p. 81

declares that the "new" legal rule will apply only to cases based on events which occur after some specified future date. Thus, similarity can be seen between prospective prospective overruling and suspended declarations in that in both cases the court declares that until some future date the law will be treated as different than what the court has decided the law actually is.

The common thread between prospective overruling doctrine and suspended declaration doctrine is the assumption by the court of a power not just to decide what the law is, but to decide that tomorrow, or a year from now, the law will be different. This takes the court out of the judicial realm of deciding what the law is, and into the legislative realm of deciding what the law should be in the future. So it has been written:

> Prospective overruling is legislative, and so courts should leave it to the legislature.[43]

> ...

> The main argument against prospective application is indeed that it "smacks of the legislative process".[44]

> ...

> [A] widespread depiction of judges who decide prospectively is that they bear too much resemblance to a legislator.[45]

---

[43] B. Juratowitch, "The Temporal Effect of Judgments in the United Kingdom," in P. Popelier, S. Verstraelen, D. Vanheule and B. Vanlerberghe (eds.), *The Effects of Judicial Decisions in Time*, (Cambridge: Intersentia Publishing, 2014) 159 at p. 178

[44] T. Koopmans, "Retrospectivity Reconsidered" (1980) 39 *Cambridge L.J.* 287 at p. 296, quoting P.J. Mishkin, "The High Court, the Great Writ and the Due Process of Time and Law" (1965) 79 *Harvard L. Rev.* 56 at p. 65

[45] E. Steiner, "Judicial Rulings with Prospective Effect – From Comparison to Systemization," in E. Steiner, ed., *Comparing the Prospective Effect of Judicial Rulings Across Jurisdictions* (Switzerland: Springer, 2015) 1 at p. 13

Courts throughout the common law world have expressed grave misgivings about the concept of prospective overruling. These same misgivings should apply with even greater force to suspended declarations, which essentially amount to prospective overruling on steroids.[46]

The conventional Canadian position against prospective overruling was articulated by the Saskatchewan Court of Appeal:

> The practice of giving prospective effect to law is endemic to legislatures. By deciding an existing case under the old rule but warning that future cases will be decided under a new rule now being announced, a court is really usurping the function of the legislature.[47]

Notwithstanding the close kinship of prospective overruling and suspended declarations of invalidity, the Supreme Court of Canada paradoxically refused to recognize the concept of prospective overruling in 2000: "Only the Legislature has the power to create a prospective change in the law."[48] By 2006, however, it reversed course and carved out an exception for prospective overruling in constitutional cases.[49]

The objection that courts cannot prospectively overrule because it is essentially legislative action has been voiced by numerous

---

[46] It was noted by the Hong Kong Court of Final Appeal in *HKSAR v. Hung Chan Ha*, [2006] HKCFA 85 at para 30 that a declaration of temporary validity is even more far-reaching than prospective overruling: "It should be noted that such a remedy is even more far reaching than prospective overruling. With prospective overruling, the court's judgment would take effect from the date of the judgment. But where a declaration of temporary validity is made, the judgment would not even take effect at that time. It would only take effect after the expiry of the period as specified in the declaration sometime after the judgment."

[47] *Re Edward & Edward* (1987), 39 D.L.R. (4th) 654 at p. 664

[48] *Friedman Equity Developments Inc. v. Final Note Ltd.*, [2000] 1 S.C.R. 842 at para. 51

[49] *Canada (Attorney General) v. Hislop*, [2007] 1 S.C.R. 429. See further discussion of *Hislop* in section 7 below.

courts and commentators.[50] Among the doctrine's strongest critics has been the U.S. Supreme Court. Although prospective overruling temporarily came into vogue in the U.S. in the 1960's, it was never completely accepted by that court (especially not by Justice John Harlan), and by the mid-1990's prospective overruling had been substantially discredited and essentially abandoned.[51] In his dissenting decision in *Mackey v. U.S.*, Justice Harlan (whose views were eventually adopted by a majority of the Court) wrote as follows about the legislative nature of prospective overruling:

> What emerges from today's decision is that, in the realm of constitutional adjudication in the criminal field, the Court is free to act, in effect, like a legislature, making its new constitutional rules wholly or partially retroactive or only prospective as it deems wise. I completely disagree with this point of view. While I do not subscribe to the Blackstonian theory that the law should be taken to have always been what it is said to mean at a later time, I do believe that whether a new constitutional rule is to be given retroactive or simply prospective effect must be determined upon principles that comport with the judicial function, and not upon considerations that are appropriate enough for a legislative body.
>
> …
>
> In truth, the Court's assertion of power to disregard the law in adjudicating cases before us that have not already run the full course of judicial review, is quite

---

[50] Although now almost 100 years old, an excellent theoretical analysis of the issues involved in prospective overruling is found in R. Von Moschzisker, "Stare Decisis in Courts of Last Resort" (1924) 37 *Harv. L. Rev.* 409

[51] See: *Griffiths v. Kentucky* 479 U.S. 314 (1987); *Harper v. Virginia Dep't of Taxation* 509 U.S. 86 (1993); *Reynoldsville Casket Co. v. Hyde*, 514 U.S. 749 (1995). For a good overview of the ebb and flow of U.S. case law dealing with prospective overruling, see, R.S. Kay, "Retroactivity and Prospectivity of Judgments in American Law" (2014) 62 *Am. J. of Comp. Law Supp.* 37

> simply an assertion that our constitutional function is not one of adjudication but in effect of legislation.[52]

This followed upon Justice Black's earlier rejection of the concept:

> Once the Court determines what the Constitution says, I do not believe it has the power, by weighing "countervailing interests," to legislate a timetable by which the Constitution's provisions shall become effective.[53]

Justice Black's criticism that prospective overruling involves the court in legislating a timetable for when the Constitution's provisions shall become effective, is directly applicable to the Canadian practice of suspending declarations of invalidity, whereby the court announces a future date when the Constitution shall be allowed to apply with respect to an impugned provision. Allowing prospective overruling in the constitutional context is especially problematic because "it surrenders in part the basic principle that the constitution is the supreme law."[54]

Justice Scalia was also troubled by prospective overruling's legislative character: "[P]rospective decision-making is incompatible with the judicial role which is to say what the law is, not to prescribe what it shall be."[55] In a later case he referred to prospective overruling as "the handmaid of judicial activism, and the born enemy of *stare decisis*.... [P]rospective decisionmaking is quite incompatible with the judicial power, and ... courts have no authority to engage in the practice."[56] He went

---

[52] *Mackey v. U.S.*, 401 U.S. 667 (1971) at pp. 677, 679

[53] *Stovall v. Denno*, 388 U.S. 293 (1967) at p.304

[54] J.A.C. Grant, "The Legal Effect of a Ruling that a Statute is Unconstitutional" (1978) *Det. Coll. of L. Rev.* 201 at p. 202. However, as will be discussed in section 7 below, the Supreme Court of Canada approved of prospective decision-making in *Canada (Attorney General) v. Hislop*, [2007] 1 S.C.R. 429

[55] *American Trucking v. Smith*, 496 U.S. 167 (1990) at p. 201

[56] *Harper v. Virginia Dep't of Taxation,* 509 U.S. 86 (1993) at pp. 105, 106

on to quote this description of the difference between the judicial and legislative roles from T. Cooley, *Constitutional Limitations*:

> [I]t is said that that which distinguishes a judicial from a legislative act is, that the one is a determination of what the existing law is in relation to some existing thing already done or happened, while the other is a predetermination of what the law shall be for the regulation of all future cases.[57]

Prospective overruling has also met opposition in other common law jurisdictions. It has been described as "constitutionally impermissible" by an Australian author,[58] who added elsewhere: "A Court has no business applying one rule to the case before it and simultaneously announcing a new rule for future cases, inconsistent with the rule being applied."[59] The High Court of Australia rejected prospective overruling in brief but pointed terms, holding that a court "has no power to overrule cases prospectively ... [and that if] an earlier case is erroneous and it is necessary to overrule it, it would be a perversion of judicial power to maintain in force that which is acknowledged not to be the law."[60]

In the U.K., although the House of Lords expressed, in *obiter*, a "never say never" attitude towards prospective overruling in one case,[61] the practice has not really caught on. The preponderant judicial view in the U.K. remains one of extreme skepticism as reflected in Lord Goff's statement that prospective overruling "has no place in our legal system."[62] Thirty years earlier, Lord

---

[57] *ibid.* at p. 107

[58] B. Juratowitch, *Retroactivity and the Common Law*, (Oxford and Portland: Hart Publishing, 2008) at p. 217. The constitutional illegitimacy of prospective overruling was also commented on in a 2000 House of Lords decision (see *infra*, footnote 64).

[59] B. Juratowitch, "Questioning Prospective Overruling" (2007) *N.Z.L. Rev.* 393 at p. 414

[60] *Ha v. New South Wales* (1997), 189 CLR 465 at pp. 503-504

[61] *Re Spectrum Plus*, [2005] 2 AC 680 at para. 41

[62] *Kleinwort Benson v. Lincoln County Council*, [1999] 2 AC 349 at p. 379

Reid had flatly rejected prospective overruling: "We cannot say that the law was one thing yesterday but is to be something different tomorrow."[63] And Lord Devlin, writing extra-judicially, added his voice to the criticism of prospective overruling's legislative nature: "I do not like it. It crosses the Rubicon that divides the judicial and legislative powers. It turns judges into undisguised legislators."[64] This was joined by a rebuke of prospective overruling *via* the pen of Lord MacKay:

> I would argue that it is *not the business of judges* to weigh up competing claims beyond the boundaries of the dispute, such as the effect retroactive application might have on the administration of justice. The parties before the court are in my view entitled to a decision which deals with the problems revealed in their case, not with those of imaginary litigants and their advisors.[65] (emphasis added)

It is also not the business of judges to legalize the illegal which is what happens, in effect, when a court employs prospective overruling: "To do otherwise [than to give retroactive effect to the court's decision] will in effect legalize the illegal and the courts are not in business to do that."[66]

---

[63] *Birmingham v. West Midland,* [1969] 3 All ER 172 at p. 180

[64] P. Devlin, "Judges and Lawmakers" (1976) 39 *Mod. L. Rev.* 1 at p. 11. See also Lord Hobhouse's comments in *R. v. Governor of Brockhill Prison, ex parte Evans (No. 2),* [2000] 4 All ER 15 at p. 39:

> It is a denial of the constitutional role of the court for courts to say that the party challenging the *status quo* is right, that the previous decision is overruled, but that the decision will not affect the parties and only apply subsequently. They would be declining to exercise their constitutional role and adopting a legislative role deciding what the law shall be for others in the future.

[65] J.P.H. MacKay, "Can Judges Change the Law?" (1987) 73 *Proceedings of the British Academy* 285 at p. 306

[66] *Percy v. Hall,* [1997] Q.B. 924 at p. 951 (C.A.)

5. Constitutions, Not Courts, Invalidate Laws

As noted earlier, many judges have come to believe that they have the power to strike down or invalidate constitutionally infirm provisions, and thereby effectively remove them from the statute books, much as a legislature does when it repeals a statute. This has resulted from a fundamental misunderstanding of the process of constitutional invalidation, and the respective roles of courts and legislatures in that process.

The "striking down" metaphor appears to have caused many lawyers and judges to misunderstand the legal principle that it is the Constitution itself, rather than a court order, which brings about the invalidity of a law that is inconsistent with the Constitution. The notion of a court "striking down" a statute, like Zeus hurling bolts of lightning, is a colourful and engaging metaphor, but, like all figures of speech, it does not describe a literal truth. In fact, it only very loosely, and inaccurately, describes the process of constitutional invalidation. The truth is that courts play only a secondary role in the process. The court identifies an inconsistency between a statute and the Constitution, and the Constitution then directs the court to ignore the statute to the extent of the inconsistency. The court has no choice in the matter.[67] It is merely doing its job of figuring out what the law is and applying that law to the facts of the case before it. Thus, contrary to popular legal belief, there is no such thing as a remedy of statutory invalidation.

Professor John Harrison, referring to American practice which accords with that of other common law jurisdictions, has recognized that while it may appear that courts strike down or invalidate unconstitutional statutes, this is actually a figurative description of the actual process:

---

[67] Canada's then Chief Justice appears to have recognized this when she wrote in a unanimous 2008 decision that s. 52(1) (Canada's constitutional supremacy clause) "confers no discretion on judges." *R. v. Ferguson*, [2008] 1 S.C.R. 96 at para. 35

> [T]he Constitution produces invalidity and the courts recognize that invalidity in deciding particular cases. Judicial invalidation on constitutional grounds is not an accurate description of American constitutional practice. It describes that practice roughly at best, and is no more than a metaphor. The same is true of judicial law-making. Metaphors can be useful, but they can also be fatally misleading.[68]

As will be revealed below, the danger of judges actually believing that they can strike down unconstitutional laws is that they may, and in fact have, come also to believe that they have the power to keep unconstitutional laws in force by refraining from striking them down or by purporting to suspend or delay the effects of their strike-down orders. This has led to the train wreck (metaphorically speaking) that is the Canadian suspended declaration of constitutional invalidity.

A relatively early statement of the principle that court orders do not cause statutes to become invalid was made by Chief Justice Latham of the High Court of Australia in 1942:

> Common expressions, such as: "The courts have declared the statute invalid," sometimes lead to misunderstanding. A pretended law made in excess of power is not and never been a law at all. Anybody in the country is entitled to disregard it. Naturally he will feel safer if he has a decision of a court in his favour – but such a decision is not an element which produces invalidity in any law. The law is not valid until a court pronounces against it – and thereafter invalid. If it is beyond power it is invalid ab initio.[69]

---

[68] J. Harrison, "The Relations Between the Courts and the Law" (2016) 35 *Univ. of Queensland L. J.* 99 at pp. 113-114; see also, J. Harrison, "Severability, Remedies, and Constitutional Adjudication," (2014) 83 *Geo. Wash. L. Rev.* 56

[69] *South Australia v. The Commonwealth* (1942), 65 CLR 373 at 408

To similar effect is a 1984 decision of the High Court of Australia[70] regarding the effect of s. 109 of Australia's Constitution which provides for supremacy of Commonwealth law over inconsistent State law.[71] Murphy J. described the provision's effect as follows: "Section 109 is invalidating or destructive; it has no reconstructive aspect. Its operation is automatic and does not require a judicial order."[72] Justice Deane added:

> According to its terms, its operation is *immediate*. Its terms are unqualified and *self-executing*. If there is inconsistency between an otherwise valid law of a State and a valid law of the Commonwealth the State law shall be, to the extent of the inconsistency, invalid.[73] (emphasis added)

The fundamental principle is that when a court purports to quash or invalidate an unlawful act, it is elucidating, but not causing, its invalidity. So Mark Elliott says: "[Q]uashing unlawful measures merely demonstrates – but does not procure – their invalidity. They are invalid because they are unlawful, not because they have been quashed."[74]

The automatic and self-executing nature of constitutional supremacy provisions is often reflected in the text of such provisions, in that they speak to the current status of an inconsistent law and contain no suggestion that the overriding effect of the Constitution depends upon a declaration or order of

---

[70] *University of Wollongong v. Metwally* (1984), 158 CLR 447
[71] Section 109 states: "When a law of a State is inconsistent with a law of the Commonwealth, the latter shall prevail, and the former shall, to the extent of the inconsistency, be invalid."
[72] *University of Wollongong v. Metwally* (1984), 158 CLR 447 at para 7
[73] *ibid* at para. 6
[74] M. Elliott, "The Legal Status of Unlawful Legislation" [2013] *Public Law for Everyone*, available online, quoted in T. Adams, "The Standard Theory of Administrative Unlawfulness" (2017) 76 *Cambridge L.J.* 289 at p. 292

a court. Accordingly, s. 52(1) of Canada's Constitution (of 1982) reads:

> (1) The Constitution of Canada is the supreme law of Canada, and any law that is inconsistent with the provisions of the Constitution is, to the extent of the inconsistency, of no force or effect.

Article 15 of Ireland's Constitution (of 1937) similarly provides:

> Every law enacted by the Oireachtas [Parliament] which is in any respect repugnant to this Constitution or to any provision thereof, shall, but to the extent only of such repugnancy, be invalid.

Thus, the Supreme Court of Ireland in holding that unconstitutional provisions of a taxation statute were void and not merely voidable, stressed that this result was *ordained* by the Constitution:

> Such [unconstitutional] enactments are, and have been consistently held to be, invalid from the time of their purported enactment because *the Constitution*, truly read and duly accorded the necessarily implied consequences of a breach of its legislative limitations, *so ordains*.[75] (emphasis added)

And Article 4 of Singapore's Constitution (of 1963) states:

> This Constitution is the supreme law of the Republic of Singapore and any law enacted by the Legislature after the commencement of this Constitution which is inconsistent with this Constitution shall, to the extent of the inconsistency, be void.

The authors of an especially insightful article had this to say in rejecting the applicability of prospective overruling to a finding of unconstitutionality of a Singaporean law:

---

[75] *Murphy v. Attorney General*, [1982] 1 I.R. 241 at p. 313

It should be noted that a law which is unconstitutional conflicts not so much with the declaration of the court but rather with the Constitution. One of the major fallacies of the doctrine of prospective overruling is that the courts assume that it is their declaration of unconstitutionality rather than the Constitution itself that strikes down an unconstitutional law. The true state of affairs is that the declaration by the courts that a law is unconstitutional is a mere prelude to the unravelling of the unconstitutional law. It does not strike down the impugned law but rather sets in motion the mechanism inherent in the Constitution that strikes down the same.[76]

This has also been recognized by the Constitutional Court of South Africa: "The Court's order does not invalidate the law; it merely declares it to be invalid."[77] And, similarly, it was said in another South African case: "The court order merely declares the law or conduct invalid. In contrast it is the Constitution itself which invalidates laws or conduct inconsistent with it."[78]

The same analysis has been applied to the process of invalidation under Hong Kong's Constitution (Basic Law).[79] And, as noted

---

[76] K. Low Fatt Kin, K. Loi Chit Fai, S. Wee Ai Yin, "Towards a Maintenance of Equality (Part I): A Study of the Constitutionality of Maintenance Provisions that Sexually Discriminate" (1998) 19 *Sing. Law Rev.* 45 at 67

[77] *Ferreira v. Levin NO,* [1995] ZAAC 13 at para. 27;

[78] *Merafong City Local Municipality v. Anglogold Ashanti Limited*, [2016] ZAAC 35 at para. 136.

[79] This is how one author described in process under Hong Kong law:

The better view therefore is that judgments of the Court of Final Appeal holding a legislative provision unconstitutional carry no general effect; they indicate but not rule. The holdings of unconstitutionality at most operate as precedents in like subsequent cases, so long as their precedential value is maintained and not removed by, say, an interpretation of the NPCSC [Standing Committee of the National People's Congress] of a provision of the Basic Law. Courts thereafter neither enforce nor sanction consequences under legislation held to be unconstitutional. Hence, strictly, it is incorrect to speak of the Courts having "struck down" legislation on constitutional grounds.

earlier, in the United States it is also recognized that the constitutional invalidity of a statute results from the operation of the Constitution itself and does not depend on judicial orders or declarations.[80]

The view that constitutional adjudication involves the invalidation or striking down of statutes implies that courts are thereby interfering with the will of elected officials. This is an inaccurate and unfortunate characterization of the judicial review process. Courts do not and cannot cause statutes to become invalid or ineffective. They merely decide if a statute is inconsistent with the Constitution. The identification of such inconsistency is not a matter of remedy or of discretion.[81] It is simply the result of courts doing their jobs of deciding what the law is. Thus, as ubiquitous as reference to the so-called remedy of constitutional invalidation may be, this is actually the result of fuzzy thinking and poor expression.

P.Y. Lo, *Judicial Consideration of the Basic Law*, PhD Thesis, University of Hong Kong, 2011, at p. 127

[80] John Harrison explains it as follows:

> Constitutional invalidity of federal statutes thus is produced by the Constitution itself, not by the order of a court. Invalidation is not a remedy, and the principles that govern constitutional invalidity are not part of the law of remedies. Those principles are a feature of the Constitution, and courts apply them in the process of identifying the applicable primary law so that they can apply it to the parties.

J. Harrison, "Severability, Remedies, and Constitutional Adjudication" (2014) 83 *Geo. Wash. L. Rev.* 56 at p. 87; See also: J. Harrison, "The Relations Between the Courts and Law" (2016) 35 *U. Queensland L. J.* 99; B.C. Lea, "Situational Severability" (2017) 103 *Va. L. Rev.* 735

[81] A court finds inconsistency between a statute and the Constitution, but does nothing to the statute itself. Thus, judicial review is a matter of interpretation, not remedy:

> [J]udges determine where the Constitution supersedes a statute, but they do not actually do anything to the statute itself. Consequently, judicial review is simply a matter of interpretation, and not a matter of remedy.

E. Fish, "Choosing Constitutional Remedies" (2016) 63 *U.C.L.A. Law Rev.* 322 at p. 330 (referring to other authors with whom Professor Fish disagrees).

It was more than a century ago that this was recognized by Everett V. Abbot, writing as a member of a Select Committee of the New York Bar Association in a memorandum examining a 1913 New York Supreme Court decision:[82]

> There has been a confused notion that a court in adjudging that a statute is unconstitutional somehow interferes with the powers of a coordinate branch of the government, and exercises a nullifying influence upon its acts. This is utterly erroneous. The court does nothing of the kind. It does not veto the enactment. It does not annul the statute. It does not take away any validity or quality that the statute may possess. It does not usurp any function which does not belong to it. It does not exercise any power that is not judicial.... Now we can see the fundamental misconception which underlies the views of those who are disturbed because a court declares that a statute is unconstitutional. They think that the court has exercised some mysterious function which is not confided to it and which invades the function of another branch of the government. The view is radically erroneous. The man who can, even by inadvertence, use such a phrase as "the veto power of the court," "judicial annulment of legislative acts," "judicial power over statutes," "judicial control of the legislature," convicts himself of ignorance of the rudimentary principles of the matter under discussion. He has not learned even the alphabet of the language which he uses.
>
> The principle is simple: When a legislature has exceeded its powers, its act has never attained the status of a law. The court in declaring the unconstitutionality of such an act has merely refrained from fictitiously giving it a validity which it never possessed and which

---

[82] *Lewkowicz v. Queen Aeroplane Company*, 207 N.Y. 290 (1913)

the people have denied. The court has done nothing to the act itself.[83]

In summary, the court cannot deprive a statute of any validity that it otherwise possesses; nor can the court confer on a statute any greater validity than it otherwise possesses.

Against this background, Canada, with its Supreme Court's statement in 2016 referred to above: "[A] law [that] does not conform to the Constitution .... remains in full force or effect, absent a formal declaration of invalidity by a court of inherent jurisdiction,"[84] would seem to be very much a common law outlier. Indeed, it is difficult to conceive of how a law that is contrary to the Constitution can remain in full force or effect given that s. 52(1) of Canada's Constitution, speaking as the supreme law of Canada, stipulates that "any law that is inconsistent with the Constitution is, to the extent of the inconsistency, of no force or effect." How can a law simultaneously be "in full force or effect" as the Supreme Court describes the situation in the absence of a formal judicial declaration of invalidity, and "of no force or effect" as Canada's Constitution prescribes?

As noted earlier, Chief Justice McLachlin's 2016 description of the legal vitality of unconstitutional laws prior to their formal judicial reprobation, is completely at odds with a 2003 decision in which she concurred:

> The invalidity of a legislative provision inconsistent with the *Charter does not* arise from the fact of its being declared unconstitutional by a court, but from the operation of s. 52(1).[85] (emphasis added)

---

[83] E.V. Abbot, quoted in L.B. Boudin, "The Problem of *Stare Decisis* in our Constitutional Theory" (1931) 8 *N.Y.U.L.Q. Rev.* 589 at p. 639

[84] *R v Lloyd*, [2016] 1 S.C.R. 130 at para. 19

[85] *Nova Scotia (Workers' Compensation Board) v. Martin*, [2003] 2 S.C.R. 504 at para. 28

Moreover, in a 1996 decision she explained, completely in line with conventional common law analysis, that judges have no power to strike down or invalidate laws:

> It is common to speak of courts or tribunals "striking down" or invalidating laws, regulations and government actions, suggesting action that transcends mere application of the law and hence, must be reserved for the highest courts. This view of the *Charter* is, with respect, inaccurate. The *Charter* confers no power on judges or tribunals to strike down laws. The *Constitution Act, 1982*, however, provides that all laws are invalid to the extent they are inconsistent with the *Charter*. Laws are struck down *not by judicial fiat*, but by operation of the *Charter* and s. 52 of the *Constitution Act, 1982*. … The *Constitution Act, 1982* does not speak in terms of bodies possessing power to invalidate laws. Rather *it pronounces* laws invalid, to the extent of their inconsistency with the *Charter*.[86] (emphasis added)

Writing extra-judicially in 2002, Chief Justice McLachlin repeated her appreciation of the fact that courts do not strike down unconstitutional laws: "While the Courts do not actually strike the law down (the Charter deems it void), the result is the same."[87] And finally, writing for a unanimous Court in 2008, she again acknowledged the metaphorical nature of the concept of courts "striking down" laws:

> When a litigant claims that a law violates the *Charter*, and the court rules or "declares" that it does, the effect of s. 52(1) is to render the law null and void. It is common to describe this as the court "striking down" the law. In fact, when a court "strikes down" a law, the

---

[86] *Cooper v. Canada (Human Rights Commission),* [1996] 3 S.C.R. 854, at para. 83. While this was a dissenting judgment, it was substantially adopted by the Court in 2003, see *Martin* cited in the footnote immediately above.

[87] B. McLachlin "Bill of Rights in Common Law Countries" (2002) 51 *Int. & Comp. Law Quarterly* 197 at 200

law has failed by operation of s. 52 of the *Constitution Act, 1982*.[88]

However, by the next year, 2009, her thinking on the subject appears to have taken a sharp and unexplained turn, as she wrote: "[T]he law becomes invalid only after the court decision declaring it inconsistent with the *Charter*."[89] This then became part of Supreme Court jurisprudence in 2016 when the Chief Justice wrote as follows in her decision for the majority: "[A] law [that] does not conform to the Constitution ... remains in full force or effect, absent a formal declaration of validity by a court of inherent jurisdiction."[90]

Of course, judges are entitled to change their minds; indeed, it would be a problem if they never did so. Nonetheless, some explanation for a dramatic shift in thinking on such a fundamental point of constitutional law would ordinarily be provided. However, we are left to speculate.[91] The best explanation may be that the Chief Justice and other members of the Court eventually realized that their jurisprudence on suspended declarations could not be reconciled with the accepted common law view that courts'

---

[88] *R. v. Ferguson*, [2008] 1 S.C.R. 96 at para. 35

[89] B. McLachlin, "Rights and Remedies – Remarks" Conference of the Canadian Institute for the Administration of Justice" Ottawa, October 2, 2009, at p. 28

[90] *R. v. Lloyd*, [2016] 1 S.C.R. 130 at para. 19

[91] It is not always easy to understand why judges decide cases as they do. Their reasons should be, but are not always, apparent from their published decisions. Access to court documents can be difficult. It was recently reported that in June, 2017 the Supreme Court of Canada placed a 50-year embargo on public access to files related to the deliberations of the judges, from the time they rule on the case. Moreover, the Court can order that such access be denied permanently. Leading Canadian political scientist on judicial affairs issues, Peter Russell, said: "I don't know any other constitutional democracy that puts the lid on it for so long." (Sean Fine, "Supreme Court of Canada to Keep Records of Deliberations Secret for at Least 50 Years." *The Globe and Mail*, Toronto, May 14, 2018.) The length of this period of embargo became the subject of critical comment by two retired Supreme Court justices who regarded it as unnecessarily long. (Sean Fine, "Retired Top Court Judges Object to 50-year Embargo," *The Globe and Mail*, Toronto, May 15, 2018.)

declarations of invalidity do not actually affect the validity or invalidity of impugned laws. A purported suspension of the effects of a declaration obviously presupposes that the declaration has effects capable of being suspended.

Of course, the Court's new Zeus-like approach to invalidation requires rejection of the idea that s. 52(1) of the Constitution means what is says – that inconsistent laws are, to the extent of the inconsistency, of no force or effect. It requires acceptance of the opposite proposition – that judicial declarations of invalidity are a necessary prerequisite to the engagement of s. 52(1) – even though there is no textual support for such a view.[92] In fact, Professor Kent Roach, who is generally a champion of suspended declarations, has conceded that they not only lack textual basis in the Constitution, but that they are actually at odds with s. 52(1):

> This novel remedy has no textual basis in the Canadian Constitution. Indeed, it is at odds with section 52(1) which mandates that laws inconsistent with the Constitution are or no force or effect to the extent of their inconsistency.[93]

Yet, despite having just described suspended declarations of invalidity as being at odds with s. 52(1), Professor Roach goes on

---

[92] Grant Hoole recognized this:
> Canada's constitutional text makes no provision for suspended declarations of invalidity. Section 52 of the *Constitution, 1982* simply affirms the supremacy of the Constitution relative to ordinary statutes ... On a plain reading of this provision, the invalidation of any law found to be ultra vires the Constitution should be immediate.

G.R. Hoole, "Proportionality as a Remedial Principle: A Framework for Suspended Declarations of Invalidity in Canadian Constitutional Law" (2011) 49 *Alta. L. Rev.* 107 at p. 110

[93] K. Roach "Remedies for Laws that Violate Human Rights" in J. Bell, M. Elliott, J. Varuhas, P. Murray, *Public Law Adjudication in Common Law Systems*, (Oxford and Portland, Oregon: Hart Publishing, 2016) 269 at p. 277

a few pages later to describe them as "remedies … awarded under section 52."[94]

It will now be argued, contrary to Canadian constitutional orthodoxy, that s. 52(1) does not authorize the granting of any remedies. None.

6. Courts Cannot Remedy Statutes

It is an accepted wisdom of Canadian constitutional law that courts can grant remedies under s. 52(1) which will somehow fix or repair a statute's constitutional deficiency. The concept of s. 52(1) remedies is now so deeply entrenched in the case law and academic writings that only heresy or lunacy could prompt the contention that Canadian courts have no legal authority or ability to remedy unconstitutional statutes. That is the contention made here.

Although s. 52(1) was first enacted as part of Canada's package of constitutional amendments in 1982, it did not add anything of substance to pre-existing constitutional arrangements. Thus wrote the Federal Court of Appeal:

> It is true that the adoption of the *Charter* in 1982 added
> a multitude of qualitative limitations on the exercise of
> power but it is difficult to ascertain any change in the
> principle that the Constitution of Canada was and is
> supreme over ordinary laws.[95]

According to Peter Hogg: "[Subsection 52(1)] states a principle that has always been part of Canadian constitutional law."[96] Similarly, Barry Strayer, a former Federal Court of Appeal justice who, as Deputy Attorney General of Canada in the early 1980's, actually drafted s. 52, has described it as follows: "All that section 52 does is to maintain the continuity of our system, which has

---

[94] *ibid.* at p. 280

[95] *Singh v. Canada (Attorney General)*, [2000] 3 FC 185 at para. 16

[96] P.W. Hogg, *Constitutional Law of Canada*, looseleaf (Toronto: Thomson Reuters, 2007) at para. 58.1

known judicial review to enforce constitutional limitations on our legislatures and executives since before Confederation [in 1867]."[97] Another author writes: "Rather than enlarge the role of the courts in constitutional affairs, section 52(1) was included to preserve the status quo in relation to the supremacy of the Canadian Constitution."[98]

In *Schachter*,[99] the Supreme Court proposed the following remedial options for a court that identifies an inconsistency between a statutory provision and the Constitution: (1) strike down the provision in its entirety; (2) read down or sever from the provision its constitutionally objectionable parts; or, (3) read in additional language in order to supplement a constitutionally underinclusive provision. In addition, of course, *Schachter* recognized a supposed power of the court to suspend the effectiveness of its remedy in order to protect public safety, preserve the rule of law, or to prevent a deserving person losing a benefit under an underinclusive provision. The Court identified s. 52(1) as the source of its authority to provide these remedies. It did not explain how any remedial powers could be derived from a provision which on its face does not speak to remedies, but rather declares the supremacy of the Constitution in the event of inconsistency with other laws.

Once again, at the risk of tedium, it is important that the full text of s. 52(1) be set out in order to illustrate that it deals with substantive law, and not remedies:

---

[97] B.L. Strayer, *Canada's Constitutional Revolution*, (Edmonton: Univ. of Alberta Press, 2013) at p. 164

[98] B. Bird, "The Unbroken Supremacy of the Canadian Constitution" (2018) 55 *Alta. L. Rev.* 755 at p. 773. See also, *Operation Dismantle v. The Queen*, [1985] 1 S.C.R. 441 at para. 86; and G.V. La Forest, "The Canadian Charter of Rights and Freedoms: An Overview" (1983) 61 Can. B. Rev. 19 at p. 28: "[The situation with s. 52] is exactly the same situation we have always had with respect to the British North America Act, although that was by virtue of its being a British statute."

[99] [1992] 2 S.C.R. 679

> 52(1) The Constitution of Canada is the supreme law
> of Canada, and any law that is inconsistent with the
> provisions of the Constitution is, to the extent of the
> inconsistency, of no force or effect.

This section tells courts what to do when inconsistency is
identified between a subordinate law and the Constitution – the
supreme law. That is all it does. It is an interpretation provision.[100]
The court is instructed to ignore the inconsistent law to the extent
of its inconsistency with the Constitution. It confers no power on
the courts to strike out, invalidate, repeal, subtract from, add to,
vary, or amend a statute. All of those actions would involve
changing the statute, and that power is reserved under the
Constitution to the legislative branch of government. Indeed,
sections 91 to 95 of the *Constitution Act, 1867,* contain an
exhaustive listing of legislative powers in Canada. All such
powers are vested either in the federal Parliament or the provincial
Legislatures. Nowhere in those sections, or elsewhere in the
Constitution, is there a hint of any power given to the judiciary to
enact, repeal, vary or amend legislation. Certainly, nothing in the
language of s. 52(1) suggests that courts possess such powers.[101]

---

[100] Professor Pierre-André Coté, one of Canada's pre-eminent statutory
interpretation scholars, argued in 1984 that s. 52(1) is an interpretation
provision in that it renders laws inoperable to the extent they are inconsistent
with the Constitution. The inconsistent laws are not necessarily invalidated, but
rather are left in a moribund state capable of operation if circumstances change
so as to remove the inconsistency. See, P-A. Coté, "La Preseance de la Charte
Canadienne des Droits et Libertes" (1984) 18 *R. J. T. n.s.* 105. Comparing the
differences in the English and French language versions of s. 52(1), Alain
Gautron, argued that the French version buttressed the view that the effect of
s. 52(1) was to hold the inconsistent law in abeyance rather than to nullify it.
See, A. Gautron, "French/English Discrepancies in the Canadian Charter of
Rights & Freedoms" (1982) 12 *Man. L.J.* 220 at p. 231. However, neither
author suggested that these inoperative laws were capable of having legal force
or effect prior to judicial identification of their inconsistency with the
Constitution, i.e., that they were merely voidable.

[101] It might be argued that s. 24(1) of the *Charter*, which empowers courts of
competent jurisdiction to grant "appropriate and just" remedies to persons
whose *Charter* rights or freedoms have been infringed or denied, allows the
courts to legislatively fix constitutionally infirm statutes. However, this
provision has been interpreted, correctly it is submitted, as restricting courts to

Indeed, it would be contrary to the "basic rule that no part of the Constitution can abrogate or diminish another part of the Constitution"[102] to find within the Constitution a judicial power to enact, repeal or amend legislation given that the Constitution clearly and expressly assigns those powers *exclusively* to Parliament and the provincial Legislatures. This point was made emphatically by Justice Southin of the British Columbia Court of Appeal in a 1988 case (although hers became a lonely voice in the Canadian judicial wilderness):

> To do what was done in *R. v. Hamilton* [an Ontario Court of Appeal decision in which the court effectively proclaimed in force in Ontario certain *Criminal Code* amendments which the federal government had deliberately not proclaimed in force in that province] is to amend the 1985 Act [which expressly allowed the government to proclaim the amendments in force in certain provinces only]. To amend is to legislate. To legislate is to usurp the function of Parliament.

> Our political system as it is found in the *Constitution Act, 1867*, confers the power to legislate only upon Parliament and the Legislatures.

> ...

> The executive power is vested in the Sovereign and the power to legislate is vested in Parliament. Neither is vested in the courts.

---

remedies of a judicial nature. Also, as will be explained, the existence, *per se*, of an unconstitutional statute does not infringe or deny any rights or freedoms under the *Charter*. It is *conduct* pursuant to such a statute which may trigger a right to a remedy under s. 24(1).

[102] *Doucet-Boudreau v. Nova Scotia (Minister of Education)*, [2003] 3 S.C.R. 3 at para. 42

> The Charter has not conferred the powers of ss. 91 and 92 upon the courts but has conferred only the power to strike down legislation.

> One ought not to construe the Charter as if it were intended to undo 900 years of constitutional development. I say 900 years for the constitutional history of Canada runs back to the time of William the Conqueror. I do not accept that the framers of the Charter intended that the power to make statutes, which by 1688 the Sovereign could no longer exercise without the concurrence of the Houses of Parliament, should be exercised, 300 years later, by the judges without the concurrence of the Sovereign or either House.

> ...

> What the judges now have, by s. 52 is a power to "dispense" with laws but only if inconsistent with the Charter. That is the extent of the new order.

> With the greatest respect, I say that the judgment of the Ontario Court of Appeal [*in R. v. Hamilton*] is as offensive to our constitutional system as was the King's assertion that, by Divine Right, he could do as he pleased.

> *The power to amend and repeal could have been given to the courts. It was not.* (emphasis added)[103]

Admittedly, when courts properly apply s. 52(1), and refuse to give effect to laws that are inconsistent with the Constitution, the result often *resembles* what would flow from an amendment or repeal of the statute. Resemblance, however, is not identity. Only legislatures can amend or repeal statutes, and it is dangerously misleading to speak of a judicial power to do so.

---

[103] *R. v. Van Vliet,* 1988 Can LII 3281 (BCCA) at para's 106-107, 109-111, 115-117

One of the first (and it appears the last) of Canada's judges to recognize that s. 52(1) is not remedial was Justice Mahoney of the Federal Court of Appeal, writing in dissent in the *Schachter* case:

> In my opinion, s. 52(1) does not provide a "remedy" in any real sense of that word. It states a constitutional fact which no court can ignore when it is invoked in a proceeding and found to apply.[104]

Inexplicably, however, an interpretation provision has been conscripted to serve as the fountainhead for a body of jurisprudence empowering courts to amend – not interpret, but amend – statutes.[105] This body of jurisprudence has been made from whole cloth. It finds no support in the text of the Constitution or in pre-*Charter* case law.[106] It is pure judicial fabrication. The idea of suspending a declaration of constitutional invalidity is also something that the Supreme Court of Canada has invented, notwithstanding its fundamental incongruity with accepted common law principles and authority, and – even more significantly – notwithstanding its inconsistency with the text of the Constitution.

---

[104] [1990] 2 F.C. 129 at p. 164 (FCA)

[105] In distinguishing between interpretation of a statute and its amendment, Lord Hope explained: "Amendment is a legislative act. It is an exercise which must be reserved to Parliament." *R. v. Lambert,* [2002] 2 AC 545 at para. 81

[106] Prior to enactment of the *Charter* in 1982, Canadian courts employed the techniques of severance and reading-in in constitutional cases, but only as a means of interpreting statutes. See, R. Sullivan, *Statutory Interpretation,* (Toronto: Irwin Law, 2nd ed., 2007) at pp. 238-239. Thus, every reasonable effort was made to interpret the impugned statute so as to render it consistent with the Constitution. This, however, is entirely different than what courts have purported to do with their supposed s. 52 remedial powers. They have been used to add or subtract language from a statute with the evident purpose of giving it a meaning different than what was intended by the legislators. An example of this approach is the Supreme Court's decision in *Vriend v. Alberta,* [1998] 1 S.C.R. 493, where the Court purported to add "sexual orientation" to the prohibited grounds of discrimination under Alberta's human rights statute, notwithstanding clear evidence of a legislative intention to exclude such coverage.

6.1   *Responding to Constitutionally Under-Inclusive Laws*

A few case studies will illustrate the conceptual unsoundness of the view that s. 52(1) empowers courts to amend statutes. Take, for example, a statute that is inconsistent with the Constitution's guarantee of equality under the law (s. 15 of the *Charter*) because it denies benefits to a particular group of persons on discriminatory grounds. Such a case came before the Nova Scotia Court of Appeal in *Nova Scotia (Attorney General) v. Phillips.*[107] A statute provided for the payment of welfare benefits to single mothers, but not to single fathers. This was held to be contrary to s. 15, and the issue for the court, at least as it saw it, was whether to strike down the provision entirely, or to read up "mother" to mean "parent." The court held that it would not be appropriate to read up the statute, as this would amount to an improper judicial usurpation of the legislative role. Therefore, it purported to strike down the section, with the anomalous result that single mothers were thereby denied the benefits which the legislature had clearly intended that they receive.

The Supreme Court of Canada, in the *Schachter* case, referred disapprovingly to the result reached by the court in *Phillips*, describing it as "equity with a vengeance." A preferable approach, in its view, would have been either to extend the benefits to single fathers, by reading up the statute, or to declare the section to be invalid, but then to suspend the declaration of invalidity so as to allow the legislature time to decide how to amend the statute to bring it into compliance with the *Charter* (while at the same time preserving the entitlements of single mothers). It is submitted, however, that neither of these alternatives was conceptually sound. Reading up the statute was not a legally supportable option. No authority exists under the Constitution or the common law for a court to amend a statute. Was the court then left with no option but to declare the statute invalid in its entirety, with the anomalous result of depriving single mothers of their benefits? That draconian result clearly was not dictated, nor permitted, by

---

[107] 1986 CanLII 3941 (NSSC)

s. 52(1), which provides that a law is of no force or effect only to the extent of its inconsistency with the Constitution.

There was nothing inconsistent with the Constitution about providing welfare benefits to single mothers. The inconsistency arose out of what was omitted from the statute – the provision of equal benefits to single fathers. To that extent, and that extent only, the law was inconsistent with the Constitution. However, this provided no basis for invalidating the benefits provided to mothers which were themselves perfectly legal. What it did provide was a basis for single fathers to complain that the government had infringed or denied their constitutional right to equal protection and benefit of the law, thus giving them grounds for application for relief under s. 24(1) of the *Charter*:

> 24 (1) Anyone whose rights or freedoms, as guaranteed by this Charter, have been infringed or denied may apply to a court of competent jurisdiction to obtain such remedy as the court considers appropriate and just in the circumstances.

Great care must be taken not to confuse or conflate rights and remedies. The denial of benefits to single fathers constituted a denial of their *Charter* rights, and this provided the fathers with grounds to request a remedy, but it did not entitle them to any specific remedy or any remedy at all. There are several recognized doctrines which limit remedies against officials who act in good faith reliance on what they believe is a valid law, but which is later adjudged invalid.[108] Also, the case law tells us that it is usually not appropriate to give s. 24(1) remedies to victims of rights violations until after the unconstitutionality of the relevant law has been identified in accordance with s. 52(1).[109] However, a person whose rights have been violated should either be granted

---

[108] See, for example, *Welbridge Holdings Ltd. v. Greater Winnipeg*, [1971] S.C.R. 957; *Central Canada Potash Co. v. Gov't of Saskatchewan*, [1979] 1 S.C.R. 42 at p. 90; *Guimond v. Quebec (Attorney General)*, [1996] 3 S.C.R. 347; *Mackin v. New Brunswick (Minister of Finance)*, [2002] 1 S.C.R. 405
[109] See Part 3 of this essay, "Trying to Right the Ship" at pp. 183-184.

or not granted a remedy in an open and honest manner. A court should not rationalize and obscure its decision not to grant a remedy by denying on spurious and unjustifiable grounds the very existence of the violated right. A decision to deny fathers a remedy, whether for violations of rights occurring before or after the court identified the constitutional infirmity, is fundamentally different than a decision that a rights violation did not occur. The job of s. 52(1) is to guide the court in ascertaining the law. Does a right exist and has it been violated? Only after that question has been answered – after s. 52(1) has done its work – does the Court need to consider what remedy, if any, should be provided for any rights violation so found.

Given the unavailability of a power to amend the statute by reading up, and the anomaly of striking down the law entirely with attendant "equity with a vengeance" consequences, could a court give the "remedy" of striking down the law, but suspending its declaration of invalidity for a temporary period while the legislature decided what to do about the law's constitutional infirmity? When carefully examined, it can be seen that this would represent not the grant, but rather the denial of a remedy. A court that deals with an underinclusive statute, like the one in *Phillips*, by declaring it invalid and then suspending its declaration of invalidity, provides no remedy.[110] To the contrary, it turns on its head the time-honoured maxim: where there's a right, there must be a remedy. Its answer to a person who has

---

[110] One author, writing from the perspective of Hong Kong constitutional law, says this about suspended declarations: "This can hardly be considered as a remedy but rather the withholding, and, in the expectation, denial in due course, of a remedy." P.Y. Lo, *Judicial Consideration of the Basic Law*, PhD Thesis, University of Hong Kong, 2011, at p. 194. Professor Roach captured the point nicely in this description of what the court effectively says to the successful litigant when granting the "remedy" of a suspended declaration:

> Congratulations, you have won your case. Even though it has taken many years and yours savings, you will not receive an immediate remedy because we are going to give the government a year to decide what to do.

K. Roach, *The Supreme Court on Trial: Judicial Activism or Democratic Dialogue*, (Toronto: Irwin Law, rev'd ed., 2016) at p. 226

established a violation of a constitutional right is to deem the relevant substantive law to be different than it actually is. Thus, the substantive right is effectively extinguished (at least during the suspension period and permanently if the legislature enacts "remedial" legislation to that effect). The new maxim becomes – where there's a right, deem the right not to exist and let the legislators decide if there should be a remedy. As will be argued later, this is an abdication by the courts of their duty under s. 24(1) to provide such remedies to victims of rights violations as it – the court hearing the particular case – considers appropriate and just in the circumstances.[111]

To be clear, there may be good reasons not to provide remedies for rights violations in certain circumstances, but that result should not be accomplished by twisting the law to fit the more comfortable or convenient conclusion that no rights were violated. The only purpose served by the suspension of a declaration of invalidity is to provide the government with a judicial hall pass allowing it to continue violating rights during the suspension period, and allowing it to decide what, if any, recourse should be made available to victims of such rights violations. This is not a remedy at all.

6.2   Reading Down Statutes

Courts also speak of using s. 52(1) to provide a remedy of severance or reading down, whereby words are removed from a statute to make it conform to the Constitution. This suggests that a court is able to excise words from a statute, which, of course, only a legislative body can actually do. "Amendment is a legislative act. It is an exercise which must be reserved to Parliament."[112] This, again, illustrates the difficulties that can arise when metaphorical shortcuts are used to describe processes and events. When it is said that words are severed from a statute, this is not literally true. What actually happens is that the court

---

[111] See Part 3 of this essay, "Trying to Right the Ship" at pp. 185-189
[112] *R. v. Lambert*, [2002] 2 AC 545 at para. 81 per Lord Hope

ignores the language of a statute to the extent that it purports to require or permit a result that would be inconsistent with what the Constitution requires. This is not a remedial exercise. It is simply what courts do when they ascertain what the law is and then apply it accordingly. Kevin Walsh of the University of Richmond has described the process as follows:

> "Excision" is, of course, only a metaphor. There is no judicial Exacto knife that courts use to excise words from the statute books. When a court holds part of a statute unconstitutional, it issues a judgment saying so (and, in some cases, an injunction against its future enforcement). By virtue of precedent and preclusion, this judgment and the reasoning in support of it prevent the unconstitutional part of the statute from having legal effect going forward. Nothing about the actual text of the statute changes as a direct consequence of judicial action.[113]

Consider, for example, the case of *R. v. Hess; R. v. Nguyen*,[114] where the Court decided that a provision of the *Criminal Code* which purported to take away a *mens rea* defence from the accused was contrary to the guarantee of fundamental justice under s. 7 of the *Charter*. The impugned provision made it an offence for a male person to have sexual intercourse with a female person under the age of fourteen years "whether or not he believes she is fourteen years of age or more." Having decided that deprivation of a *mens rea* defence based on mistaken belief as to age was unconstitutional, the Court then turned its mind to what it characterized as a question of remedy. Rather than declare the entire section invalid, which would have resulted in the absurdity of it not being a crime for a man to knowingly have intercourse with an underaged female, the Court referred to s. 52(1) as the basis for its declaration that the words "whether or not he believes

---

[113] K.C. Walsh, "Partial Unconstitutionality" (2010) 85 *N.Y.U.L. Rev.* 738 at p. 747
[114] [1990] 2 S.C.R. 906

that she is fourteen years of age or more" are of no force or effect, and so should be shorn from the section.

The correctness of the result in *Hess/Nguyen* cannot be doubted. However, the Court's analysis of the issue as one of remedy was unsatisfactory. No question of remedy arose in that case. The issue was simply one of deciding which of two inconsistent laws should be followed. One law was section s. 7 of the *Charter* and its guarantee of fundamental justice. The other law was the direction in the subject section that a *mens rea* defence be denied. Given this inconsistency, s. 52(1) directed that primacy be given to the Constitution. This required the Court to ignore the statute's direction to deny the accused's *mens rea* defence. This was not a question of remedy, but of ascertaining the law. By characterizing the issue as one of remedy, the Court perpetuated the myth that s. 52(1) empowers courts to amend statutes.

The Supreme Court has from time to time made contradictory statements about a judicial power to amend statutes in order to make them consistent with the Constitution. Notwithstanding decisions, such as *Hess/Nguyen*, which apparently recognize such a power, the Court has also denied that it can do this:

> Although this Court *must not add anything to legislation or delete anything from it* in order to make it consistent with the *Charter*, there is no doubt in my mind that it should also not interpret legislation that is open to more than one interpretation so as to make it inconsistent with the *Charter* and hence of no force or effect. (emphasis added)[115]

---

[115] *Slaight Communications Inc. v. Davidson*, [1989] 1 S.C.R. 1038 at p. 1078. This statement has been repeated by the Court in numerous other cases: *Committee for the Commonwealth of Canada*, [1991] 1 S.C.R. 139 at p. 163; *R. v. Swain*, [1991] 1 S.C.R. 933 at p. 1010; *Osborne v. Canada (Treasury Board)*, [1991] 2 S.C.R. 69 at p. 102; *Symes v. Canada*, [1993] 4 S.C.R. 695 at pp. 751-752; *Ontario v. Canadian Pacific Ltd.*, [1995] 2 S.C.R. 1031 at para. 12; *Eldridge v. British Columbia (Attorney General)*, [1997] 3 S.C.R. 624 at para. 22; *R. v. Monney*, [1999] 1 S.C.R. 652 at para. 31; *R. v. G(B)*, [1999] 2

6.3   Reading In or Adding to Statutes

Another instructive case is *Vriend v. Alberta*,[116] where the Supreme Court purported to add "sexual orientation" to the prohibited grounds of discrimination under Alberta's human rights statute. It did so notwithstanding clear evidence of a legislative intent to exclude such coverage.[117] This reading-in remedy was a clear example of judicial statutory amendment, ostensibly pursuant to s. 52(1). "For all intents and purposes, the Court amended the statute."[118] The Court framed the issue as a choice, either to read "sexual orientation" into the statute, or to strike down the statute in its entirety, leaving Alberta with no human rights law. This is another example of the "equity with a vengeance" dichotomy which courts often present as justification for adding things to constitutionally underinclusive statutes.[119] It

---

S.C.R. 475 at para. 42; *Winko v. British Columbia (Forensic Psychiatric Institute)*, [1999] 2 S.C.R. 625 at para. 124; *Lavallee, Rackel & Heintz v. Canada (Attorney General)*, [2002] 3 S.C.R. 209 at para. 55

[116] [1998] 1 S.C.R. 493

[117] In *Winnipeg School Division No. 1 v. Craton*, [1985] 2 S.C.R. 150 at para. 8, the Court referred to the special nature of human rights legislation and opined that "it may not be altered, amended, or repealed, nor may exceptions be created to its provisions, save by clear *legislative* pronouncement." (emphasis added)

[118] B. Bird, "The Unbroken Supremacy of the Canadian Constitution" (2018) 55 *Alta. L. Rev.* 755 at p. 771

[119] Sharpe and Roach presented *Vriend* as involving an all or nothing choice between adding sexual orientation or invalidating Alberta's entire human rights statute:

> Reading in is a controversial technique as the Court appears to be exercising a legislative role. However, given the alternative of striking down the law in its entirety, it seems inevitable that reading in should be permitted in certain situations. To strike down an entire statute because it fails to extend its benefit to a group that is relatively small in relation to the overall purpose and application of the statute would seem to constitute an even more serious interference by the judiciary with legislative choice. Another alternative, examined below in Section B(4)(f), is to strike down the under-inclusive benefit, but to suspend the effect of the declaration for six to eighteen months in order to give the

is always a false dichotomy – an *in terrorem* constitutional bogeyman. The text of s. 52(1) does not require or permit an all or nothing approach. It states that a law is of no force only to the extent of its inconsistency with the Constitution. To the extent a law is not inconsistent with the Constitution, s. 52(1) has nothing to say about it. It must be allowed to operate in accordance with its terms.[120] The subject Alberta statute prohibited discrimination on many grounds – race, religion, age, and so forth – and allowing those prohibitions to operate violated no provisions of the Constitution. The statute's infirmity was that it did not prohibit discrimination on the basis of sexual orientation and to that extent, and that extent only, it was of no force or effect.

However, what does it mean to say that something that does not exist (a prohibition against discrimination because of sexual orientation) is of no force or effect? It means nothing at all in terms of the content of the statute. The instruction of s. 52(1) is to ignore law that is inconsistent with the Constitution, but that instruction simply has nothing to bite on in situations of omission because it is surrealistic to speak of ignoring that which does not

---

legislature an opportunity to decide whether to extend or reduce the benefit or to repeal the benefit altogether.
R.J. Sharpe and K. Roach, *The Charter of Rights and Freedoms* (Toronto, Irwin Law, 2013) at p. 423

[120] This, however, has not been the practice of the Supreme Court of Canada in cases involving mandatory minimum sentences. Instead of asking whether application of the statutory mandatory minimum would contravene the particular accused's constitutional rights, the Court asks whether there are any reasonably foreseeable situations where the statute could operate unconstitutionally vis-à-vis a hypothetical accused. If such a reasonable hypothetical is identified, the statute is not applied to anyone, even to those whose rights clearly would not be infringed or denied. See, for example: *R. v. Nur*, [2015] 1 S.C.R. 773; *R. v. Smith*, [1987] 1 S.C.R. 1045. This line of cases is very difficult to square with the language of s. 52(1) which directs that laws are of no force or effect *to the extent* of their inconsistency with the Constitution. To the extent that laws are not inconsistent with the Constitution, no authority is given to courts to refuse to apply them. A case in which the Court actually understood and properly applied s. 52(1) to a statute which was capable of both constitutional and unconstitutional applications is *R. v. Sharpe*, [2001] 1 S.C.R. 45.

exist. This point was clearly recognized in the 1970's by Wiltraut Rupp-v. Brunneck, a justice of Germany's Federal Constitutional Court, who observed that in the case of an underinclusive statute "it is technically impossible to declare a Nothing void."[121] She went on to explain that in one case a court did "choose the surrealistic way of declaring the statutory gap itself void, but later corrected itself."[122] The same point was made in 1987 by the President of the German Federal Constitutional Court who commented that "it is rather difficult to construe an omission as 'void'."[123]

However, this does not mean that the Court's determination that it was unconstitutional to omit sexual orientation from the human rights statute was of no legal consequence. To the contrary, it provided the necessary foundation for applications by aggrieved persons for appropriate and just remedies under s. 24(1) of the *Charter*. The power of s. 24(1) is vast. As Justice McIntyre stated in *R. v. Mills*: "It is difficult to imagine language which could give the court wider and less fettered discretion."[124] Although the courts could not have directly ordered Alberta to amend its statute, as this would have offended the Constitution's division of powers and, thus, not been a proper judicial remedy, they could have given a broad range of other remedies, including damage awards on a class action basis. These powerful and readily

---

[121] W. Rupp-v. Brunneck, "Admonitory Functions of Constitutional Courts – Germany" (1972) 20 *Am. J. Comp. L.* 387 at p. 393

[122] *ibid.* at p. 393

[123] W. Zeidler, "The Federal Constitutional Court of the Federal Republic of Germany: Decisions on the Constitutionality of Legal Norms" (1986) 62 *Notre Dame L. Rev.* 504 at p. 511. Justice Southin of the British Columbia Court of Appeal also recognized this in *R. v. Van Vliet*, 1988 Can LII 3281 (BCCA) at para. 101, where she rejected the argument that courts have the power to ameliorate the inequality arising from the absence of a law by deeming the law to exist: "But when as here what is said to be inconsistent with the Charter is not law but lack of law, how can the courts grant a remedy such as the one sought?" See further quotations from *Van Vliet, supra,* at pp. 37-38.

[124] *R. v. Mills*, [1986] 1 SCR 863 at para. 278. This has been repeated by the Court on numerous occasions: *Doucet-Boudreau v. Nova Scotia (Minister of Education)*, [2003] 3 S.C.R. 3 at para's 24, 50, 52; *R. v. Bjelland*, [2009] 2 S.C.R. 651 at para. 53; *Vancouver (City) v. Ward*, [2010] 2 SCR 28 at para. 17.

available remedies would have made the Alberta government painfully aware of the cost of not bringing its laws into line with the Constitution.[125]

The crucial point is that s. 52(1) speaks only to the substantive content of the law, and not to remedies. It concerns the ascertainment of the law, and not the creation of new or different laws. Remedies, on the other hand, only become relevant after s. 52(1) has done its work. By interpreting s. 52(1) as a remedial provision, however, courts have arrogated to themselves a power to change the substantive content of the law. Courts are not allowed to do this under Canada's Constitution. Nonetheless, they do just that in a number of ways, including through the issuance of so-called suspended declarations of invalidity.

7. Rights are Rights are Rights

The law relating to constitutional invalidity in Canada is in a woeful state of confusion. A great deal of the confusion arises from the fact that courts engage in results-oriented analysis of the issues. They conclude, often for good reasons, that a remedy is not appropriate in the circumstances, and then backfill their way to a justifying conclusion that no rights violation has occurred. Sometimes this is accomplished by prospective decision-making. Often it results from the court's use of a so-called suspended declaration of invalidity which effectively ordains the law to be different than it actually is. By declining to give their decisions retroactive effect, courts create a mirage wherein it appears that complainants' rights have not been denied.

This can be illustrated by looking at *Canada (Attorney General) v. Hislop*,[126] where the Supreme Court considered whether the government was entitled to deny survivors of same-sex relationships benefits under the Canada Pension Plan for the

---

[125] Of course, Alberta might have chosen, as the Constitution permits, to exercise its s. 33 override powers so as to exclude its human rights statute from the reach of the *Charter*.

[126] [2007] 1 S.C.R. 429

period between the effective date of s. 15 of the Charter in 1985, and the Court's decision in a 1999 case which recognized same-sex partners as constitutionally entitled to equal protection and benefit of the law. The Court concluded that the government was lawfully entitled to deny such benefits. The majority tried mightily to explain its decision on the basis that the Court's decision in the earlier case, *M. v. H.*[127] – that sexual orientation is a *Charter*-protected right – was not retroactive. For the majority, the question was whether the *M. v. H.* decision represented a sufficient shift or change in the law to justify treating it as prospective only. In other words, the majority asked whether there was a denial of the *Charter* rights of a person whose same-sex partner died in 1985 but who received no survivor benefits until remedial legislation was enacted in 2000, whereas a similarly situated heterosexual survivor would have received such benefits since 1985 (or earlier). The answer to this relatively easy question was made difficult by the majority judges because they conflated rights and remedies. Instead of acknowledging that there had been a rights violation – and going to the heart of the matter which was whether the government's refusal to provide retroactive relief was "appropriate and just" under s. 24(1) – they asked, and answered "yes" to the question of whether the Court's decision in *M v. H.* was prospective only. That was not the correct question.

As Justice Bastarache recognized in his concurring decision, s. 52(1) mandates that an unconstitutional law is invalid from the moment of its enactment. "The Constitution exists independently of judicial decisions and, as such, any law which is inconsistent with it is invalidated from the moment the law came into effect."[128] The Court has no say about it – no discretion.[129] That is

---

[127] [1999] 2 S.C.R. 3

[128] [2007] 1 S.C.R. 429 at para. 138

[129] In fact, this was recognized by a unanimous court in the following year when it was written by Chief Justice McLachlin that s. 52(1) "confers no discretion on judges." *R. v. Ferguson*, [2008] 1 S.C.R. 96 at para. 35. But *contra* see the British Columbia Court of Appeal's 2016 decision in *Jaswal* which is discussed *infra* at footnote 136, page 53, where s. 52 was (dubiously) regarded as conferring discretion on judges.

what s. 52(1) requires. The proper question for the Court was not whether there had been a rights violation – clearly there had been – but whether in all of the circumstances the government should be required to pay retroactive benefits to same-sex survivors. In the result, both the majority and Justice Bastarache agreed that the government should not be required to do so. However, the majority arrived at this result by concluding, erroneously, that its decision in *M. v. H.* was prospective only, so that the plaintiff's constitutional rights had not been violated. In this way, the existence of a constitutional right was improperly relegated to the region of judicial remedial discretion. The question of whether the constitutional rights of same-sex surviving spouses had been infringed or denied was made to depend on whether the Court considered itself to be operating inside or outside the so-called Blackstonian paradigm. In disagreeing with the majority's approach, Justice Bastarache explained that the Constitution exists independently of judicial interpretations. Therefore, rights under the Constitution do not come into existence only if, as, and when courts decide to recognize them:

> For these reasons, I cannot accept my colleagues' critique of the declaratory approach as a basis for denying retroactive relief. As will be explained below, there are important reasons for denying retroactive relief in certain circumstances. I am largely in agreement with my colleagues on what they are. But I cannot agree that they have anything to do with the success or failure of the "Blackstonian paradigm" in the context of constitutional law.
>
> The dangers of my colleagues' approach are adequately evidenced when applied to the claimants in this appeal. The starting point of their analysis is that there was a substantial change in the law between 1985, when s. 15(1) of the *Charter* came into force, and this Court's decision in *M. v. H.,* 1999 CanLII 686 (SCC), [1999] 2 S.C.R. 3. The implication is that the right of same-sex spouses not to be excluded from survivor benefits did not form part of the Constitution until 1999. To put it bluntly, s. 15(1) of the *Charter* did not extend to same-

sex couples until this Court said it did. I note that my colleagues are not simply saying that this Court's *interpretation* of the Constitution had changed between 1985 and 1999. If that were the case, it would be sufficient to base their denial of retroactive relief solely on the good faith reliance of the government. Instead, by relying on a critique of the declaratory theory and the "living free" doctrine, my colleagues assert, in essence, that the Constitution actually changed between 1985 and 1999 and that the claimants, unlike other Canadians, were not entitled to its protection in 1985. Such an approach runs counter to the spirit of the *Charter* and should not be countenanced.[130]

Concern about the conflation of rights and remedies is not merely a question of form versus substance. It matters a great deal that courts have fallen into a habit of responding to remedial questions by denying the existence of rights. This is a dubious practice because it leads the courts down the treacherous path of mistaking judgment and discretion. Everyone interested in understanding the concept of the rule of law should read, and then read again, Professor Christopher Forsyth's 2013 paper "The Rock and the Sand: Jurisdiction and Remedial Discretion."[131] The title of Forsyth's paper pays homage to Lord Shaw's famous warning that: "To remit the maintenance of constitutional right to the region of judicial discretion is to shift the foundations of freedom from the rock to the sand."[132] Quoting from Professor Wade's classic administrative law treatise,[133] Forsyth begins his article by juxtaposing the question of whether a right exists with the question of whether a court, often as a matter of discretion, should give a remedy for violation of the right:

> This article emerges from the tension between two conflicting fundamental propositions in modern

---

[130] [2007] 1 S.C.R. 429 at para's 145-146
[131] Paper No. 31/2013 of the University of Cambridge Faculty of Law Legal Research Paper Series, retrievable at www.law.cam.ac.uk/ssrn
[132] *Scott v. Scott*, [1913] AC 417 at p. 477
[133] H.W.R. Wade and C. Forsyth, *Administrative Law* (10th ed., 2009) at p. 599

administrative law. On the one hand there is the proposition summed up in these words: "There are grave objections to giving the courts discretion to decide whether governmental action is lawful or unlawful: the citizen is entitled to resist unlawful action as a matter of right, and to live under the rule of law, not the rule of discretion." And on the other hand there is the proposition that all the remedies available in the application for judicial review – the quashing order, the mandatory order, the prohibiting order, the declaration and the injunction – are discretionary. It follows that an applicant who establishes that an impugned decision is legally flawed may, none the less, be denied the fruits of that victory by the judge's refusal to grant an appropriate remedy.[134]

The question of whether a right exists is one of legal judgment; the court exercises no discretion as to what the law is. Rights are rights are rights. That is the rock. Then there is discretion, which may come into play with respect to remedy if a rights violation is found. That is the sand. Professor Wade explained it in this way:

> The true scope of discretion is in the law of remedies, where it operates within narrow and recognized limits and is far less objectionable. If the courts were to undermine the principle of *ultra vires* by making it discretionary, no victim of an excess or abuse of power could be sure that the law would protect him.[135]

It is very dangerous to allow the sand of discretion to erode and supplant the rock of the law. Remedial discretion should not be allowed any role in the determination of substantive rights. There is an immense difference between withholding a remedy for breach of a constitutional right, and refusing to recognize the existence of the right.[136] A person whose rights are being violated,

---

[134] C. Forsyth, "The Rock and the Sand", *supra*, footnote 131 at para. 1

[135] H.W.R. Wade, *Administrative Law*, 6th edn. (Oxford, 1988) at p. 354

[136] In *Jaswal v. British Columbia (Superintendent of Motor Vehicles)*, 2016 BCCA 245 (CanLII) at para. 71, the British Columbia Court of Appeal held (dubiously) that the court below had exercised a discretion as to whether its

but is refused a remedy by the court, deserves an honest explanation. This is a matter of fundamental justice. It is an emanation of the rule of the law. By baldly declaring that it is suspending its declaration of invalidity (with the unspoken further incident of a declaration of deemed validity), the court seeks to sweep the constitutional violation under the rug. It obfuscates the true nature of its actions.

Once a court convinces itself that it has a discretion to decide that the law should be one thing yesterday or today, and another thing tomorrow – as when prospective overruling is employed – it is but a small step to decide that it also has the discretion to decree that the law shall temporarily be different than it actually is. That is the Canadian suspended declaration of invalidity.

8. In Rem versus In Personam – Down the Rabbit Hole

Upon whom is a finding of inconsistency with the Constitution binding? Does it bind only the parties to the proceeding (*in personam* and with *inter partes* effect), or does it bind the world at large (*in rem* and with *erga omnes* effect)?

First, it is important to be clear in differentiating decisions' *stare decisis* and *res judicata* effects.

The doctrine of *stare decisis* or precedent provides that decisions of a court higher up the judicial hierarchy will bind lower courts within the same jurisdiction. The lower court will be required to follow the higher court's decision in subsequent cases unless the subsequent case can be meaningfully distinguished.

---

declaration of invalidity was retroactive, i.e., whether the petitioners' constitutional rights had been violated. Kent Roach appears also to accept the notion that courts acting under s. 52(1) are able to exercise discretion as to existence of rights. (K. Roach, "Principled Remedial Discretion Under the Charter," (2004) 25 *S.C.L.R. (2d)* 101 at p. 105). It is submitted that by (erroneously) viewing s. 52(1) as a remedial provision, the idea of courts exercising discretion as to whether a person's rights have been violated becomes more palatable (though no less wrong).

Res judicata, on the other hand, operates as an estoppel to preclude relitigation of questions already finally determined by a court of competent jurisdiction. The reach of *res judicata* may depend on whether the decision in question was *in personam* or *in rem*. An *in personam* decision binds only the parties to the proceeding and their privies (i.e., persons associated with the parties). It is said to have *inter partes* effect. An *in rem* decision, on the other hand, binds the world at large. It is said to have *erga omnes* effect. A decision is generally regarded as *in rem* when it concerns the legal status of a person or thing. This is how the Supreme Court of Canada has described it:

> A judgment *in rem* is an adjudication pronounced upon the status of some particular subject-matter by a tribunal having competent authority for that purpose. Such an adjudication being a solemn declaration from the proper and accredited quarter that the status of the thing adjudicated upon is as declared, concludes all persons from saying that the status of the thing adjudicated upon was not such as declared by the adjudication.[137]

Some examples of judgments that have been held to be *in rem* relate to: the ownership of land; determination of an interest in a matrimonial home; an easement; location of a boundary; declaration of paternity or maternity; a divorce decree; and, validity of a treaty.[138]

Are decisions as to the constitutionality of statutes *in personam* or *in rem*, and why does it matter? Let us first consider the second question. It matters whether a final decision of a court is *in rem* because, if it is, it will potentially have more effect than merely as a precedent under *stare decisis* doctrine; it will bind everyone in the jurisdiction, and all courts, including courts at the same level and even a higher level in the judicial pecking

---

[137] *Sleeth v. Hurlburt* (1896), 25 S.C.R. 620 at p. 630
[138] D. Lange, *The Doctrine of Res Judicata in Canada*, (Toronto: LexisNexis, 4th ed., 2015) at pp. 487-488

order. Remember that *stare decisis* is only binding on lower courts. An *in rem* determination of a matter, on the other hand, if it is final and not set aside on appeal, binds all courts. This is of much practical importance in the constitutional field because it often happens that one judge declares that a statute either is or is not inconsistent with the Constitution, and the question arises whether other judges in the same jurisdiction are bound to follow that decision even if they disagree with it. Under *stare decisis* doctrine, the judge of co-ordinate jurisdiction would not be bound (although as a matter of judicial comity they will generally follow it unless they consider it to be plainly wrong). However, *in rem* determinations are more powerful. Not only do they bind courts of co-ordinate jurisdiction, they also bind higher courts (except for a court acting on appeal from the specific *in rem* determination in question). Therefore, if a judge of a provincial superior court makes an *in rem* decision, which is not appealed, that decision, regardless of its merits, will bind not only the province's court of appeal, but also the Supreme Court of Canada. Thus, it can matter a great deal whether a decision on the constitutionality of a statute is *in rem* or *in personam*.

There is no clear answer in Canada to the question of how constitutional decisions should properly be characterized. The traditional view seems to have been that unlike decisions on the validity of municipal by-laws which are often regarded as *in rem*, decisions on the constitutionality of statutes should be regarded as *in personam*. Thus, except for the parties to the particular proceeding, they have force only as precedents under *stare decisis* doctrine.

This issue arose before the Supreme Court of Canada in *Emms v. The Queen.*[139] A section of the *Public Service Employment Regulations,* upon which the government's appeal to the Supreme Court of Canada depended, had been declared invalid in another case (*Ouimet v. The Queen*).[140] The declaration of invalidity in

---

[139] [1979] 2 S.C.R. 1148
[140] [1979] 1 F.C. 55

Ouimet had been affirmed on appeal to the Federal Court of Appeal, but the government had not sought to appeal that decision to the Supreme Court of Canada. Thus, the question in *Emms* was whether for *res judicata* purposes, the Federal Court of Appeal's decision in *Ouimet* was final and binding on the world at large (*in rem*), or just on the parties to that particular proceeding (*in personam*).

The Court in *Emms* concluded that it did not have to decide the point because it was convinced that the Federal Court of Appeal was correct in its decision that the impugned regulation was invalid. Only if it had doubted the correctness of that decision would it have been necessary for it to decide whether it was in any event bound by it because of a presumed *in rem* quality. After referring to authorities holding that decisions quashing municipal by-laws are *in rem*,[141] Justice Pigeon posed the question of whether declarations of invalidity of subordinate regulations should be treated as by-laws are treated or as declarations relating to statutes are treated, i.e., *only as precedents*:

> Should the situation be viewed in the same way as in the case of declarations of invalidity of statutes which seem to have always been considered only as precedents?

> After anxious consideration, I find it unnecessary to express an opinion on this difficult question because, assuming the respondent is entitled to ask that the judgment in *Ouimet* be overruled, I find no reason to do so.[142]

Emms was followed by the Federal Court of Appeal in a 1989 case:

> The principle that judgments bind only the parties to them applies to declaratory judgments as to others. As

---

[141] *Corporation du Village de Deschenes v. Loveys*, [1936] S.C.R. 351; *Dilworth v. Town of Bala*, [1955] S.C.R. 284
[142] *Emms v. The Queen*, [1979] 2 S.C.R. 1148 at pp. 1161-1162

> far as third parties are concerned, a judgment has only the force of a precedent, and in this regard its *ratio decidendi* has as much authority as its disposition: see in this regard the remarks of Pigeon J. in the case of *Emms v. The Queen* (1979), 1979 CanLII 245 (SCC), 102 D.L.R. (3d) 193 at pp. 201-2, [1979] 2 S.C.R. 1148, 29 N.R. 156.[143]

Justice Pigeon cited no authority in *Emms* for his view that declarations of invalidity of statutes are to be considered only from the perspective of *stare decisis* (and, thus, not as *in rem*). A review of the authorities provides no clear answer to this question, but it is submitted that if the Court were to think the issues through, it would likely conclude that the implications of viewing such decisions as *in rem* would be intolerable. Several courts and commentators have noted the potential anomalies which could result if such decisions were *in rem*. In a British Columbia case, the judge refused to treat as *in rem* a previous decision in a case involving different parties where an enactment had been held constitutionally valid:

> If a judicial decision deciding the constitutionality of taxing legislation is to be considered as a judgment *in rem*, the results could be remarkable. If I, as a trial judge, make such a determination and that judgment is not appealed, then it would stand against all persons not privy to the decision and the decision could not thus be later tested at the appellate level. While the definition of a judgment *in rem* appears straight forward, the determination of whether a judgment is a judgment *in rem* or *in personam* is not clear. There has been no decision cited to me by counsel or of which I have been able to locate as to whether a judgment on constitutional issues can be a judgment *in rem*.... In these circumstances, I am not prepared to find that the decision of the Supreme Court of Canada in *Allard* to

---

[143] *Poirier v. Canada (Minister of Veteran Affairs)*, 1989 CanLII 5208 (FCA) at para. 18

be a judgment *in rem*. Rather it is a binding decision
unless it can be distinguished on its facts.[144]

If constitutional decisions are *in rem*, a decision of any judge of a
provincial superior court adjudging a law valid or invalid,
regardless of the merits of the decision or the quality of counsels'
arguments, would be binding upon all other courts within the
province, including the court of appeal (other than on direct
appeal from that specific decision). Indeed, even the Supreme
Court of Canada would be bound by an incorrect *in rem*
constitutional decision which had not been appealed. The
anomaly of such a situation was commented on very critically by
one author: [translation] "[I]t would be unacceptable for the
Supreme Court to be muzzled by the decision of a lower court on
a constitutional question".[145] Donald Lange has said this on the
point:

> One factor in considering whether a decision is a
> judgment *in rem* may be the actual appeal review of
> that determination. If the parties themselves do not
> appeal the decision, which determines an earlier
> decision to be a judgment *in rem*, then the earlier
> decision is conclusive against the whole world. The
> validity of that judgment *in rem* cannot later be tested
> at the appellate level by nonparties who have no right
> to appeal. With this proposition in mind, one court has
> held that a judgment on constitutional issues is not a
> judgment *in rem*.[146]

Similarly, while acknowledging that authority could be found
both for and against characterizing constitutional decisions as *in*

---

[144] *Coquitlam (City of) v. Construction Aggregates Ltd.*, 1998 CanLII 1910
(BCSC) at para. 17, aff'd 2000 BCCA 301 (CanLII), and followed in *Withler
v. Canada (Attorney General)*, 2002 BCSC 820 (CanLII) at para's 43-48
[145] S. Letourneau, "L'Autorite d'Un Jugement Prononcant
l'Inconstitutionnalite d'Une Loi" (1989) 23 *R.J.T. n.s.* 173 at p. 182
[146] D. Lange, *The Doctrine of Res Judicata in Canada*, (Toronto: LexisNexis,
4th ed., 2015) at p. 487, citing *Coquitlam (City of) v. Construction Aggregates
Ltd.*, 1998 CanLII 1910 (BCSC)

rem, an Australian author expressed concerns about the troubling implications of *in rem* characterization:

> While it may be possible to characterize a judgment in a suit for a declaration as to the validity of legislation as a judgment *in rem* ... the consequences of so characterising the judgment would be that, subject to the exercise of any rights of appeal, the judgment would be unassailable, no matter how inadequately the case had been argued and no matter whether the resolution of it was "right" or "wrong".[147]

On the assumption that the estoppel effects of decisions cannot cut across Canada's provincial borders,[148] another anomaly that arises from the *in rem* characterization of constitutional decisions is the prospect of federal laws – in particular, criminal laws – being different in different provinces.[149] Not only would this be inconsistent with s. 8 of the *Criminal Code* of Canada: "The provisions of this Act apply throughout Canada ...", it would also seem incongruent with the very concept of federalism which the Supreme Court has identified as one of the fundamental underlying principles of Canada's Constitution.[150] Although it is recognized that, in the absence of a Supreme Court of Canada decision on the point, *interpretations* of federal law may vary between provinces,[151] this is different than substantive federal law

---

[147] E. Campbell, "Relitigation in Government Cases: A Study of the Use of Estoppel Principles in Public Law Litigation" (1994) 20 *Monash Univ. L. Rev.* 21 at p. 36

[148] Although it is debatable, as a matter of principle, whether the *res judicata* effects of decisions on questions of federal law should stop at provincial borders, this seems to be the accepted view. (See, *R. v. Pete,* 1998 CanLII 6016 (BCCA); *R. v. Moraes,* 1998 CanLII 15094 (BCSC))

[149] While it has been recognized that Parliament is competent to establish different rules in different provinces (see, *R. v. Turpin,* [1989] 1 S.C.R. 1296), this would be the result of deliberate legislative policy-making. It is another matter entirely for the courts in the various provinces to be entitled to establish, otherwise than through the operation of *stare decisis,* criminal law that is uniquely applicable in just one province.

[150] *Reference re Secession of Quebec,* [1998] 2 S.C.R. 217 at para's 55-60

[151] *Wolf v. the Queen,* [1975] 2 S.C.R. 107 at p.109

actually *being* different from province to province as a result of judicial decisions.[152] The Quebec Court of Appeal has described such a situation as "legally unacceptable":

> It is true that, as a general rule, the judgments of the courts of a province have no extraterritorial effect. It would be legally unacceptable, however, in a constitutional area involving the Attorney General of Canada regarding a matter within the jurisdiction of the federal Parliament, for a provision to be inapplicable in one province and in force in all of the others.[153]

Moreover, although it seems to be assumed that when the Supreme Court of Canada finally determines the constitutional question, its decision would then apply throughout Canada (as no doubt would be the case according to *stare decisis*), it is actually not at all clear conceptually how the Supreme Court could undo the conclusive effects of an *in rem* decision which had never been appealed. The whole idea behind *in rem* determinations is that they are not open to challenge (otherwise than by direct appeal) regardless of their merits or lack thereof.[154]

Although the question of *in rem* or *in personam* characterization was not directly in issue, the reasons of Chief Justice Lamer in *R. v. Laba*[155] strongly support the *in personam* characterization of constitutional determinations. He expressly contemplates the scenario where a superior court judge declares a law unconstitutional, which decision is not appealed, and another superior court judge in a subsequent case declares the same law

---

[152] This distinction was, in fact, noted by the Yukon Supreme Court in *Dunbar & Edge v. Yukon (Government of) & Canada (Attorney General)*, 2004 YKSC 54 CanLII at para. 22.

[153] *Ligue catholique pour les droits de l'homme c. Hendricks*, 2004 CanLII 76590 (QCCA) at para. 28

[154] Cyr and Popescu have contended that constitutional decisions are *in personam*, although *stare decisis* may extend their reach to other cases as well (H. Cyr and M. Popescu, "The Supreme Court of Canada" in A. Jakab, A. Dyevre and G. Itzcovich, ed's, *Comparative Constitutional Reasoning*, (Cambridge: Cambridge Univ. Press, 2017) pp. 154-198 at p. 164

[155] [1994] 3 S.C.R. 965 at para. 21

to be constitutional. That scenario, of course, would not be possible if the original declaration of invalidity had been *in rem*.

However, notwithstanding the support, both in the cases and in principle, for *in personam* characterization, there has been a recent wave of cases in Canada holding or suggesting that decisions as to constitutionality are *in rem*. Often the courts mix up the *stare decisis* and *res judicata* effects of decisions. A case which appears to have given rise to considerable confusion is *R. v. Scarlett*.[156] At one point, the judge appears to embrace an *in rem* characterization (at para. 36): "Where legislation is declared unconstitutional, the declaration applies not merely to the parties immediately before the court, but to the whole world". However, he goes on (at para's 43-44) to analyze the issue in *stare decisis* terms, by stating that as a matter of judicial comity courts should follow decisions of courts of co-ordinate jurisdiction unless they consider them to be plainly wrong. This confusion has resulted in judges approaching the issue from an *in rem* perspective,[157] a *stare decisis* perspective,[158] or an amalgam of the two.[159] In other cases, courts seem not to have considered themselves bound by either *res judicata* or *stare decisis* to follow other courts' declarations of invalidity.[160]

In addition to considerations of judicial efficiency and the desirability of courts applying the law in a consistent manner, the impetus for *in rem* characterization of constitutional decisions appears to have been driven by the Supreme Court's conception of s. 52(1) as a remedial provision. *In rem* characterization is

---

[156] 2013 ONSC 562 (CanLII)
[157] *R. v. Sarmales*, 2017 ONSC 1869 (CanLII); *R. v. Ali*, 2017 ONSC 4531 (CanLII); *R. v. McCaw*, 2018 ONSC 3464 (CanLII), where the judge made valiant efforts to reconcile the conflicting case law.
[158] *R. v. Millard*, 2018 ONSC 1299 (CanLII) at par. 45; *R. v. Sauve*, 2018 ONSC 7375 (CanLII) at para. 18; *R. v. Hussein*, 2017 ONSC 4202 (CanLII) at para. 28; *R. v. Gill*, 2015 ONSC 6184 (CanLII) at *R. v. J.N.*, 2015 ONSC 6849 (CanLII) at para's 28-33; *R. v. J.A.A.*, 2018 ONSC 3285 (CanLII) at para. 6
[159] *R v. M.*, 2018 ONSC 746 (CanLII) at para's 45-46
[160] *R. v. Scofield*, 2018 BCSC 91 (CanLII); *R. v. Hussain*, 2015 ONSC 7115 (CanLII) at para. 95

consistent with the (erroneous) belief that s. 52(1) empowers courts to change the substantive content of statutes. Accordingly, Justice Gonthier wrote in *Martin*: "Only by obtaining a formal declaration of invalidity by a court can a litigant establish the general invalidity of a legislative provision *for all future cases*."[161] (emphasis added) *Stare decisis* was, thus, not seen as sufficiently powerful. In *R. v. Ferguson*, Chief Justice McLachlin described s. 52 as being able effectively to remove a provision from a statute, not merely for purposes of the case at hand, but for all cases:

> In either case, the remedy is a s. 52 remedy that renders the unconstitutional provision of no force or effect to the extent of its inconsistency. To the extent that the law is unconstitutional, it is not merely inapplicable for the purposes of the case at hand. It is null and void, and is effectively removed from the statute books.[162]

The *in rem* nature of s. 52's supposed remedial powers was then expressly stated by the Court in a 2009 decision:

> It is important to distinguish between the appellant's personal, or *in personam*, remedies, brought by her as an individual, from an *in rem* remedy flowing from s. 52 that may extend a benefit to the appellant and all similarly affected persons.[163]

Of course, as argued above, s. 52 is not actually a remedial provision at all, but that has not deterred the courts from using it as such.

---

[161] *Nova Scotia (Workers' Compensation Board) v. Martin*, [2003] 2 S.C.R. 504 at para. 31

[162] *R. v. Ferguson*, [2008] 1 S.C.R. 96 at para. 65. This led an Ontario Superior Court judge to state that "once a declaration is made ... that the law contravenes the Constitution, the offending section ceases to exist and is of no force and effect." *R. v. Sarmales*, 2017 ONSC 1869 (CanLII) at para. 20. See also, *Re Starz*, 2015 ONCA 318 (CanLII) at para. 103

[163] *Ravndahl v. Saskatchewan*, [2009] 1 S.C.R. 181 at para. 27

As a matter of principle, it is difficult to square the idea that constitutional decisions are *in rem*, with the concept of constitutional supremacy. If the Constitution is the supreme law, courts must have the ability to decide cases in accordance with the Constitution, and they cannot be constrained from doing so by judge-made doctrines such as *res judicata*. To the extent that there is a conflict between the Constitution and a previous judicial decision, the Constitution must prevail. It can be no answer that the previous decision was *in rem* and, thus, not open to challenge. Indeed, if decisions as to the constitutional validity or invalidity of statutes were *in rem*, how could any court, even the Supreme Court, overrule a prior final decision on the point? *Stare decisis* provides the requisite flexibility (because the Supreme Court is not strictly bound by its own decisions), but *res judicata* doctrine does not.

It is submitted that the Supreme Court's recent efforts to give *in rem* characterization to constitutional decisions – contrary to earlier Supreme Court authority[164] and academic commentary,[165] and contrary also to what appears to be the preponderate view in other jurisdictions,[166] – is a classic case of bootstrapping. Of

---

[164] *Emms v. The Queen*, [1979] 2 S.C.R. 1148 at pp. 1161-1162

[165] S. Letourneau, "L'Autorite d'Un Jugement Prononcant l'"Inconstitutionnalite d'Une Loi" (1989) 23 *R.J.T. n.s.* 173; H. Cyr and M. Popescu, "The Supreme Court of Canada" in A. Jakab, A. Dyevre and G. Itzcovich, ed's, *Comparative Constitutional Reasoning*, (Cambridge: Cambridge Univ. Press, 2017) pp. 154-198 at p. 164

[166] Doubt as to the applicability of *res judicata* doctrine to decisions on the constitutionality of legislation were expressed by Chief Justice Barwick of the High Court of Australia in *Queensland v. Commonwealth*, [1977] HCA 60 at para's 7-8. The American authorities seem to point to *in personam* rather than *in rem* characterization: "The function of the judicial department, with respect to legislation deemed unconstitutional, is not exercised *in rem*, but always *in personam*." *Allison v. Corker*, 67 N.J.L. 596 at p. 600 (1902), quoted in *Re Borg*, 123 N.J.L. 104 (1939) at pp. 108-109; F.G. McKean, "Border Lines of Judicial Power" (1943) 48 *Dick. L. Rev.* 1 at p. 6; Note, "What is the Effect of a Court's Declaring a Legislative Act Unconstitutional?" (1926) 39 *Harvard L. Rev.* 373 at p.p. 376-377: "When a court has once decided that the statute cannot be applied in the case before it because it is contrary to a constitutional provision, it will follow this decision on established principles when the same

course, if courts could do all the things to constitutionally infirm statutes which they claim to be able to do – strike out, invalidate, repeal, subtract from, add to, vary or amend – then their judgments would, indeed, have to operate *in rem*. No doubt about it. That simply begs the question, however. How did the judiciary acquire these astonishing legislative powers? Certainly, there is nothing in the text or the legislative history of s. 52(1) to explain it. Simply stated, the judge-made doctrine of *res judicata* cannot supersede s. 52(1)'s unequivocal declaration that no law – including no judicial decision – can prevail over the Constitution.

9. The Problematic Concept of Suspending a Declaration of Invalidity

There are two possible ways to look at declarations of invalidity and their suspension. One way is to view a declaration as a necessary prerequisite to depriving an unconstitutional provision of its legal force and effect. On this view of things, by delaying or suspending the effective date of the declaration, the unconstitutional law is allowed to continue to operate with full force and effect. There is virtually no common law support for this approach, although the Supreme Court of Canada seems to be trying to move in that direction. The constitutions of some countries expressly allow for this result by providing, for example, that an unconstitutional law is not nullified until the court publishes its decision, and by further allowing courts to delay nullification for specified periods.[167] Canada's Constitution, however, contains no such provisions. To the

---

point is raised under analogous situations, but the statute itself is not destroyed." The view in Hong Kong is similarly that: "The holdings of unconstitutionality at most operate as precedents in like subsequent cases..." (P.Y. Lo, *Judicial Consideration of the Basic Law*, PhD Thesis, University of Hong Kong, 2011, at p. 127). It has also been noted that the decisions of the European Court of Human Rights "have no *erga omnes* effect, it has come to be accepted that the Court's interpretations have *res interpretata* or 'force of interpretation'." J. Gerards, "The European Court of Human Rights" in A. Jakab, A. Dyevre and G. Itzcovich, ed's, *Comparative Constitutional Reasoning*, (Cambridge: Cambridge Univ. Press, 2017) pp. 237-276 at p. 248
[167] See Part 3 of this essay, "Trying to Right the Ship" at pp. 177-182.

contrary, as noted earlier, s. 52(1) of Canada's Constitution, by stipulating that an inconsistent law "is ... of no force or effect," is at odds with the concept that an unconstitutional law is of full force and effect until a formal judicial declaration becomes effective.

The other way to view a declaration of invalidity – and this is the view that accords with accepted common law authority – is that the declaration itself does nothing more than describe the law as it exists independently of the declaration. It does not affect the substantive content of the law. It follows that if a purported suspended declaration carries no legal significance, then judges who issue these orders must actually have something else in mind. What they call a suspended declaration of invalidity is really intended to operate as a declaration of deemed validity. However, calling it what it is – a declaration of deemed validity – starkly raises the issue of how a court acquires a power to make law in this way. Unable to answer this question, or unwilling to admit to the true nature of their actions, courts euphemistically describe it as a suspended declaration of invalidity which seems less obviously legislative.

Thus, it can be seen that each of these two ways of looking at suspended declarations is problematic. The first view is based on an illogical supposition that a constitutionally infirm law can simultaneously be "of no force or effect" (because that is what the Constitution says), and "of full force and effect" (because a court has not yet formally declared it to be invalid, as the Supreme Court of Canada has said). The second view seeks to disguise judicial law-making by describing it figuratively as the suspension of a declaration of invalidity.

9.1   *The Legal Nature of a Declaration: Nothing Changes*

A declaration is a formal judgment by a court pronouncing upon the existence or non-existence of a legal state of affairs.[168] "As

---

[168] H.K. Woolf and J. Woolf, *Zamir & Woolf - The Declaratory Judgment* (London: Sweet & Maxwell, 3d ed., 2002) at para 1.02

their name indicates, the essence of declaratory remedies is that they do not change anything, but only clarify what is already the law."[169] Justice La Forest of the Supreme Court of Canada recognized the purely descriptive nature of declaratory relief: "[T]he declaration by its nature merely states the law without changing anything."[170] Edwin Borchard, a pioneering scholar on declaratory judgments, explained that unlike conventional remedies, they are substantively non-creative:

> [Declaratory judgments] do not constitute operative facts creating new legal relations of a secondary or remedial character; they purport merely to declare preexisting relations and create no secondary or remedial ones. Their distinctive characteristic lies in the fact that they constitute merely an authentic confirmation of already existing relations.[171]

Although it is referred to as a remedy, a declaration is a weak remedy, at best, as it does not impose any obligations on the parties and cannot be enforced by the courts. It cannot be breached, and thus is incapable of supporting a finding of contempt.[172] As Peter Hogg puts it: "The declaration is a remedy that declares the legal position, but does not actually order the defendant to do anything."[173] Unlike other remedies, a declaration does not change anything in terms of the rights or obligations of the parties. "[T]he declaratory judgment merely declares and goes no further in providing relief to the applicant than stating his

---

[169] J. Harrison, "Severability, Remedies and Constitutional Adjudication" (2014) 83 *Geo. Wash. L. Rev.* 56 at p. 83, note 131

[170] *Kourtessis v. M.N.R.,* [1993] 2 S.C.R. 53 at p. 86, citing B.L. Strayer, *The Canadian Constitution and the Courts* (Canada: Butterworth, 3rd ed., 1988)

[171] E.M. Borchard, "The Declaratory Judgment – A Needed Procedural Reform" (1918) 28 *Yale L.J.* 1 at p. 5

[172] K. Roach, "Remedial Consensus and Dialogue Under the *Charter*: General Declarations and Delayed Declarations of Invalidity" (2002) 35 *U.B.C. Law Rev.* 211 at p. 221, note 29; O.M. Fiss "Dombrowski" (1977) 86 *Yale L.J.* 1103 at p. 1122; *Perez v. Ledesma*, 401 U.S. 82 (1971) at p. 126

[173] P. Hogg, *Constitutional Law of Canada*, looseleaf (Toronto: Thomson Reuters, 2007) at para. 40.2(g.1)

rights."[174] This is to be contrasted with a judgment for damages in a tort or breach of contract action which results in a change in the substantive legal relations between the parties, as the rights embedded in the plaintiff's cause of action are effectively transformed or merged into a legally enforceable money judgment. The only legal effect of a declaration is to define the existence or non-existence of a legal state of affairs, and thus to give rise to an estoppel (*res judicata* or issue estoppel) between the parties to the action and their privies.[175]

The legal effect of declarations of statutory invalidity has been described as follows by Professor Harrison:

> Declaratory judgments concerning invalidity may seem like invalidation, but a declaration cannot make a previously valid law invalid, precisely because of its declaratory nature. A declaratory judgment clarifies existing legal relations; it does not make new ones. Only if a legal rule was invalid before the declaratory judgment was issued can a judgment declaring it invalid be correct.[176]

In Canada, only courts of inherent jurisdiction (superior courts) are able to issue declaratory judgments.[177] Statutory courts of limited jurisdiction (including the Supreme Court of Canada except where it is acting on appeal from a court of inherent

---

[174] L. Sarna, *The Law of Declaratory Judgments*, 3rd ed. (Toronto: Thompson Carswell, 2007) at p. 1

[175] As explained in the previous section, only where a declaration is *in rem*, will it be capable of supporting an estoppel against strangers to the action, i.e., *erga omnes* operation. A judgment *in rem* is as to the legal status of the *res*, that is, a person or thing. The preponderance of authority is to the effect that a declaration of unconstitutionality of a statute is not a judgment *in rem*, but Canadian courts have recently been taking the opposite view, a position which is difficult to justify in terms of principle.

[176] J. Harrison, "Severability, Remedies and Constitutional Adjudication" (2014) 83 *Geo. Wash. L. Rev.* 56 at pp. 82-83

[177] *R v Lloyd*, [2016] 1 SCR 130

jurisdiction)[178] are not able to issue formal declarations.[179] However, this should be of little practical significance given that all courts are required to decide cases in accordance with the law and to ignore any law that is inconsistent with the Constitution. In other words despite suggestions to the contrary from the Supreme Court of Canada,[180] the law is the law is the law, and no court, regardless of its place in the judicial pecking order, is either required or permitted to enforce any law to the extent of its inconsistency with the Constitution. This is so whether or not the law has been formally declared invalid by a court of inherent jurisdiction. Notwithstanding the Supreme Court's opinions to the contrary, this is so even in the face of orders purporting to suspend such declarations of invalidity.

9.2   *Suspension of a Declaration: Empty Vessel, Fun House Mirror, or Trojan Horse?*

The conceptual impossibility of a suspension or stay of declaratory relief has been explained as follows:

> The effect of a declaratory order is to authoritatively indicate a legal state of affairs as they exist at that time. The effect of the court's order is not to create or negate rights but to merely identify the existence or

---

[178] It has been pointed out in a Federal Court of Canada decision that the Supreme Court has not always been true to its own prescriptions as to the jurisdictional limits on statutory courts to grant declaratory relief, as it has in a number of cases granted such relief on appeal from Federal Court decisions (see, *Bilodeau-Massé v. Canada (Attorney General)*, 2017 F.C. 604 (CanLII) at para. 62).

[179] Given that the Supreme Court of Canada cannot issue declaratory judgments except when it is acting on appeal from a court that can grant such judgments, it is difficult to understand the grounds upon which, according to popular belief, it found the jurisdiction to grant declaratory relief in the *Manitoba Language Rights* case. That case involved a statutory reference on which the Court had no power to grant any remedy at all, and certainly not a declaration. A deeper dig into *Manitoba Language Rights* will follow in Part 2 of this essay, "Fidelity to the Law: The Good, the Bad, and the Ugly".

[180] *R. v. Lloyd*, [2016] 1 S.C.R. 130 at para. 19. See further, Part 3 of this essay, "Trying to Right the Ship" at pp. 155-160.

non-existence of rights or duties. For instance, a court may declare that a certain interpretation of a contract is the correct construction or that a licence was invalidly issued. Declarations tell it as it is. As a result, a declaratory order is non-executory; it cannot be enforced. The logical extension, from a conceptual perspective, is that there can be no stay of declaratory relief. A stay operates to prevent the execution of an order and with declaratory relief there is no execution to stay; the declaration has already done its work.[181]

To similar effect, another author writes: "The effect of the court's order is not to create rights but merely to indicate what they have always been …. [B]ecause of this, if an appeal is lodged against a declaratory order, conceptually, there can be no stay of proceedings."[182] As Christopher Forsyth has put it: "[I]f the grant of the remedy changes nothing, the denial of the remedy changes nothing either."[183]

The very notion of suspending a declaration is rather odd. One must first ask what it is that would be suspended? At most, suspension of a declaration would involve a deferral of the effects of the declaration. As the declaration itself does not create any rights or obligations, but rather merely recognizes a legal state of affairs that already exists, a suspension of the declaration will be

---

[181] Jeremy Birch, "Staying Declaratory Relief" in K. Dharmananda and A. Papamatheos, ed's, *Perspectives on Declaratory Relief,* (Sydney: The Federation Press, 2009) at p.163. The same author goes on to explain that while it is not possible to stay a declaration, there may be other techniques available to achieve a similar result (in terms, for example, of preserving rights pending appeal). Thus, a court may make an order restraining a party from exercising a right the existence of which is recognized in the declaration. Or the court may delay formal pronouncement or issuance of the declaration so as to delay the estoppel effects of the declaration taking force. However, in neither of those situations would the court purport to alter the existing legal relations of the parties as reflected in the declaration.

[182] P.W. Young, *Declaratory Orders*, (Sydney: Butterworth-Heinemann, 2nd ed., 1984) at para. 2408.

[183] C. Forsyth, "The Rock and the Sand: Jurisdiction and Remedial Discretion", Paper No. 31/2013 of the University of Cambridge Faculty of Law Research Series, retrievable at www.law.cam.ac.uk/ssrn at para. 48.

pretty much a non-event, an empty vessel.[184] At most, the suspension of a declaration might delay a person from taking advantage of the estoppel which would otherwise arise from the declaration.

However, the suspended declaration's vague and amorphous quality gives it the capacity to mislead people, including lawyers and judges, into believing that it can affect the substantive content of the law.[185] That is the fun house mirror. As discussed in Part 2 of this essay, several courts have commented critically on the tendency of the purported suspension of an order to mislead people into believing that it has legal significance that it lacks.[186] The suspension of a declaration, in itself, is of little, if any, legal significance. In its true form, a suspended declaration is really just window dressing or cosmetics. Accordingly, Australian judge Sir Anthony Mason, who served on a Hong Kong Final Court of Appeal panel which in one case granted a suspended declaration of invalidity in its true form, has frankly admitted in extra-judicial writings that "its effect may be no more than cosmetic".[187] Cosmetics, of course, are by their very nature intended to deceive.

Then there is the Trojan horse. It is not uncommon for lawyers to ask that a declaration be suspended, not merely to give the impression that is has legal significance, but in order actually to avert or delay the legal consequences which flow from the existence or non-existence of the legal state of affairs that the

---

[184] On the basis of similar reasoning, courts have also refused to grant interim declarations. See, *Armstrong v. The West Vancouver Police Board*, 2007 BCSC 164 (Can LII) at para's 22-23; *Shaw v. British Columbia*, 1982 Can LII 596 (BCSC) at para. 4; *Kaiser Resources Ltd. v. Western Canada Beverage Corp.*, 1992 Can LII 517 (BCSC)

[185] The U.K. Supreme Court rejected a proposal that it should purport to suspend a declaration of invalidity out of concern that doing so would mislead people about the true legal situation by obfuscating the effects of the court's judgment. (*Ahmed v. Her Majesty's Treasury*, [2010] UKSC 5)

[186] "Fidelity to the Law: The Good, the Bad, and the Ugly" at pp. 85-89.

[187] A. Mason, "The Common Law" in S.N.M. Young and Y. Ghai, ed's, *Hong Kong's Court of Final Appeal*, (Cambridge: Cambridge Univ. Press, 2014) pp. 327-351 at p. 343

declaration recognizes. Thus, when people speak of suspending a declaration, they often mean something different – something more. Rather than a suspended declaration in its true form, which is an empty legal vessel, they mean a declaration of deemed validity; that is, a judicial fiat that for a temporary period the law will be different than it actually is. The deemed law can even be contrary to the dictates of constitutional provisions which are stated to have supreme and overriding effect. How a court acquires this remarkable power is a mystery, although Canadian judges seem to have convinced themselves that they possess it.

9.3   Declarations of Deemed Validity: Judicial Legislation by Another Name

When a court deems the law to be different than it actually is, it makes law – it legislates. However, rather than call it what it is, the more judicial-sounding term "suspended declaration of invalidity" is used. The very fact that courts which purport to grant declarations of deemed validity rarely describe them accurately, but rather conceal their true quality behind the euphemistic term "suspended declaration," may belie a basic jurisprudential discomfort with what they are doing. Judges are not supposed to prescribe laws; that is the job of legislators. "[T]he judicial role... is to say what the law is, not to prescribe what it shall be."[188] It is true that judges in a real sense do make law when they contribute to the development of the common law, but they do so in a particular and limited way – as judges.[189] This was recognized by Justice Scalia:

> I am not so naive (nor do I think our forebears were) as to be unaware that judges in a real sense "make" law. But they make it *as judges make* it, which is to say *as though* they were "finding" it – discerning what the law

---

[188] *American Trucking v. Smith*, 496 U.S. 167 (1990) at p. 201
[189] A list of more than thirty examples of changes in the law brought about by judges developing the common law is found in P. Perell, "Changing the Common Law and Why the Supreme Court of Canada's Incremental Change Test Does Not Work" (2003) 26 *Advoc. Q.* 345 at pp. 348-351

is, rather than decreeing what it is today *changed* to, or
what it will *tomorrow* be.[190] (emphasis in the original)

However, by pretending that they are merely suspending or
delaying the coming into force of a declaration, it becomes easier
for judges to rationalize what is, in reality, patently legislative
action.[191] It excuses them from engaging in deep and serious
analysis of what they are doing. It allows pragmatism to prevail
over principle.

---

[190] *James M. Beam Distilling Co. v. Georgia*, 501 U.S. 529 (1991) at p. 549
[191] Peter Hogg understates matters when he suggests that "the making of a
suspended declaration of validity is *close* to a legislative function." (emphasis
added) P.W. Hogg, "Judicial Amendment of Statutes to Conform to the Charter
of Rights" (1994) 28 *R.J. T., n.s.* 533 at p. 543. In fact, it is demonstrably
legislative. Moreover, the court effectively relieves the legislature of the
trouble and inconvenience of using its legislative override powers under s. 33
of the *Charter* (see Part 3 of this essay, "Trying to Right the Ship" at pp. 207-
210).

PART 2 –FIDELITY TO THE LAW: THE GOOD, THE BAD, AND THE UGLY

SUMMARY

In *Manitoba Language Rights*, a 1985 case, the Supreme Court of Canada decided that substantially all of Manitoba's statutes enacted in English only since 1890 – although invalid and of no force or effect – should be deemed valid and enforceable for a temporary period pending translation and re-enactment in French. The Court identified an emergency situation and, in the spirit of German political theorist Carl Schmitt, effectively declared itself sovereign to deal with such state of exception. This decision is now the wellspring for what has become a routine, though unlawful, practice of courts purporting to breathe life into invalid and ineffective laws through the issuance of so-called suspended declarations of invalidity. It is argued that the jurisprudential legacy of *Manitoba Language Rights* has been an erosion of the fidelity of Canadian courts to the rule of law. Courts in other common law jurisdictions have generally refused to follow the lead of Canadian courts in assuming a power to deem the unlawful to be lawful.

1. Introduction

As explained in Part 1 of this essay,[1] suspended declarations of invalidity are premised on the erroneous notion that the court's declaration causes the invalidation of the impugned enactment. Thus, by refraining from making a declaration, or by suspending or delaying its effectiveness, the court can somehow allow the unconstitutional law to continue in operation. The truth, however, is that constitutionally infirm laws are invalid from the moment of their enactment as a result of the automatic operation of the Constitution. The court finds that the law is invalid, but it does not make it so. Once this truth is revealed, proponents of suspended declarations are forced to admit that the term "suspended declaration" is a euphemism for the actual process which involves the court deeming the law to be different than it actually is.

A review will be made first of some decisions of courts in various common law jurisdictions, other than Canada, which for the most part have refused requests to deem the law to be what it is not. They have confined themselves to a judicial role and shown fidelity to the law. That will be the good part. The bad part will be the Supreme Court of Canada's problematic decision in *Manitoba Language Rights*. The ugly part will be the jurisprudential legacy of *Manitoba Language Rights*.

2. New Zealand Decisions

Courts in New Zealand have strongly resisted the thinking that underlies suspended declarations of constitutional invalidity. Although New Zealand does not have an entrenched constitution, the same issues arise whenever there is inconsistency between a superior law and a subordinate law, practice or policy. Can a court, having determined the subordinate law, practice or policy to be invalid due to inconsistency with a superior law, accord temporary validity to what it has determined to be invalid?

---

[1] "Some Misconceptions About Constitutional Invalidation" at pp. 22-30.

In *Willowford Family Trust v. Christchurch City Council*,[2] the court had found a by-law regulating the location of brothels in Christchurch under the *Prostitution Reform Act 2003*, to be invalid. The City applied for a stay of proceedings pending appeal of this order under a rule that allowed the court to "grant any interim relief" pending appeal. The admitted purpose of this stay was to allow the City to continue to enforce the impugned by-law pending the appeal, notwithstanding that the court had found it to be invalid. The court, in rejecting the City's application, held that having decided that the by-law was invalid, there remained nothing capable of being stayed. Moreover, the court accepted the respondent's submission that reinstating the by-law in this case, thereby maintaining in force a provision found to be invalid, would involve "an exercise of judicial power irreconcilable with the rule of law."[3] It quoted with approval[4] this statement by the High Court of Australia in *Ha v. State of New South Wales*, in relation to unlawful taxation provisions: "[I]t would be a perversion of judicial power to maintain in force that which is acknowledged not to be the law."[5] In refusing to allow enforcement of the Christchurch by-law pending appeal, Pankhurst J. said:

> To contemplate the revival at this point of a bylaw which I have found to be invalid impresses me as conceptually wrong.
>
> ... Once a Court has determined that a particular provision is invalid, it is antithetical to that determination to contemplate the recognition of the provision as lawful, even in the short term.[6]

---

[2] [2006] 1 NZLR 791
[3] *ibid.* at para. 20
[4] *ibid.* at para. 19
[5] (1997), 189 CLR 465 at 504
[6] *supra,* footnote 2, at para's 22-23

Yet, that is precisely what the Supreme Court of Canada purports to do when it makes suspended declarations of constitutional invalidity.[7]

Another New Zealand case in which a court refused to allow the temporary enforcement of what it had determined to be illegal is *A.G. on behalf of Ministry of Health v. Spencer*.[8] The Human Rights Review Tribunal had declared that a restrictive Ministry of Health policy (the "Policy") was inconsistent with the New Zealand's *Human Rights Act* ("HRA"). The Ministry, pending its appeal, sought and obtained from the Tribunal an order that its declaration of invalidity "is suspended until further order of the Tribunal."[9] The applicant, Mrs. Spencer, relying on the Tribunal's declaration that the Policy was invalid, made an application for benefits under the statutory scheme. Her application was refused by the Ministry on the basis that the effect of the Tribunal's suspension order was to allow it to continue to enforce the Policy notwithstanding the Tribunal's earlier declaration of invalidity. Justice Winkelmann of the New Zealand High Court, affirmed by the Court of Appeal, held that "Even if the Tribunal had power to stay or suspend a declaration, this would not render the policy lawful."[10] In particular, Justice Winkelmann recognized the Tribunal's declaration for what it was – a statement of the law. Thus, the declaration identified the Policy as being illegal, but it did not *make* it illegal. It was the fact of the inconsistency between the Policy and a superior law, the HRA, that rendered the Policy invalid:

> In this case the declaration issued by the Tribunal was merely a statement of the law. It did not prevent the operation of the policy it dealt with; it was not an injunction. It did not compensate the parties for the breach of law declared in the order; it was not an award

---

[7] *Willowford Family Trust* was followed in *Independent Fisheries Limited v. The Minister for Canterbury Earthquake Recovery*, [2012] NZHC 1810, and in *Jackson v. Te Rangi*, [2015] NZHC 1149
[8] [2015] NZCA 143
[9] [2013] NZHC 2580
[10] *ibid.* at para. 71

of damages. It was merely the formal order encapsulating the legal reasoning set out in the judgment. Without the declaration the law would still be as it is expressed in the reasoning of the Tribunal, and indeed, as it was expressed by the High Court and Court of Appeal.[11] Even if the declaration was stayed (or "suspended", to use the language of the order), that would leave the law unchanged. The policy would still be unlawful, as a breach of s. 19.[12]

On appeal, in affirming Winkelmann J's decision, the Court of Appeal reiterated that the illegality of the Policy arose not from the Tribunal's formal order, but from the law, and no order staying or suspending the Tribunal's formal order could change the law:

> [Ministry counsel submits that] the suspension order effectively rendered lawful what the Tribunal had declared to be unlawful or altered the declaration's temporal effect by deeming the policy to be valid. However, as Winkelmann J observed, a declaration is merely a formal order encapsulating the consequences of the legal reasoning set out in the preceding reasons for decision. The existence of the remedy makes no difference to the law as found in the judgment. While the formal order may be notionally suspended, its substance – the reasoning process and its result – remains unchanged.
>
> ... The Tribunal had already found the policy was unlawful: its substance cannot be altered by an order purporting to suspend its formal embodiment.[13]

---

[11] By the time the judicial review application from the Ministry's refusal of Mrs. Spencer's application for benefits reached Winkelmann J., both the High Court and the Court of Appeal had affirmed the correctness of the Tribunal's original declaration of the Policy's invalidity.

[12] *ibid.* at para. 70

[13] [2015] NZCA 143 at para's 36-37

To underscore the point, the Court of Appeal went on to say: "Putting it another way, it was not the Tribunal's declaration that has the effect of making the Policy unlawful: The unlawfulness arose from the breach of the HRA."[14]

The same is true of Canada's Constitution. It is not the court's declaration that renders the inconsistent law of no force or effect. The Constitution does that. Therefore, in the absence of a power to suspend or abridge the Constitution, the illegality identified by the court in its reasoning – not in its formal order, but in its reasoning – cannot be done away with by any further order of the court. Significantly, in rejecting the Ministry's argument that the Tribunal's order suspending its declaration of invalidity rendered the impugned Policy lawful and enforceable during the period of suspension, the New Zealand courts had before them the Supreme Court of Canada's decision in *Manitoba Language Rights,* and a full array of its suspended declaration cases. Justice Winkelmann devoted several pages of her analysis to these Canadian cases but found them unpersuasive on the core issue of the legal effect of an order purporting to suspend a declaration of invalidity.[15]

3. Hong Kong Decisions

In *Koo Sze Yiu v. Chief Executive of the HKSAR,*[16] the issue was whether the Hong Kong court could make an order giving

---

[14] *ibid.* at para. 43

[15] She did, however, recognize the potential power of a court in exceptional circumstances to deem an invalid law valid, but only (in apparent reference to the state of emergency identified by the Supreme Court in *Manitoba Language Rights*) in cases of constitutional necessity: "The Tribunal has no power to deem a policy it has found unlawful, lawful. Deeming an invalid Act or policy valid is an exceptional remedy, utilized by constitutional courts in cases of necessity." ([2013] NZHC 2580 at para. 71) As argued elsewhere in this essay, the facts and circumstances of the *Manitoba Language Rights* case were exceptional and extreme, involving a state of emergency resulting from an impending collapse of Manitoba's entire legal system. It is impossible to draw from it a general authority for courts to deem invalid law valid in the absence of circumstances threatening the very existence or survival of the state.

[16] [2006] 3 HKLRD 455

temporary validity to a law which it had already declared to be unconstitutional. Alternatively, could the court suspend such a declaration in order to postpone its coming into effect? (Note that whereas the approach of the Supreme Court of Canada is to treat a suspension of a declaration of invalidity as involving both a delay of the declaration's effects and a conferral of deemed validity on the law throughout the period of suspension, the Hong Kong courts treat these as two different matters. In other words, the Hong Kong courts do not obscure the issues with euphemistic tropes.)

The trial court had declared invalid, as contrary to the Basic Law (Hong Kong's Constitution), an Ordinance and Executive Order which purported to authorize certain covert surveillance operations. However, the court went on to make a temporary validity order to the effect that notwithstanding its declaration of invalidity, the "Ordinance and Executive Order, are valid and of legal effect for a period of six months from the date hereof." An appeal to the Court of Appeal was dismissed. On further appeal to Hong Kong's Final Court of Appeal, the temporary validity order was set aside. The Final Court of Appeal expressly left open whether there might ever be a case where a court could make an order of deemed validity – for example in a case of state emergency such as existed in *Manitoba Language Rights* – but it stated that this clearly was not such a case.[17]

The Court then considered the government's alternative request for an order suspending the effectiveness of the declaration. While the Court was persuaded to make a suspension order for a period of six months, it made clear that the suspension order would have very limited effect; that is, it would merely permit the government to function as it had before, without being in breach of the Court's declaration. It was specifically stated that "the Government is not shielded from legal liability for functioning

---

[17] In 2013 the Hong Kong Court of Final Appeal did make an order delaying for 12 months the effectiveness of its declaration that transsexual persons have a constitutional right to marry (*W. v. The Registrar of Marriages*, [2013] HKCFA 39 at para. 150)

pursuant to what has been declared unconstitutional."[18] In other words, the only comfort provided to the government during this period of suspension was that it could not be held in contempt for acting contrary to the Court's declaration. That was small, if any, comfort, especially given that the prevailing common law view seems in any event to be that a declaration, being merely declaratory of the law and creating no obligations, is not capable of being breached or violated in a contumacious manner.[19] Thus, Sir Anthony Mason, who sat as one of the Final Court of Appeal judges in *Koo Sze Yui,* writing extra-judicially, expressed doubt about the propriety of a court granting temporary validity to legislation which it had held invalid, and further suggested that the effect of the suspension order granted in *Koo Sze Yui* may have been no more than cosmetic:

> In a concurring judgment, I pointed out the difficulties of making an order giving temporary validity to legislation that a court holds to be invalid despite the existence of Pakistan and Canadian authorities seemingly supporting such a course. The CFA has left open the question whether it could make such an order. The judgments in *Koo Sze Yui* make it very clear that suspending the operation of a declaration of invalidity of a statute does not entail, as some Canadian authority might seem to suggest, the valid operation of the statute in the period of suspension. Acts (including omissions) and transactions occurring in that period will ultimately be determined for legality by reference to the law as declared by the court. The suspension does not affect the rights of the parties; indeed its effect may be no more than cosmetic.[20]

---

[18] *Koo Sze Yiu*, [2006] 3 HKLRD 455 at para. 63
[19] See Part 1 of this essay, "Some Misconceptions About Constitutional Invalidation" at p. 67.
[20] A. Mason, "The Common Law" in S.N.M. Young and Y. Ghai, ed's. *Hong Kong's Court of Final Appeal*, (Cambridge: Cambridge Univ. Press, 2014) pp. 327-351 at pp. 342-343

In another case, the Hong Kong Court of Appeal had decided that the detention of certain persons by immigration authorities was unlawful. The Director of Immigration intended to appeal to the Court of Final Appeal, but was concerned that pending the appeal, other detained persons would rely upon the Court of Appeal's reasons in support of their own *habeus corpus* applications. Thus, the Director asked the Court of Appeal for an order staying the effects of its judgment. The Court of Appeal refused this request on the basis that having made a decision as to what the law is, it could not issue an order undoing or suspending the law as so found:

> It is clear that the court has the power to stay an order and that includes the power to stay a declaration. But is seems to me that a stay would not make the judgment a nonjudgment: as if it had never been made. I do not believe it is possible for this court to say that it should not be assumed that our judgment does not represent our view of the law. Of course it may be that the Court of Final Appeal will eventually overturn our decision, but in the meantime, our judgment must have effect as a judgment so far as our statements of the law and their implications are concerned.[21]

These statements are pertinent to suspended declarations of constitutional invalidity in Canada. The significance of a finding by a court that a law is inconsistent with the Constitution lies in its reasons, not in any formal order it might make. Once a court decides that a law is unconstitutional, no further order of the court can undo the precedential value or effects of its decision, nor deem the law not to be as reflected in that decision. Put another way, no court can enjoin another court from deciding cases in accordance with its best judgment as to what the law is. This includes the Supreme Court of Canada. It has no right and no power, by the issuance of suspended declarations or otherwise, to require or permit lower courts to decide cases otherwise than in accordance with the dictates of the Constitution. The Supreme

---

[21] *A v. Director of Immigration*, [2008] HKCA 330 at para. 8

Court is supreme over other courts. It is not supreme over the Constitution. To repeat: The Supreme Court is not supreme over the Constitution.

4. Australian Decisions

In *Ha v. State of New South Wales*,[22] the High Court of Australia found certain taxation provisions to be unconstitutional. The government urged the Court to allow these unconstitutional provisions to remain in force for a twelve-month transition period, by applying the doctrine of prospective overruling. The Court ultimately concluded that its finding of invalidity did not require it to overrule any earlier cases. However, its *dicta* forcefully rejected the proposition that a court could maintain in force that which is acknowledged not to be the law:

> The Court was invited, if it should come to that conclusion, to overrule the franchise cases prospectively, leaving the authority of those cases unaffected for a period of 12 months. This Court has no power to overrule cases prospectively. A hallmark of the judicial process has long been the making of binding declarations of rights and obligations arising from the operation of the law upon past events or conduct. The adjudication of existing rights and obligations as distinct from the creation of rights and obligations distinguishes the judicial power from the non-judicial power. Prospective overruling is thus inconsistent with judicial power on the simple ground that the new regime that would be ushered in when the overruling took effect would alter existing rights and obligations. If an earlier case is erroneous and it is necessary to overrule it, it would be a perversion of judicial power to maintain in force that which is acknowledged not to be the law.[23]

---

[22] (1997), 189 CLR 465
[23] *ibid.* at pp. 503-504

Put plainly, Australia's highest court would regard Canadian-style suspended declarations of invalidity as "a perversion of judicial power."

The decision of the Supreme Court of South Australia in *Roosters Club Inc. v. The Northern Tavern Pty Limited*,[24] is another strong rejection by an Australian court of the idea that a court, by staying a declaration, can temporarily cause the law to be different than what it has determined the law to be. A judge had declared that the appellant's gaming machine licence was void. The appellant sought a stay of the declaration pending appeal, with the apparent goal of being able to continue operating its gaming business pending the appeal without being in violation of the law. The Court held that it had no such power and expressed concern that granting the stay order requested could mislead the appellant as to its true legal position:

> Conceptually, it is difficult to see how the Court can stay what it has already declared, namely that the grant of the licence is void.
>
> ....
>
> The appellant wishes to continue to operate its gaming machines until its application to the High Court for special leave to appeal has been disposed of. The appellant appears to believe that the grant of a stay will mean that it is to be treated as holding a licence meantime, even though the Court has declared it does not. The appellant may also believe, although this is not clear, that the effect of the stay will be that even if its application to the High Court is unsuccessful, or even if it gets leave to appeal and an appeal is ultimately unsuccessful, the appellant will be treated in the meantime as holding a gaming machine licence under the *Act*. In short, the application for a stay seems to be premised on the assumption that a stay would have the effect of deeming the appellant to hold a licence under

---

[24] [2003] SASC 143

the Act, even if ultimately the decision of the judge stands.

…

Accordingly, the Court should not grant a stay that might create the impression that the continued operation of the gaming machines in question is lawful, and will be lawful even though the appellant's application or appeal to the High Court ultimately fails.

If my view is correct, there is no point in ordering a stay. The appellant must decide whether it will continue to operate the gaming machines in question, and must accept whatever consequences flow from that decision. The Court is unable to protect it against the consequences that will flow, in respect of the period pending an ultimate decision, by the grant of a stay.

I realize that this puts the appellant in a difficult position. The point I make is that there is nothing that the Court can do about that, and the grant of a stay would be misleading if it were taken by the appellant to be providing protection to it.[25]

As will be seen, the potential misleading effects of purported suspensions of declaratory orders has also been the subject of comment by the United Kingdom's highest court.

5. United Kingdom Decisions

A very important case is *Ahmed v. Her Majesty's Treasury,*[26] where the U.K. Supreme Court was asked to suspend its declaration that certain anti-terrorism orders, which were designed to freeze the assets of terrorists, were *ultra vires* the empowering Act. The purpose of the government's request was to prevent assets from being released prior to the enactment of valid replacement orders. It was accepted by everyone that the court had no power to grant validity to the impugned orders for a

---

[25] *ibid.* at para's 18, 20, 23, 24, and 25
[26] [2010] UKSC 5

temporary period. One commentator summed it up simply: "Given that the orders were void, remedial discretion could not be used to breathe life into invalid orders."[27] Thus, what is routinely done by Canadian courts was not even considered to be arguable in the U.K.. Rather, what was sought was an order purporting to suspend the declaration of invalidity apparently in the hope that the banks holding the targeted assets would not be inclined to release them if the court had suspended its order, even though such suspension would actually have no effect on the legality or illegality of the banks' actions. In other words, as the government frankly conceded, its objective was to cause the banks to believe that the impugned orders possessed some validity that they in fact lacked (a posture which leading administrative law scholar, Christopher Forsyth termed "disconcertingly authoritarian").[28] The six to one majority of the Supreme Court would have none of it (per Lord Phillips):

> Mr. Swift [government counsel] urged the court to suspend the operation of its judgment because of the effect that the suspension would have on the conduct of third parties. He submitted that the banks, in particular, would be unlikely to release frozen funds while the court's orders remained suspended. I comment that if suspension were to have this effect this would only be because the third parties wrongly believed that it affected their legal rights and obligations.
>
> The ends sought by Mr. Swift might well be thought desirable, but I do not consider that they justify the means that he proposes. This court should not lend itself to a procedure that is designed to obfuscate the

---

[27] C. Forsyth "Blasphemy Against Basics: Doctrine, Conceptual Reasoning and Certain Decisions of the UK Supreme Court" in J. Bell, M. Elliott. J. Varuhas and P. Murray ed's, *Public Law Adjudication in Common Law Systems*, (Oxford and Portland, Oregon: Hart Publishing, 2016) pp. 145-163 at p. 161
[28] *ibid.* at pp. 160-161

> effect of its judgment. Accordingly, I would not
> suspend the operation of any part of the court's order.[29]

Consistent with the Hong Kong Court of Final Appeal's decision in *Koo Sze Yiu,* discussed above, government counsel conceded that any suspension by the court of its order would provide no shield from liability for those who acted during the suspension period in accordance with the anti-terrorist orders which the court had declared *ultra vires*. The government relied in its argument, apparently to no avail, on a number of Supreme Court of Canada decisions, including *Manitoba Language Rights* and several leading suspended declaration cases.[30] It bodes well for the rule of law in the U.K. that its Supreme Court did not accede to the allure of pragmatism or cower to public opinion,[31] but instead rendered a principled decision which reflected, according to Professor Forsyth, "deep fidelity to the law".[32]

Ahmed was recently followed in a 2017 case where the court, having determined that certain rules relating to the determination of asylum claims (the "FTR 2005") were *ultra vires*, was asked by the government not to make a formal declaration to that effect due to concerns about the impact of such a declaration on other pending cases. In rejecting that request, the court held that the difference between determining the rules to be *ultra vires* and making a formal declaration to that effect was merely formal:

> The difference between holding that the FTR 2005
> were ultra vires for the purposes of then considering the
> lawfulness of the appeal decisions, and the

---

[29] *supra*, note 26 at para's 7-8

[30] See P.Y. Lo, "Impact of Jurisprudence beyond Hong Kong" in S. Young and Y. Ghai, *Hong Kong's Court of Final Appeal* (Cambridge: Cambridge Univ. Press, 2014) 579 at 590

[31] The majority's decision was pilloried in the British press. The author of one article stated: "It takes a truly ludicrous sense of judicial self-importance to think that the critical issue is not dead bodies on the streets, but that the Supreme Court should 'not lend itself to a procedure designed to obfuscate the effect of its judgment'," quoted in PY Lo, *ibid.* at p. 590

[32] C. Forsyth, *supra*, footnote 27 at p. 161

consequences if those decisions were held unlawful, and granting a declaration that the FTR 2005 were ultra vires, is no more than formal.[33]

In addition, declining to make a declaration would lead to uncertainty as to the legal effect of the court's determination that the rules were invalid:

> The decision of the Supreme Court in *Ahmed v. HM Treasury* [2010] UKSC 2 and 5, [2010] 2 AC 534 at 690 [5-8] on whether to suspend a declaration that two terrorism asset freezing orders were invalid, and quashing them, is also of some assistance. The declaration had been made; the issue was whether it should be suspended until valid replacement orders could be made. Lord Phillips said that suspension would not alter the position in law but a stay, on a declaration that the Order was unlawful, would leave doubt as to whether the Order was lawful meanwhile, and so conflict with and muddle the clear decision that it was unlawful. That is not exactly the same problem as here, since I am being asked not to make a declaration at all. But what Lord Phillips said is also apposite in this case. A holding that the FTR 2005 were ultra vires, yet a refusal so to declare, would lead to uncertainty as to the status of that holding for other cases, and whether I had intended different consequences to flow, as a result. That would be a very undesirable consequence of refusing to grant a declaration.[34]

Another U.K. case in which the court refused to make an order that would have allowed the government to act in a manner that the court had decided was illegal is *Secretary of State v. Payne and Cooper*[35] The court had determined that the government acted

---

[33] *TN (Vietnam) & US (Pakistan), R. (On the Application Of) v. Secretary of State for the Home Department*, [2017] EWHC 59, at para. 47
[34] *ibid.* at para. 48. To similar effect, see also: *TR (On the Application Of) v. Greater Manchester Chief Constable*, [2013] EWCA Civ. 25 at para. 83
[35] [2011] EWCA Civ. 492

unlawfully in exercising set off in respect of social security overpayments made to persons who had been granted protection from creditors under a statutory scheme (Debtor Relief Orders). That is, the court had decided that the government was not allowed to deduct previous overpayments of benefits from currently payable benefits. The Court of Appeal issued a stay which allowed the government, pending further appeal to the Supreme Court, not to repay amounts which it had to date unlawfully set off. The government subsequently returned to the Court of Appeal asking for a broader order which would allow it to continue to exercise set off pending its appeal to the Supreme Court. In other words, the government was asking the Court of Appeal for an order which would, pending the appeal, authorize the very conduct that the Court had just decided was unlawful. The government's explanation for seeking this order was a pragmatic one: that if it was ultimately successful on its appeal, it would have difficulty recovering the subject payments from the recipients who were already under creditor protection, and that this would have adverse budgetary implications for the government. The Court of Appeal characterized the issue as constitutional in nature, i.e., does a court, constitutionally, in the absence of statutory authorization, have the power to authorize actions that are contrary to the law as determined by the court? It held that it had no such power:

> What is said is that we are being asked, contrary to the decision of the court as to what the law was, to authorise the Secretary of State to do something that is not in accordance with the law. The Secretary of State wishes to continue making deductions. Cranston J and this court by a majority held that there was no power in the circumstances affecting DRO's [Debtor Relief Orders] to make these deductions, and so what the Secretary of State is in fact asking the court to do is either suspend the law, as it is declared to be, or to dispense with it, or to ask this court by express order to authorise something which it is held to be contrary to law.

> In my judgment, Mr. Drabble is right in saying that
> constitutionally this court has no power to do this. No
> powers of case management under the Civil Procedure
> Rules could authorise the court to do something that
> constitutionally it has no power to do. The court has no
> power to authorise general acts which are contrary to
> the law, unless there is some law authorizing them to
> do it, and there is nothing in the relevant legislation that
> allows the court to do this.[36]

This analysis begs the following question vis-à-vis Canadian-style suspended declarations of constitutional invalidity: What is the source of the power of judges to authorize, even temporarily, conduct under laws which the Constitution of Canada declares to be of no force or effect? No Canadian court has ever answered this question, at least other than in an *ipse dixit* manner. When explanation is attempted, it inevitably and ultimately leads to the Supreme Court of Canada's decision in *Manitoba Language Rights*. Let us now take a careful look at this much celebrated and misunderstood decision.

6. *Re Manitoba Language Rights*: Bad Decisions Make Bad Law

Just as it is said that all roads lead to Rome, all discussions of suspended declarations of constitutional invalidity lead to the Supreme Court of Canada's 1985 decision in *Manitoba Language Rights*. It involved a statutory reference by the federal government seeking an advisory opinion as to the legality of Manitoba's body of English-only statutes and regulations. The significance of this decision is hard to overstate. If it actually stands for the propositions for which it is commonly cited, it recognizes a judicial power to bestow force and effect upon laws which the Constitution of Canada declares to be of no force or effect. Not only that, these remarkable judicial powers would have emerged from the decision of a court acting in a non-judicial capacity on a statutory reference, where it was able only to give a

---

[36] *ibid.* at para's 8-9

non-binding advisory opinion. Some decision that must have been.

When Manitoba joined Canada in 1870, it was constitutionally required that its laws be enacted in both English and French. By 1890, the English-speaking majority in Manitoba decided to abandon this requirement, and so a statute was enacted purporting to allow laws to be made in English only. Despite some early decisions holding the 1890 statute to be invalid,[37] for the next almost hundred years virtually all statutes and regulations in Manitoba were enacted in English only. In the 1970's, renewed challenges to the legality of Manitoba's English-only laws began, and by 1979 the Supreme Court of Canada had definitively determined that the 1890 statute purporting to allow English-only enactment was invalid and of no force or effect.[38] This left open the question of the status in law of all of Manitoba's English-only laws enacted since 1890. In 1984, the government of Canada, concerned about the potential implications of most of Manitoba's laws being invalidated, submitted a reference to the Supreme Court of Canada.

A reference is a procedure provided for by statute in Canada which allows the federal government to ask the Supreme Court for an advisory opinion on any legal question which the government considers to be of sufficient importance. Usually, the reference procedure is employed where the government wishes to obtain clarification as to the constitutionality of existing or proposed legislation. Three points about references are important: first, they engage the court in the exercise of a non-judicial function; second, the court's decision on a reference is advisory only – it does not bind anyone, although as a practical matter the court's opinion is invariably followed; and, third, the Supreme Court, as a statutory court without any inherent powers, can grant no remedies in connection with a reference. All it can

---

[37] *Pellant v. Hebert*, Mar. 9, 1892, (Man. Co. Ct.), reported at (1981), 12 R.G.D. 242; *Bertrand v. Dussault*, Jan. 30, 1909, (Man. Co. Ct.), reported at 1977 Can LII 1635.
[38] *A-G Manitoba v. Forest*, [1979] 2 S.C.R. 1032

do is render an advisory opinion on the questions referred to it by the government.[39]

The Supreme Court did not have any difficulty in deciding that Manitoba's English-only laws were unconstitutional. Clearly, they were not enacted in accordance with the constitutionally-mandated manner and form requirement of bilingualism. Thus, they were invalid and of no force or effect.[40] In fact, not only were they invalid as of the date of the decision, they had always been invalid: "All unilingually enacted Acts of the Manitoba Legislature are, and always have been, invalid and of no force or effect."[41] The Court could have stopped there, but was concerned that this would have left the Province of Manitoba in a state of chaos. What would be the impact on citizens' and governments' rights and obligations, their contracts, their property ownership rights, and so forth, if the entirety of legislation made in Manitoba over the past ninety-five years had to be treated as invalid? Would there be no highway traffic laws? Would Manitoba's publicly administered programs for health care, motor vehicle insurance, and education, all crumble to the ground? Could citizens lawfully stop paying their property taxes? Could the provincially-constituted and operated criminal and civil courts continue to assert legitimate authority? Moreover, would the election of members to Manitoba's Legislature under invalid provincial elections laws call into question their ability to enact valid bilingual replacement legislation? The Supreme Court viewed the situation as very serious:

---

[39] See: *Reference re Secession of Quebec*, [1998] 2 SCR 217 at para's 15, 25; *Re References by Gov. Gen.* (1910), 43 S.C.R. 536, aff'd 1912 Can LII 407, [1912] AC 571 (P.C.); *Re Remuneration of Judges*, [1998] 1 S.C.R. 3; "The non-judicial powers granted to the judiciary include the government's ability to refer a question of law to the courts for an advisory opinion." Hon. J.D. Richard, "Separation of Powers: The Canadian Experience" (2009) 47 *Duq. L. Rev.* 731 at p. 744; M. St. Hilaire, "The Codification of Human Rights Canada" (2012) 42 *R.D.U.S.* 506 at p. 555

[40] *Manitoba Language Rights*, [1985] 1 S.C.R. 721 at para's. 52, 54

[41] *ibid.* at para. 108

> The conclusion that the Acts of the Legislature of Manitoba are invalid and of no force or effect means that the positive legal order which has purportedly regulated the affairs of the citizens of Manitoba since 1890 will be destroyed and the rights, obligations and other effects arising under these laws will be invalid and unenforceable.[42]

It declared that Manitoba was in a "state of emergency."[43]

Faced with this dire situation, the Court realized that it could not simply provide its opinion that Manitoba's entire system of law and government was invalid and of no legal force or effect, and leave it at that. Something more had to be done. The question was, however, what more could it do given the constitutional limitations on it as a court, especially a court acting in a mere advisory capacity in a statutory reference? Some members of the Court were inclined to leave it to the legislators to clean up their own mess, but that was ultimately rejected as too uncertain a solution. This was "clearly a politically loaded case."[44] It has been reported that Chief Justice Brian Dickson, who was from Manitoba, and who strongly supported the concept of a bilingual Canada, was affronted by the Manitoba government's refusal to live up to its constitutional obligations.[45] The first draft of the Court's opinion, prepared by the Chief Justice, went so far as to have the Court issue a mandatory order requiring "that the legislature of Manitoba act *affirmatively* to remedy its past non-compliance, by taking steps to translate and re-enact all of its unilingual legislation in both languages."[46] A number of the other justices were uncomfortable with a court ordering such a remedy against legislators, including Justice Estey who was said to be

---

[42] *ibid.* at para 61

[43] *ibid.* at para. 107. Many years later, the Saskatchewan Court of Appeal referred to Manitoba as having been in a "state of nature." *R. v. Conseil Scolaire Fransakois*, 2013 SKCA 35 (CanLII) at para. 56

[44] R. J. Sharpe and K. Roach, *Brian Dickson: A Judge's Journey*, (Toronto: University of Toronto Press, 2003) at p. 416

[45] *ibid.* at p. 416

[46] *ibid.* at p. 419

"just apoplectic" about the remedy.[47] Not only would such a remedy raise serious separation of power issues, it is difficult to see how the Court could make such an order on a reference where, as Justice Beetz correctly noted: "[The Court's] power is confined to answering the constitutional questions."[48]

And in any event, the greatest problem facing the Court was the fact that it would take considerable time for the legislation to be translated and re-enacted. The Court recognized that much of what had transpired in the past, even though pursuant to invalid laws, could be preserved through the operation of recognized common law saving doctrines such as *de facto* officer, *res judicata*, mistake of law, prescription, and necessity. These doctrines generally operate so as to allow unlawful acts to withstand subsequent challenge on the basis of reasonable reliance on what was believed to be valid law. They recognize that while Manitoba's unlingual laws did not exist as a legal matter, they did exist as a factual matter and this reality could give rise to legal consequences.[49] However, what about the immediate future while the laws were being translated? To the extent that these saving doctrines are based on reasonable belief that an invalid law was in fact valid, they would be of no on-going value following release of the Court's decision which would serve as clear notice to everyone that these laws were invalid. What mayhem would there be on the streets of Manitoba until valid replacement laws could be enacted, and who could enact such laws given the uncertainty surrounding the status of legislators who had been elected under invalid provincial elections statutes? Even Chief Justice Dickson's drastic proposed order forcing the legislators to enact valid bilingual legislation would not solve this fundamental problem. Some way would have to be devised to give validity to invalid laws. That would take some really nice pants.[50]

---

[47] *ibid.* at p. 419
[48] *ibid.* at p. 420
[49] See Part 3 of this essay, "Trying to Right the Ship" at p. 158, footnote 9.
[50] Will Smith, *The Pursuit of Happyness,* Columbia Pictures, 2006

In the end, the Court's solution was to hold that Manitoba's invalid unilingual laws would be deemed temporarily valid for the minimum period of time necessary for their translation, re-enactment, printing and publishing in both English and French. It based this result on the concept of the rule of law, which is referred to in the preamble of the *Charter* and has been recognized as "a fundamental postulate of our constitutional structure."[51] In particular, the Court held that it was essential to the rule of law that there exists a body of positive law. It was antithetical to the rule of law for there to be a legal vacuum. "The rule of law simply cannot be fulfilled in a province that has no positive law."[52] Thus, the rule of law and, indeed, the Constitution itself, demanded that Manitoba's invalid unilingual laws be temporarily recognized as valid: "In order to ensure rule of law, the Courts will recognize as valid the constitutionally invalid Acts of the Legislature."[53]

While ostensibly anchoring its decision in the rule of law, the Court spent much time examining the doctrine of state necessity, which it said provided "analogous support for the measures proposed." Peter Hogg has suggested that the Court's decision could as easily have been based on necessity rather than rule of law grounds.[54] Indeed, it has been observed that there is no small irony in the Court having relied on the rule of law as justification for giving effect to unconstitutional laws.[55] This is particularly so given that the Court decided in a rule of law case to exceed its powers under a statutory reference without even acknowledging that it was doing so.[56] Violating the rule of law to save the rule of

---

[51] *Roncarelli v Duplesssis*, [1959] S.C.R. 121 at p. 142

[52] *Manitoba Language Rights*, [1985] 1 S.C.R. 721 at para. 62

[53] *ibid.* at para. 85

[54] P.W. Hogg, "Necessity in a Constitutional Crisis" (1989) 15 *Monash Univ. L. Rev.* 253 at p. 263

[55] "[I]t is richly ironic that the rule of law was maintained by the device of imposing unlawful law." W.H. Hulburt, "Fairy Tales and Living Trees: Observations on Some Recent Constitutional Decisions by the Supreme Court of Canada" (1998) 26 *Man. L.J.* 181 at p. 194

[56] "Interestingly, in a case about the rule of law, the Court decided to deviate from its own legal constraints and issued a binding judgment on the parties rather than an advisory opinion (as required in a reference)." P.W. Hogg and

law is a difficult concept even for the most agile of legal minds to grasp. As will be explained below, it is especially difficult for disciples of liberal constitutionalism to accept that the rule of law is not inviolable.

6.1   *The Court's Decision – Fiction and Fact*

Before proceeding with an analysis of what the Court actually decided, and actually said in *Manitoba Language Rights*, it is instructive to consider how subsequent courts and commentators have interpreted and applied it. The disconnect is striking. It is now part of Canadian constitutional lore that the Court in *Manitoba Language Rights* invented the suspended declaration of constitutional invalidity. Simply by virtue of being repeated over and over again, it has become accepted wisdom that this case constitutes the jurisprudential foundation for suspending the (supposed) effects of a declaration of invalidity.

It is important not to confuse terminology by failing to distinguish between suspended declarations in their true form versus their euphemistic form. In its true form, a suspended declaration involves an order merely delaying the coming into effect of the declaration. In its euphemistic form, it involves the affirmative creation of law to cover the field which the impugned law failed ever to cover due to its invalidity. As previously explained, the euphemism disguises the true legislative character of the court's order by suggesting that it is merely allowing a pre-existing legal state of affairs to continue. When it is argued below that the Court in *Manitoba Language Rights*, contrary to popular belief, did not suspend a declaration of invalidity, the term is used in its true, rather than euphemistic, form.[57]

C.F. Zwibel, "The Rule of Law in the Supreme Court of Canada" (2005) 55 *U. Toronto L.J.* 715 at p. 721, footnote 30.

[57] What the Court did do was make law by judicial fiat. It did not merely preserve or continue pre-existing law. It had already decided that the unilingual laws were and had always been invalid and of no force or effect. Thus, to say that the Court made a suspended declaration of invalidity in *Manitoba*

If the Supreme Court had invented the suspended declaration of invalidity in *Manitoba Language Rights,* as lore would have us believe, its decision would presumably provide some support for the notion that a statute's constitutional invalidity arises as a result of the court's decision. As observed in Part 1 of this essay, it is the Constitution itself that makes the statute invalid, rather than a court's order which merely recognizes the fact of the statute's invalidity.[58] Thus, if the court's declaration changes nothing in terms of the statute's legal efficacy, a purported suspension of that declaration would be equally inefficacious. A careful reading of *Manitoba Language Rights*, in fact, reveals not a whit of evidence that the Court believed the invalidity of Manitoba's unilingual laws depended upon a judicial declaration to that effect, or that such laws possessed any validity prior to the Court making its determination. To the contrary, the Court very clearly, and purposefully, emphasized that the unilingual laws both were and had always been of no force or effect. There is not the slightest hint that the Court believed that it was invalidating the laws. They were held to be invalid and of no force or effect from their inception because they did not conform to the constitutional requirement of bilingual enactment. Thus, the Court wrote:

> To summarize, the legal situation in the Province of Manitoba *is* as follows. All unilingually enacted Acts of the Manitoba Legislature *are, and have always been*, invalid and of no force or effect.[59] (emphasis added)

If the Supreme Court had intended to suspend a declaration of invalidity in *Manitoba Language Rights* it would also be expected that it would have (a) made a declaration, and (b) indicated that it was suspending or delaying the effects of such declaration. In fact, the Court did not make any declaratory order of invalidity. To repeat: At no time did the Court issue an order declaring the

---

Language Rights is accurate only if the term is understood as a euphemism that disguises the reality of what actually happened.

[58] See "Some Misconceptions About Constitutional Invalidation" at pp. 23-34.

[59] *Manitoba Language* Rights, [1985] 1 S.C.R. 721 at para 108

unilingual statutes to be invalid.[60] Of course, such an order was unnecessary because the statutes' invalidity arose at their inception as a result of non-compliance with a constitutional requirement. No court order was necessary to bring about that result. Moreover, if the Court had intended to invent the suspended declaration of invalidity, it is reasonable to expect that it would have referred to a suspension of something. In fact, as was observed by a New Zealand judge in 2013, the words "suspend" or "suspension", appear nowhere in *Manitoba Language Rights*:

> It is of note that the Court did not in *Manitoba* purport to suspend the declaration of invalidity, but rather accompanied it with a declaration deeming the affected Acts valid as an interim measure. The words "suspend" or "suspension" were not used.[61]

Thus, the Court deemed the law to be different than it actually was. In other words, the Court legislated – it made law – not

---

[60] Possibly, the Court realized that as this was a statutory reference, it had no jurisdiction to make a declaration or any other remedial order. It could only describe the law by way of an advisory opinion. Although it does at various points in its decision speak in terms of the unilingual statutes being declared invalid, (see para's 52, 59, 67, 68, 72), this is simply the Court's description of the fact of Manitoba's non-compliance with the constitutional form and manner requirements of bilingual enactment. The Court does not make a formal declaratory order that the statues are invalid. What it did eventually do, on November 5, 1985, five months after release of its decision, was to convene a hearing and issue an order, as agreed by the parties, defining the period of temporary validity of the unilingual laws, i.e., providing temporal specificity to its earlier holding that the invalid laws "are deemed to have temporary validity and force and effect from the date of this judgment to the expiry of the minimum period required for translation, re-enactment, printing and publishing." (at para 150) Thus, the November 4, 1985 Order read as follows: "THE COURT ... ORDERS THAT the period of temporary validity for the laws of Manitoba will continue as follows: (a) to December 31, 1988, [for certain enactments] ... (b) to December 31, 1990 for all other laws of Manitoba." ([1985] 2 S.C.R. 347). By further orders of the court these periods were extended in 1990 ([1990] 3 S.C.R. 1417) and again in 1992 ([1992] 1 S.C.R. 212). However, at no time did the Court issue a declaration of invalidity.
[61] *Spencer v. Attorney-General*, [2013] NZHC 2580 at para. 53

through incremental development of the common law, but by way of judicial fiat.

The conventional characterization of *Manitoba Language Rights* as involving a suspension of a declaration of invalidity is not only unsupported by the language of the decision, it is also contrary to logic and common sense. The defect in Manitoba's unilingual laws was that they were not enacted in the manner and form required for them *ever* to become valid law. It was as though they had never been passed by the Legislature. They may have looked like law, and people may have believed them to be law, and relied on them accordingly (thus, potentially giving rise to legal consequences under various saving doctrines), but as a matter of the law, as the Court expressly stated, they were and had always been, invalid and of no force or effect. No declaration of the Court was required to bring about that legal state of affairs and the Court made no such declaration. That being so, even if the Court had purported to suspend a declaration (which it did not), there is no cognizable legal basis, and indeed no logical basis, upon which to conclude that such a suspension could have breathed life into Manitoba's unilingual statutes (given that they had never been enacted in accordance with the constitutionally-mandated manner and form requirements).

However, despite the impossibility of the occurrence, lawyers, judges, and academics have been saying for decades that the Court in *Manitoba Language Rights* made a suspended declaration of invalidity.[62] While it is true that what happened in

---

[62] Interestingly, in one of the earliest academic commentaries on *Manitoba Language Rights* (R.W. Kerr, "The Remedial Power of the Courts after the Manitoba Language Rights Case" (1986) 6 *Windsor Yearbook of Access to Justice* 252), the author indicated a clear understanding that the Court had taken two distinct actions, i.e. it had: (1) adjudged or declared Manitoba's unilingual laws to be invalid; and, (2) taken further steps to ensure the rule of law. There was no suspension of a declaration of invalidity (at p. 262):

> The Court concluded that its duty was to make a declaration of invalidity and "then to take such steps as will ensure the rule of law in Province of Manitoba." Both conclusions indicate that the Court's announced intention to give

that case may have resembled a suspended declaration in terms of practical effect, resemblance is not identity. This is not a matter of semantics. There is a world of difference between an order

---

temporary continuing effect to Manitoba's unilingual laws is a separate counterbalancing measure to a declaration of invalidity, rather than a mere suspension of such a declaration. If mere suspension of a remedy was all that the Court had in mind, its seems unlikely that the Court would have formulated its decision in these terms.

For the next several years, courts and commentators appear to have appreciated that what had happened in *Manitoba Language Rights* involved the affirmative deeming of invalid laws to be valid, as opposed to a suspension of a declaratory remedy. (See, for example, *R. v. Mercure*, [1988] 1 S.C.R. 234 at p. 280; *R. v. Brydges*, [1990] 1 S.C.R. 190; *Dixon v. British Columbia (Attorney General)*, 1989 CanLII 248 (BCSC) at p. 60). By the mid-1990's however, and onward to the present day, the mantra became that the Supreme Court of Canada had suspended its declaration in *Manitoba Language Rights* and had thereby invented what we now know as the suspended declaration of invalidity. See, A. Lamer, "The Rule of Law and Judicial Independence: Protecting Core Values in Times of Change" (1996) 45 *U.N.B.L.J.* 3 at p. 5; J.C. Tait, "Charter Remedies and Democracy," *Canadian Institute for the Administration of Justice Conference Papers*, "Human Rights in the 21st Century: Prospects, Institutions and Processes," Halifax, October 16-19, 1996, pp. 286-295 at p. 288; A.J. Duggan and K. Roach, "A Further Note on *Final Note*: The Scope and Limits of Judicial Law Making" (2002) 36 *Can. Bus. L.J.* 115 at p. 129; J. Leclair, "Canada's Unfathonable Unwritten Constitutional Principles" (2002) 27 *Queen's L.J.* 389 at p. 391; C.L. L'Heureux-Dube, "Bijuralism: A Supreme Court of Canada Justice's Perspective" (2002) 62 *La. L. Rev.* 449 at p. 452; G.R. Hall, "Preserving the Clavicle in the Cat: Stunted Reform of Common Law Rules in the Supreme Court of Canada" (2002) 36 *Can. Bus. L. J.* 89 at p. 110; P.W. Hogg and C.F. Zwibel. "The Rule of Law in the Supreme Court of Canada" (2005) 55 *U. of Toronto L.J.* 715 at p. 721; J.W. Penney and R.J. Danay, "The Embarrassing Preamble? Understanding the 'Supremacy of God' and the *Charter*" (2006) 39 *U.B.C. Law Rev.* 287 at p. 296; C. Morey, "A Matter of Integrity: Rule of Law, the *Rumuneration Reference*, and Access to Justice" (2016) 49 *U.B.C. Law Rev.* 275 at p. 291; R. Leckey, "Remedial Practice Beyond Constitutional Text" (2016) 64 *Am. J. of Comp. Law* 1 at p. 22; *Reference re Secession of Quebec*, [1998] 2 S.C.R. 217 at para. 145: *R. v. Marshall*, [1999] 3 S.C.R. 533 at para. 12; *Trociuk v. British Columbia (Attorney General)*, [2003] 1 S.C.R. 835 at para. 43; *Canadian Foundation for Children, Youth and the Law v. Canada (Attorney General)*, [2004] 1 S.C.R. 76 at para. 244; *Canada (Attorney General) v. Hislop*, [2007] 1 S.C.R. 429 at para's 90, 140.

which allows an existing state of affairs to continue temporarily, versus an order which creates a new and different state of affairs. Their effects may be similar, but they are very different things. An order allowing an existing state of affairs to continue temporarily might arguably be within the tool box of a court. However, an order bringing a legally effective body of legislation into existence, even temporarily, is something else entirely. It is hard to know exactly how to characterize it, but this much is clear: It is not the act of a court acting in a judicial capacity.

Accordingly, to accept the lore that *Manitoba Language Rights* empowers judges to impose temporary laws which the Constitution says are invalid and of no force or effect, one must wade into shark-infested waters, and ask how the judiciary, especially the Supreme Court acting on a statutory reference, managed to find the power to turn unlawful water into lawful wine.[63] It also becomes necessary to give up the pretense that the term "suspended declaration" actually means what it suggests, and to admit that it is a trope for judicial legislation.[64]

---

[63] A more generous, though revisionist, interpretation of the decision might be that the Court did not, itself, cause the temporary validity of the invalid laws, but that this was the result of the unassisted operation of the Constitution, which the Court merely recognized. Not only would this dodge the vexing question of how the Court acquired the necessary legislative powers, it would also fit the decision within the limits of the solely advisory powers of the Court on a reference. However, this is not what the Court said, and it should be expected that after having reserved its judgment for a full year it would have clearly articulated this theory of the case if this had been what it actually intended to do. Furthermore, on this view of things, *Manitoba Language Rights* would not be about constitutional remedies at all. Certainly, that is not how the case has been interpreted and applied over the past three decades.

[64] The need for judicial linguistic accuracy was commented on by Guido Calabresi:

> [L]inguistic inaccuracy has its costs. Too much of it destroys the credibility of communications in general. And too much use of it by courts destroys their credibility, especially since the major effective control on Courts stems precisely from their duty to explain what they are doing.

G. Calabresi, *A Common Law for the Age of Statutes*, (Cambridge, Mass.: Harvard Univ. Press, 1982) at pp. 175-176

Admittedly, there is a certain pragmatic appeal in the argument that the Court must have had the power to make law to fill the void resulting from the invalidity of Manitoba's unilingual statutes because *someone* had to have such power in order for public chaos to be avoided. However, this is both circular and self-serving. There is nothing that compels the conclusion that in times of public crisis the judiciary must assume the role of sovereign. Indeed, the very nature of the judicial role is disconsonant with that of law-making (apart from the limited way judges may be said to make law through incremental development of the common law). Fundamentally, the problem with allowing courts to assume the role of law-maker in times of crisis, in place of the legislative or executive branches, is that the concept of the rule of law does not sit well with judges being able to define and police the exercise of their own powers. David Dyzenhaus has made this point:

> ...it is an axiom of the rule of law that legal authority is constituted by law, hence it must be exercised within the limits of the law, which requires, that the body purporting to have authority cannot themselves decide what those limits are.
>
> ...
>
> A corollary is that some other body must have the task of policing the limits. And judges understand their role as interpreters of the law independent of other branches of government in constitutional terms, as vesting in them the authority to decide on the limits.[65]

Alexander Bickel, in his seminal work, *The Least Dangerous Branch*, noted the absurdity of inviting the legislature to set its own limits, and warned also against the even greater absurdity of the judiciary being allowed to do so:

> [B]ut the Constitution does not limit the power of the legislature alone. It limits that of the courts as well, and

---

[65] D. Dyzenhaus, *The Constitution of Law: Legality in a Time of Emergency*, (Cambridge: Cambridge Univ. Press, 2006) at pp. 75-76

> it may be equally absurd, therefore, to allow courts to set the limits. It is, indeed, more absurd, because courts are not subject to electoral control.[66]

Justice Reed of the U.S. Supreme Court also stressed that for good reasons the courts do not have power to extend their own jurisdiction; "A court does not have the power, by judicial fiat, to extend its jurisdiction over matters beyond the scope of authority granted to it by its creators."[67] The judiciary is supposed to defend the rule of law by serving as a check on the exercise of power by other branches of government. For the judiciary to arrogate to itself the power to make law in the way that legislators make it, or as the executive may do so under the royal prerogative, is alarmingly authoritarian. It is not the way democracies are supposed to work.

The best explanation for how the Court in *Manitoba Language Rights* found these astonishing powers *within the Constitution* may simply be that it did not do so. A strong case can be made that the Court, in this extraordinary situation of existential constitutional crisis, acted outside the law in an extra-constitutional manner. In fact, Antonio Lamer, one of the *Manitoba Language Rights* judges, writing extra-judicially in 1996 as the then Chief Justice of Canada, alluded to the extra-constitutional quality of the Court's decision by acknowledging that the supremacy of the Constitution *had to yield* to the demands of legal order:

> Powerful as the Court regarded the principle of the supremacy of the Constitution – itself an important aspect of the rule of law – to be, it *had to yield* to the even more fundamental principle that the relations between citizen and citizen and between citizen and the

---

[66] A.M. Bickel, *The Least Dangerous Branch: The Supreme Court at the Bar of Politics*, (New Haven: Yale Univ. Press, 1962) at pp. 3-4
[67] *Stoll v. Gottlieb*, 305 U.S. 165 (1938) at p. 171

state be governed by a positive legal order.[68] (emphasis
added)

The concept of a Constitution being supplanted in times of crisis
is not unprecedented and is not necessarily a bad thing, as will be
explained below. However, was it appropriate for the Court itself
to initiate these extra-constitutional actions, rather than to decide,
as courts typically do, on the legitimacy of another branch of
government doing so? It is one thing for a court to recognize and
give effect to unconstitutional acts of the executive or legislature,
and another thing for the court to do the acts itself. And even if it
was appropriate for the Court to do so in this exceptional case,
should its actions have been regarded as judicial in any
conventional sense? Should its decision have been received as a
legitimate precedent for use by courts in future cases involving
nothing resembling the situation in Manitoba in 1985?

It is submitted that this extra-constitutional action taken by the
Court in the context of an extreme public crisis should not have
been allowed to become juridically normalized.[69] This has, in fact,
happened in Canada where the granting of suspended declarations
of invalidity, often expressly on the authority of *Manitoba
Language Rights*, has become commonplace.[70]

---

[68] A. Lamer, "The Rule of Law and Judicial Independence: Protecting Core
Values in Times of Change" (1996) 45 *U.N.B.L.J.* 3 at p. 5

[69] Mark Tushnet advances an interesting argument that emergency powers
should not be normalized, but rather regarded as extraconstitutional and, as
such, regrettable: "Treating emergency powers as extraconstitutional has
another advantage. Decision-makers can then understand that they should
regret that they find themselves compelled to invoke emergency powers." M.
Tushnet, "Defending Korematsu: Reflections on Civil Liberties in Wartime"
(2003) *Wis. L. Rev.* 273 at p. 306

[70] For example, in one case, the Ontario Court of Appeal found a municipal by-
law unconstitutional in that its blanket prohibition of commercial signs in
residential areas was an impermissible restriction on freedom of expression.
(*Vann Media Group Inc. v. Oakville (Town)*, 2008 ONCA 752 (CanLII)) It
declared the by-law invalid, but then purported to suspend its declaration for
six months in order to give the municipality time to enact a constitutionally-
compliant replacement by-law. During the suspension period the

It is now time to examine the circumstances where courts will countenance public officials acting outside the Constitution, and even contrary to it, during times of emergency.

6.2 *"Sovereign is He Who Decides on the Exception"* [71]

Two months before the Supreme Court released its decision in *Manitoba Language Rights*, the German legal and political theorist, Carl Schmitt, died at age 96. Notwithstanding the ignominy of his early association with the Nazis,[72] Schmitt became and remains one of the leading political thinkers of the twentieth century. His signature contribution was his critique of liberalism and its inherent contradictions, particularly its inability to contend with the exception – emergency situations where the very survival of the state is imperiled.[73] This is how David Dyzenhaus explains Schmitt's critique of liberalism's assumption that all political power can be confined by the rule of law:

> Liberalism aspires to banish the state of emergency or exception from the legal order because it wants a world where all political authority is subject to law. But liberals have to recognize that legal norms cannot apply in a state of emergency. A state of emergency is a

---

unconstitutional bylaw was deemed valid so that citizens could be prosecuted for breaching what the court had found to be an unconstitutional law. It is difficult to draw a comparison between the impending chaos in Manitoba in 1985 due to the imminent collapse of the province's legal system, and the inconvenience that might have resulted from some commercial signage being erected in the Town of Oakville's quaint residential areas pending enactment of a constitutionally valid law.

[71] Carl Schmitt, *Political Theology, Four Chapters on the Concept of Sovereignty*, G. Schwab (trans.), (Chicago: University of Chicago Press, 2005) at p. 5

[72] According to David Dyzenhaus, Schmitt became disillusioned with Nazi policies because he was too intellectual for the Nazis, and too academic to express properly the visceral basis of Nazi ideology. Thus, he fell from official favour. D. Dyzenhaus, ed., *Law as Politics: Carl Schmidt's Critique of Liberalism*, (Durham and London: Duke Univ. Press, 1998) at p. 2

[73] The author is indebted to Jamie Peltomaa (Columbia University and Sciences Po, class of 2020) who introduced him to the writings of Carl Schmitt.

lawless void, a legal black hole, in which the state acts unconstrained by law.[74]

Another writer adds these thoughts:

> According to Schmitt, the existence of exceptional situations refutes the formal face of legal liberalism, which argues that pre-established general norms cover and apply to all possible situations. The need to decide the exceptional, concrete situation per force catapults the judge into the role of a law-maker.[75]

Kim Lane Scheppele explains that, according to Schmitt, liberal constitutionalism actually depends on governments being able to fool their citizens to believe that legal norms can govern in emergencies:

> For Schmitt, liberal constitutions fool their citizens if it appears that these constitutions could have accounted for everything. There will always be moments outside the constitutional range of legitimate expectation, and legitimate constitutional action under unanticipated and extreme threats can never be fully elucidated within a constitution's terms. This is a clear challenge to the idea that the rule of law must constrain rulers and ruled alike, for if the rule of law constrains the sovereign entirely, then the sovereign should not be

---

[74] D. Dyzenhaus, "*Schmitt v. Dicey*: Are States of Emergency Inside or Outside the Legal Order?" (2006) 27 *Cardoza L. Rev.* 2005 at p. 2006

[75] O. Gross, "The Normless and Exceptionless Exception: Carl Schmitt's Theory of Emergency Powers and the 'Norm-Exception' Dichotomy" (2000) 21 *Cardoza L. Rev.* 1825 at p. 1827. According to Victor Ramraj who has written extensively about law in the states of emergency:

> For Schmitt, emergencies expose a fundamental weakness in liberalism; the most the law could do is to spell out *who* may exercise emergency powers. It cannot, however, set out in advance what would be a necessary or permissible response. And so, in an emergency, "the state remains, whereas the law recedes."

V.V. Ramraj, "Emergency Powers and Constitutional Theory" (2011) 41 *Hong Kong. L. J.* 165 at p. 166

able to claim exception to the rules. But an emergency makes visible the incompleteness of the constitutional design because by its very nature, it cannot be predicted in its particulars in advance. In practice, Schmitt seems to say, a liberal constitution can therefore never be complete.[76]

The situation in Manitoba in 1985 was of true Schmittian proportions. A legal and political crisis loomed for which the Constitution provided no solution. Almost all of Manitoba's laws *were* invalid and of no force or effect, but simply recognizing that fact, without more being done *by someone*, would have led to chaos. Some way had to be found to give temporary force and effect to these invalid unilingual laws. *But who*, if anyone, had the power to do this? The idea of a court being able to give life to non-law is, to say the least, novel. No precedent for the exercise of such a power was provided, and it is doubtful that any such precedent existed. All the Court was able to say was that the rule of law required that there be an enforceable body of positive laws, and therefore that such laws must be deemed to exist for the minimum period of time required for the Legislature to bring them into existence through constitutional means. *Ipse dixit.*

Strangely, the Court did not squarely address the fundamental point of its institutional competence to give temporary force and effect to the invalid and ineffectual unilingual laws. This omission is strange for several reasons. First, one would think that the Court's instinctive reaction to the suggestion that it should confer validity on what is legally invalid would be to question its power to do so. Second, in the absence of any clear power for the Court thus to turn water into wine, it might be expected that the Court would inquire into whether another person or body possessed these remarkable powers. Third, one would have expected the Court to be especially reticent about exercising such astonishing and unprecedented powers in the context of a

---

[76] K. Lane Schleppele, "Law in a Time of Emergency: States of Exception and the Temptations of 9/11" (2004) 6 *U. Pa. J. Const. L.* 1001 at pp. 1009-1010

statutory reference where it could lawfully do nothing more than provide an advisory opinion.[77]

The closest the Court came to wrestling with these issues was to conclude that since, in other cases, the executive or the legislature had acted to fill a legal vacuum resulting from a determination of constitutional invalidity, it must also be open to the Court to do so itself (rather than just decide on the legality of executive or legislative actions). Thus, the Court wrote as follows:

> The *Special Reference No. 1 of 1955, supra,* [a decision of the Federal Court of Pakistan under the state necessity doctrine] stands for the proposition that a situation of state necessity can arise as a consequence of judicial invalidation of unconstitutional laws, leaving a legal void. The difference between that case and the present is that in the present case it is the *judicial* branch that is retrospectively recognizing unconstitutional laws as temporarily valid and enforceable, while in the *Special Reference No. 1 of 1955* case it was the *executive* branch of government which proclaimed that laws were retrospectively valid and enforceable, and that the role of the judiciary was simply to condone the actions of the executive. (emphasis in the original)

> Thus, the *Special Reference No. 1 of 1955* case, *supra,* cannot be directly applied to the present set of circumstances. It is, however, illustrative of the broader principles which justify this Court's actions in the present case: namely that otherwise invalid acts may be recognized as temporarily valid in order to preserve the normative order and rule of law. The Federal Court of Pakistan allowed an unconstitutional exercise of executive power since the effects of *not* allowing such

---

[77] The Court did not address the issue of its limited competence on a statutory reference. Several years later, Chief Justice Lamer explained, circuitously, that in *Manitoba Language Rights*: "The rule of law gave this Court constitutional authority to provide a binding remedy in this unique situation." *Reference re Remuneration of Judges of PEI et al*, [1998] 1 S.C.R. 3 at para. 10.

an exercise of power would have been anarchy and
chaos and thereby a violation of the rule of law.
(emphasis in the original)

...

In every case in which the doctrine of state necessity
has been applied it has been *either the executive or the
legislative branch of government* which has responded
to the necessitous circumstances, later to have its
actions tested in the courts. This fact does not,
however, detract from the general relevance of these
cases in demonstrating that courts will not allow the
Constitution to be used to create chaos and disorder.[78]
(emphasis added)

Two points of significance jump out from these passages. First,
the Court recognized as legitimate the executive branch
responding to a situation of state necessity by means of "an
unconstitutional exercise of executive power." Second, it
essentially conflated the judicial branch with the executive and
legislative branches in terms of competence to take
unconstitutional actions in response to situations of state necessity
which threaten the rule of law. The first point is unremarkable;
the second is breathtaking. Both points identify *Manitoba
Language Rights* as an outlier – a case involving an
unconstitutional, or extra-constitutional, judicial response to a
situation of public crisis. As such, it is a dubious authority for the
purportedly constitutional exercise by courts of a general power
to sanctify unlawful conduct under authority of the suspended
declaration of invalidity.

Was it necessary for the Supreme Court in *Manitoba Language
Rights* to give temporary effect to Manitoba's invalid and
ineffective unilingual laws in order to avert public chaos?
Probably it was not. There were various options open to the Court
which would not have required it to invent for itself a power to
impose non-law.

---

[78] *Manitoba Language Rights*, [1985] 1 S.C.R. 721 at para's 102, 103 and 106

Most obviously, as Justice O'Sullivan of the Manitoba Court of Appeal noted in a case argued the day after release of the *Manitoba Language Rights* decision, the Supreme Court could have acknowledged the executive or royal prerogative power. This is the power of Her Majesty in right of Manitoba (that is, the Lieutenant Governor of Manitoba acting on the advice of the Premier and Cabinet) to bring into effect laws necessary to deal with a public emergency.[79] That very power was, in fact, recognized by the Supreme Court in *Manitoba Language Rights* in its discussion of the Federal Court of Pakistan's decision in *Special Reference No. 1 of 1955*, referred to above. In that case, the Governor General of Pakistan reacted to a constitutional emergency by issuing a proclamation conferring on himself the power to validate and enforce all laws necessary to preserve the State and maintain the government of the country during the period of emergency. Although the Pakistani court's decision was framed in terms of the state necessity doctrine, it could as well have been explained as an exercise of the royal prerogative to act extra-legally in order to deal with situations of public crisis.

This royal prerogative has a long and venerable history. John Locke, though considered the father of modern liberalism, was an early proponent. He contended that the formal powers of the executive set out in the law must be supplemented with "prerogative", that is: "Power to act according to discretion, for the publick good, without prescription of the Law, and sometimes even against it."[80] More recently, the House of Lords adopted Locke's formulation of the emergency prerogative:

> The essence of a prerogative power, if one follows Locke's thought, is not merely to administer the existing law – there is no need for any prerogative to execute the law – but to act for the public good, where

---

[79] *Yeryk v. Yeryk,* [1985] 5 WWR 705

[80] C. Fatovic, *Outside the Law: Emergency and Executive Power*, (Baltimore, John Hopkins Univ. Press, 2009), at p. 4, quoting J. Locke, *Two Treatises of Government*, ed. P. Laslett (Cambridge: Cambridge University Press, 1988) at para. 160

there is no law, or even to dispense with or override the law where the ultimate preservation of society is in question.[81]

The principle that survival of the state supersedes all other laws was clearly and candidly expressed in 1918 by Chief Justice Fitzpatrick of the Supreme Court of Canada:

Our legislators were no doubt impressed in the hour of peril with the conviction that the safety of the country is the supreme law against which no other law can prevail. It is our clear duty to give effect to their patriotic intention.[82]

Even the strong advocate for limited government, Thomas Jefferson, recognized the need to allow deviation from the written law in order to protect the country:

The laws of necessity, of self-preservation, of saving our country when in danger, are of higher obligation. To lose our country by a scrupulous adherence to written law, would be to lose the law itself, with life, liberty, property and those who are enjoying them with us; thus absurdly sacrificing the end to the means.[83]

Similarly, Alexander Hamilton wrote: "The circumstances that endanger the safety of nations are infinite, and for this reason, no constitutional shackles can wisely be imposed on the power to which the care of it is committed."[84] And Abraham Lincoln, who

---

[81] *Burmah Oil Co. (Burmah Trading) v. Lord Advocate*, [1965] AC 75 at p. 118 , per Viscount Radcliffe

[82] *Re Gray* (1918), 57 SCR 150 at p. 160

[83] P.F. Ford, ed., *The Writings of Thomas Jefferson* (New York: G.B. Putnam's Sons, 1893) at pp. 279-80, quoted in V. Iyer, "Courts and Constitutional Usurpers: Some Lessons from Fiji" (2005) 28 *Dalhousie L.J.* 27 at p. 37

[84] "The Federalist No. 23 – The Necessity of a Government as Energetic as the One Proposed to the Preservation of the Union", in I. Kramnick (ed.) A. Hamilton, J. Madison and J. Jay, *The Federalist Papers* (London: Penguin, 1987) at 185-85

controversially suspended *habeas corpus* during the Civil War without the prior authority of Congress, is said to have "subscribed to a theory that in a time of emergency, the President could assume whatever legislative, executive, and judicial powers he thought necessary to preserve the nation, and could in the process break the 'fundamental laws of the nation, if such a step were unavoidable'."[85]

Oliver Cromwell is quoted as having said: "If nothing be done but what is according to the law, the throat of the nation might be cut while we send for someone to make the law."[86] As it has sometimes been put, "the Constitution is not a suicide pact,"[87] and in situations of crisis, where the Constitution or other positive law does not provide the necessary tools for survival of the state, the executive may act in extra-legal or extra-constitutional ways. This has been described as "political realism":

> But the core of political realism is not a mere dismissal of law. It is the claim that recognizes the authority and binding force of law, yet argues that the law may be violated for the sake of law itself. This is the idea of reason of state. The state is a legal order and to preserve that legal order those charged with its preservation may find it expedient to perform illegal acts.[88]

Thus, it would appear that the Supreme Court in *Manitoba Language Rights* could have left it to the executive branch of government to deal with the impending emergency arising from

---

[85] D. Dyzenhaus, *"Schmitt v. Dicey:* Are States of Emergency Inside or Outside the Legal Order" (2006) 27 *Cardozo L. Rev.* 2005 at p. 2013, quoting C. L Rossiter, *Constitutional Dictatorship*, 1948 (Princeton: Princeton Univ. Press, 1979) at p. 229

[86] Quoted in M.M. Stavsky, "The Doctrine of State Necessity in Pakistan" (1983) 16 *Cornell Int'l L.J.* 341 at p. 368

[87] *Kennedy v. Mendoza-Martinez*, 372 U.S. 144 (1963) at p. 160, per Goldberg, J.; R.A. Posner, *Not a Suicide Pact: The Constitution in a Time of National Emergency* (New York, Oxford: Oxford Univ. Press, 2006)

[88] T. Nardin, "Emergency Logic: Prudence, Morality and the Rule of Law" in V.V. Ramraj, ed., *Emergencies and the Limits of Legality*, (Cambridge: Cambridge Univ. Press, 2008) 97-117 at pp. 114-115

the determination that Manitoba's unilingual laws were invalid and of no force or effect. Alternatively, it could have left it to the federal Parliament to legislate a temporary solution pursuant to its powers to legislate in emergencies regarding matters of provincial jurisdiction under the Constitution's "peace, order and good government" clause.[89] Or, it could have allowed for the negotiation of a political solution; for example, an amendment to the Constitution allowing English-only enactment, retrospectively, prospectively, or both.[90]

There is no reason to believe that the political actors could not have acted effectively and with sufficient alacrity to avert the apprehended chaos. Both the Canadian and Manitoba governments were headed by parties with strong legislative majorities. While the wheels of government tend to move slowly, there is truth in the old adage that nothing sharpens the mind quite like an impending morning execution. Dale Gibson of the University of Manitoba, who served as a legal advisor to the Manitoba government on its language rights issues,[91] thought that the political actors could have dealt with the problem and that it

---

[89] *Re Anti-Inflation Act*, [1976] 2 S.C.R. 373; *Fort Frances Pulp and Paper Co. v. Manitoba Free Press Co.*, [1923] 3 D.L.R. 629 (P.C.)

[90] In fact, Professor Roach has expressed the view that this would have been the probable outcome if the Court had simply pronounced on the illegal status of the unilingual laws. K. Roach, *The Supreme Court on Trial: Judicial Activism or Democratic Dialogue*, (Toronto: Irwin Law, rev'd ed., 2016, at p. 172). A constitutional amendment that would have averted the crisis had in fact been negotiated between the federal and Manitoba governments and the Franco-Manitoba community in 1983, but failed as a result of procedural roadblocks established by the opposition party in the Manitoba Legislature (G.H.A. Mackintosh, "Heading Off Bilodeau: Attempting Constitutional Amendment" (1985) 15 *Man. L.J.* 271). See also, M. Dawson, "From the Backroom to the Front Line: Making Constitutional History or Encounters with the Constitution: Patriation, Meech Lake and Charlottetown" (2012) 57 *McGill L.J.* 955 at p. 975

[91] Gibson's role is reported in G.H.A. Mackintosh, "Heading Off Bilodeau: Attempting Constitutional Amendment" (1985)15 *Man. L.J.* 271 at pp. 274-276

was not necessary for the Court to intervene in the "spurious" way that it did:

> In my view, swift legislative remedial measures would have been possible and would have been preferable to the spurious invocation of the "rule of law" to which the Court felt driven.[92]

As well, it arguably would not have been inappropriate, in the circumstances, for the Court to have communicated its intended decision to the government in advance of its release to the general public. Although this would have been an unusual step, it must be remembered that this was a statutory reference where the Court was acting in a non-judicial capacity as a legal advisor to the Crown. And in any event, it is difficult to take seriously concerns that the Court would or should have felt constrained by judicial protocol in a case where it ultimately decided, without the support of any applicable precedent, to temporarily implement an entire body of constitutionally invalid laws. The reality, however, is that the Court had identified a problem, and had decided that it alone could fix it.

It is unclear why the Court chose not to follow the course of judicial modesty and self-restraint, but rather to assume for itself the power to declare enforceable that which it had just decided was invalid and of no force or effect. Did it not trust the politicians to solve the problem in a satisfactory manner? Was it a case of institutional hubris? Was the Court, in these early days of Canada's patriated Constitution, eager to flex its new constitutional muscles?[93] Several statements in the decision reveal

---

[92] D. Gibson, "Founding Fathers-in-Law: Judicial Amendment of the Canadian Constitution" (1992) 55 *Law & Contemp. Probs.* 261 at p. 277, footnote 48

[93] These were indeed heady times for constitutional law at the Supreme Court. It assumed with great gusto its new powers under the *Charter*. Just six months after deciding *Manitoba Language Rights*, it released its groundbreaking and controversial decision in *Reference Re s. 94(2) of* Motor Vehicle Act *(British Columbia)*, [1985] 2 SCR 486, where it decided that the "principles of fundamental justice" in s. 7 of the Charter were *substantive* as well as procedural in nature, notwithstanding clear and uncontroverted evidence that

a resolute determination that only the Court could or should solve the problem:

> The judiciary is the institution charged with the duty of ensuring that the government complies with the Constitution. We must protect those whose constitutional rights have been violated, whomever they may be, and whatever the reasons for their violation.
>
> ...
>
> Since April 17, 1982, the mandate of the judiciary to protect the Constitution has been embodied in s. 52 of the *Constitution Act, 1982*.
>
> ...
>
> A declaration that the laws of Manitoba are invalid and of no legal force or effect would deprive Manitoba of its legal order and cause a transgression of the rule of law. For the Court to allow such a situation to arise and fail to resolve it would be an abdication of its responsibility as protector and preserver of the Constitution.
>
> ...
>
> The only appropriate resolution to this Reference is for the Court to fulfill its duty under s. 52 of the *Constitution Act, 1982* and declare all the unilingual Acts of the Legislature of Manitoba to be invalid and of not force and effect and then to take such steps as

---

the framers of the *Charter* intended that it refer only to procedural fairness. See, A. Petter, *The Politics of the Charter: The Illusive Promise of Constitutional Rights*, (Toronto, Buffalo, London: Univ. of Toronto Press, 2010) at pp. 50-76. The Court's enthusiasm for the *Charter* was also reflected by these remarks by Chief Justice Antonio Lamer in 1992: "[T]he introduction of the Charter has been nothing less than a revolution on the scale of the introduction of the metric system, the great medical discoveries of Louis Pasteur, and the invention of penicillin and the laser." Quoted in R. Hirschl, *Towards Juristocracy: The Origins and Consequences of the New Constitutionalism*, (Cambridge, Mass.: Harvard Univ. Press, 2004) at p. 18

will ensure the rule of law in the Province of Manitoba.[94]

The Court refused to recognize any meaningful distinction between the powers of the judicial branch and those of the executive and legislative branches:

> The question in *Ibrahim, supra,* [a case from Cyprus involving a constitutional crisis] was whether a temporary unconstitutional law, enacted in order to meet the exigencies of a state of emergency, could be valid. The question in the present Reference is quite different. Here, the Court is concerned with whether unconstitutional laws can be given temporary validity in order to avoid a state of emergency. *It is the Court which must take steps* to avoid the deleterious consequences of the Manitoba Legislature's persistent failure to observe the Constitution. In *Ibrahim* the Court simply condoned the measures taken by the Parliament of Cyprus in response to a necessitous situation arising out of circumstances beyond its control. Thus, *Ibrahim* is not directly applicable to the circumstances of the present case. (emphasis added)
>
> ...
>
> The *Special Reference No. 1 of 1955, supra,* [a case from Pakistan discussed above] stands for the proposition that a situation of state necessity can arise as a consequence of judicial invalidation of unconstitutional laws, leaving a legal void. The difference between that case and the present is that in the present case it is the *judicial* branch of government that is retrospectively recognizing unconstitutional laws as temporarily valid and enforceable, while in the *Special Reference No. 1 of 1955* case it was the *executive* branch of government which was proclaimed that laws were retrospectively valid and enforceable,

---

[94] *Manitoba Language Rights*, [1985] 1 S.C.R. 721 at para's 47, 50, 68 and 72

and the role of the judiciary was simply to condone the actions of the executive. (emphasis in the original)[95]

It is evident that the Court, while fully aware of the primary role played by the legislative and executive branches in the precedent cases referred to, was not prepared to cede any ground to the other governmental branches in this case. This calls to mind the famous opening line in Carl Schmitt's seminal work on the state of emergencies, or the exception: "Sovereign is he who decides on the exception."[96] The Court asserted in clear and unmistakable terms its sovereignty over the state of emergency that existed in Manitoba consequent upon its determination that Manitoba's unilingual laws were and had always been invalid and of no force or effect. It had no time for the idea that the executive or legislative branches should be allowed to perform their usual roles, with the Court restricting itself to judicial functions.

Professor Jacques Frémont found unconvincing the Court's efforts to distinguish the *Ibrahim* case[97] (where the Parliament of Cyprus enacted constitutionally unauthorized legislation to deal with an emergency), and observed that even though there were alternatives available to it, "the Court refused to play a passive role":

> In the *Manitoba Reference* case, the reasons of the Court indicate clearly that other avenues were open to ensure the existence of the principle of legality despite the effect of an eventual ruling. It is striking that, in discussing the doctrine of necessity in this case, the Court indicated clearly, with Commonwealth case law in support, that the concept of rule of law fully justified the judiciary to maintain the validity of otherwise unconstitutional statutes in exceptional circumstances

---

[95] *ibid.* at para's 96 and 102

[96] Carl Schmitt, *Political Theology, Four Chapters on the Concept of Sovereignty*, George Schwab (trans.), (Chicago: University of Chicago Press, 2005) at p. 5

[97] *Attorney General of the Replubic v. Mustafa Ibrahim*, [1964] Cyprus Law Reports 195

where the principle of the rule of law is threatened. The most interesting case discussed is that of *Attorney General of the Republic v. Mustafa Ibrahim* where *Parliament had taken upon itself the task* of remedying an emergency by using an ordinary statute to modify a provision of the constitution. That measure *was approved by the Court* of Appeal under the doctrine of necessity. In *In Re Manitoba Language Rights* the Court took great pains to distinguish *Ibrahim* from the instant case but it is very difficult to actually do so.

Can it be said, however, that the situation would have been similar if the Court had simply invalidated the Manitoba statutes and if the Manitoba Legislature or the Federal Parliament had intervened legislatively or otherwise to protect public order and the rule of law in the province? Although alternatives existed it is significant that *the Court refused to play a passive role.* The crucial conclusion to draw in the light of these two cases is that the Court considered the judiciary to be the guardian, protector and, in some cases, the saviour of the constitution and of the constitutional order.[98] (emphasis added)

Similarly, Peter Hogg has commented upon the important difference between the *Ibrahim* case and *Manitoba Language Rights*, in that in the former case:

> … the Cypriot Court was not the author of the measures necessary to preserve the legal order. The Court's role was confined to upholding a measure promulgated by another institution of government, in this case, the Parliament of Cyprus.[99]

---

[98] J. Frémont, "The Dickson Court, the Courts, and the Constitutional Balance of Powers in the Canadian System of Government" (1991) 20 *Man. L.J.* 451 at pp. 468-469

[99] P.W. Hogg, "Necessity in a Constitutional Crisis" (1989) 15 *Monash Univ. L. Rev.* 253 at p. 262

The highly political, indeed Schmittian, nature of the Court's decision in *Manitoba Language Rights* was also recognized at an early stage by Professor Robert Kerr of the University of Windsor, who commented on the Court's acceptance for itself of the authority to take emergency action:

> There is no discussion in the judgment of the possibility of the Court simply recognizing the applicability of the doctrine of state necessity to the Manitoba situation and leaving it to the legislature and executive to take appropriate action under that doctrine. However, this would seem to suggest itself as a natural and simple alternative to the proposal for correction by way of amendment, particularly in light of the precedents of emergency legislative or executive action reviewed by the Court. The fact that the Court does not suggest this alternative reinforces the conclusion that *the Court accepted for itself the authority to take emergency action*. (emphasis added)[100]

It has been observed that politics "hides at the backdoor of constitutional adjudication."[101] It is probably fair to say that politics was invited to sit at the kitchen table as *Manitoba Language Rights* was being decided. Justice Gerald LeDain, who participated in the *Manitoba Language Rights* decision, captured the overtly political nature of the case several years after his retirement from the Court as he described it as "a boldly creative act of judicial statesmanship."[102] Statesmanship is what politicians do. Judges are supposed to decide cases in accordance

---

[100] R.W. Kerr, "The Remedial Power of the Courts after the Manitoba Language Rights Case" (1986) 6 *Windsor Yearbook of Access to Justice*, 252 at p. 262

[101] C. Hübner Mendes, *Constitutional Courts and Deliberative Democracy*, (Oxford: Oxford Univ. Press, 2013) at p. 209

[102] G. LeDain, "Jean Beetz as Judge and Colleague" (1994) 28 *R.J.T. n.s.* 721 at p. 723

with the law, although they are sometimes drawn, and at other times drive themselves, into the realm of politics.[103]

Of course, for liberal constitutionalists, the idea of deviating from the sanctity of the rule of law is difficult to accept:

> The kind of extralegal action that executives are frequently called upon to take in response to emergencies is deeply problematic for liberal constitutionalism, which gives pride of place to the rule of law, both in its self-definition and in its standard mode of operation.[104]

Thus, there followed a perceived need to fit what the Court had done in *Manitoba Language Rights* within normalized constitutional parameters. That was accomplished over the ensuing three decades by a series of Houdini-like contortions of the Canadian Constitution.

6.3   *Criticism of the Manitoba Language Rights Decision*

There is relatively little academic commentary that is critical of what the Supreme Court did in *Manitoba Language Rights.*[105] The

---

[103] S.A. de Smith once described legal analyses by judges of unconstitutional action as "fundamentally political judgments dressed in legalistic garb." S.A. de Smith, "Constitutional Lawyers in Revolutionary Situations" (1968) 7 *W. Ontario L. Rev.* 93 at p. 94

[104] C. Fatovic, *Outside the Law: Emergency and Executive Power*, (Baltimore: John Hopkins Univ. Press, 2009) at p. 2

[105] Outside the mainstream were the views expressed by Dale Gibson who contended that the Court effectively amended the Constitution and "fashion[ed] constitutional supplements from whole cloth." D. Gibson, "Founding Fathers-in-Law: Judicial Amendment of the Canadian Constitution" (1992) 55 *Law & Contemp. Probs.* 261 at p. 276. See also, D. Gibson, "The Real Laws of the Constitution" (1990) 28 *Alta. L. Rev.* 358 at pp. 371-373. Hugo Cyr and Monica Popescu also referred to the "intellectual contortion" the Court was required to perform in order to be able to claim that it was not suspending the Constitution. H. Cyr and M. Popescu, "The Supreme Court of Canada" in A. Jakab, A. Dyevre and G. Itzcovich, ed's., *Comparative Constitutional Reasoning*, (Cambridge: Cambridge Univ. Press, 2017) pp. 154-198 at pp. 174-175

predominate view is that the Court had no choice but to do what it did in order to avert chaos and anarchy.[106] As for judicial opinions on the matter, perhaps the only questioning of the competence of the Supreme Court to cause invalid laws to become temporarily valid came from a justice of the Manitoba Court of Appeal who was promptly and publicly chastised by the Chief Justice of Manitoba.[107]

On the day following release of the Supreme Court's decision in *Manitoba Language Rights,* the Manitoba Court of Appeal heard a family law case which did not appear to raise any issues of especial difficulty or importance. However, Justice Joseph O'Sullivan, obviously perplexed by what the Supreme Court had done, took this as an opportunity to express his thoughts – in very blunt terms:

> If what appear to be her [Majesty's] laws are not really so, we can certainly declare them null and void. But I do not see how we have the power to declare them invalid at the option of the court. For that would be to assume for the courts a power that is not even recognized in the Queen, as James II found out long ago.

> I have always understood that the rule of law is quite different from the rule of lawyers. I cannot bring myself to believe that the rule of law can require the imposition by a court of null laws. There is a contradiction in terms.

---

[106] "Clearly, the elimination of all law in Manitoba would be an act of judicial lunacy and the Court reasonably deferred the remedial effect of its ruling until Parliament had a chance to remedy the defect." R. Dixon and S. Issacharoff, "Living to Fight Another Day: Judicial Deferral in Defense of Democracy" (2016) *Wis. L. Rev.* 683 at p. 701; "It is hard to criticize the Court's ruling, since the Court could hardly allow the Manitoba Legislature to ignore its constitutional obligations, and could hardly leave Manitoba with a vacuum of law." P.W. Hogg, "Canada: From Privy Council to Supreme Court," in J. Goldsworthy, ed., *Interpreting Constitutions: A Comparative Study,* (Oxford: Oxford Univ. Press, 2006) 55 at p. 98
[107] *Yeryk v. Yeryk*, [1985] 5 WWR 705 at para. 17

...

I do not understand how the Supreme Court or any other court has a power to declare judicially valid or enforceable that which is judicially invalid. I do not understand how it can be said that emergency situations justify a usurpation by a court of the royal power.

In British systems, the Queen is the one who can bring into effect laws made necessary by true emergencies. If the laws of Manitoba were really judicially invalid, I think it is the Queen in right of Manitoba who has the right to proclaim measures necessary to meet the situation, not the Supreme Court.

I do not know of anyone ever until this time disputing the Queen's royal prerogative in this respect. Courts have recognized royal proclamations declaring laws in force in time of emergency.

...

In writing as I do, I do not intend to reject the Supreme Court's judicial authority but rather to attempt to make sense of their judgment as best I can, having regard to the presumption that the court intends to follow the law and not to create it or to impose new law.[108]

This resulted in a judicial tongue-lashing from Chief Justice Alfred Monnin:

Now to another aspect. I have read the reasons for judgment of my brother O'Sullivan. The issue about which he writes was not discussed by counsel at the hearing but raised by him. It was not followed by the other members of the panel. It has nothing to do with the case at hand.

---

[108] *ibid.* at para's 28, 29, 35, 36, 37 and 42

His comments are gratuitous, unnecessary, injudicious and perhaps impertinent. I disassociate myself entirely from them.[109]

Shut up, he explained.[110]

Though Justice O'Sullivan professed not to be challenging the Supreme Court's authority, he was very clearly challenging its grasp of some very basic principles of the law. His words were certainly impolitic, but the thrust of his criticism was dead on the mark. Where did the Supreme Court, or any court, get the "power to declare judicially valid or enforceable that which is judicially invalid"? The only answer suggested by the Supreme Court was that because the executive and legislative branches were recognized as having such powers in situations of emergency where the rule of law was threatened, so too must the courts have such powers. Justice O'Sullivan had the impertinence to ask the basis on which the Supreme Court believed that it could exercise powers which heretofore had been exercised by legislatures or the executive, but never by the courts. He further asked: How could the rule of law require a court to impose null laws? These are legitimate questions which have never been answered.

Nonetheless, *Manitoba Language Rights* has become the *magna carta* of a school of constitutional thought that sees nothing wrong with judges, often in the name of the rule of law, declaring that the law should for a temporary period be that which has already been determined not to be the law. They do so notwithstanding s. 52(1) of the Constitution which stipulates that the law to which they are purporting to give temporary validity "is ... of no force or effect". To the contrary, they actually point to s. 52(1) as the *source* of their power to vivify invalid law.

---

[109] *ibid.* at para's 16-17
[110] *"Are you lost daddy?" I asked tenderly. "Shut up" he explained.* Ring Lardner, *The Young Immigrunts* (1920), in The Ring Lardner Reader 411, 426 (Maxwell Geismar, ed., 1963), quoted in M. Tushnet, "Shut Up He Explained" (2001) 95 *Nw. U. L. Rev.* 907 at p. 907

6.4 *Manitoba Language Rights as a Legal Precedent*

For what propositions of law does *Manitoba Language Rights* properly stand as authority? Strictly speaking, the answer is "none." An advisory opinion on a statutory reference is not binding on any court, and has no more authority than would an opinion of a law officer of the Crown.[111] In fact, the Court on a reference acts in a non-judicial capacity. However, the practical reality is that reference opinions are treated as though they were judicial decisions, and it is probably appropriate to assess *Manitoba Language Rights* on that basis.[112] At the same time, given its unusual context, it would also seem appropriate to be particularly careful not to read things into the decision that are not there.

On the basis that a case is only authority for what it actually decides, what did the Court in *Manitoba Language Rights* actually decide? In answering this question, let us give the Court the benefit of every doubt and assume that it, indeed, had no choice in the matter: that Armageddon would have ensued if it had not acted as it did. Assume, contrary to what is argued above, that allowing the executive or legislators to exercise their recognized emergency powers would not have averted chaos. Where would that leave us in terms of *Manitoba Language Rights* as a legal precedent? Would it support the now virtually routine issuance by courts of suspended declarations of invalidity? It is submitted that it would not, for the following reasons:

1. The Court did not suggest that the invalidity of Manitoba's unilingual laws resulted from any determination or declaration of the Court. They were found to be and to have always been invalid and no force and effect.

---

[111] *Reference re Secession of Quebec*, [1998] 2 S.C.R. 217 at para. 15
[112] *Canada (Attorney General) v. Bedford*, [2013] 3 S.C.R. 1101 at para. 40

2. The Court did not purport to suspend or delay any order, declaration or other remedy granted. The words, suspend or delay, or their variations, were nowhere used.

3. As this was a statutory reference, the Court had no jurisdiction to grant any order or remedy, and to the extent it purported to do so, it was acting extra-legally in response to a situation of extreme public crisis.

4. No authority was referred to by the Court to support *its assumption of the power* to give force and effect to invalid and ineffective laws, and to the extent it purported to do so, it was acting extra-legally in a situation of extreme public crisis.

5. Any precedential value of *Manitoba Language Rights* must be assessed in light of its exceptional context which involved the imminent collapse of Manitoba's governmental and legal systems.[113]

At its highest, *Manitoba Language Rights* stands as authority for the proposition that where a situation of public crisis arises, and it is not possible for the executive or legislative branches of government to deal with the crisis using their emergency powers and prerogatives, then the courts may step in and exercise such powers as are necessary to preserve the rule of law, including by giving force and effect temporarily to unconstitutional legislative provisions. Thus, it recognizes the existence of an exceptional power for courts to act outside the law in circumstances of grave public crisis. So viewed, it is doubtful that a case has arisen in

---

[113] "*Reference re: Manitoba Language Rights* could easily have been regarded as a unique aberration in light of the unusual and extreme circumstances of the case." G.R. Hall, "Preserving the Clavicle in the Cat: Stunted Reform of Common Law Rules in the Supreme Court of Canada" (2002) 36 *Can. Bus. L.J.* 89 at p. 110

Canada since 1985 which would have necessitated reliance on
Manitoba Language Rights.[114]

However, this is not how courts have interpreted and applied the
case. They have treated it as a licence to deem the law temporarily
to be different than it actually is, when they consider it in the
public interest to do so. It has been treated as permission to
disbelieve that s. 52(1) of the Constitution really means what it
says – that a law inconsistent with the Constitution "is ... of no
force or effect." This has resulted, among other things, in the
prosecution and conviction of persons under unconstitutional
laws, orders allowing governments to exact illegal taxes, unlawful
participation of police officers at criminal court bail hearings, and
denials of a constitutional right to medically-assisted death. More
than that, it has contributed to a general corrosion of judicial
faithfulness to the rule of law in Canada. Ironically, that is the
legacy of a decision which ostensibly was driven by a desire to
preserve the rule of law.[115]

7. The Jurisprudential Legacy of *Manitoba Language Rights*

A decision that judges have the power to cause invalid law to
become valid is a ticking juridical time-bomb. Like a loaded
weapon that should be carefully stored under lock and key, the
urge to play with it will surely prove irresistible. David
Dyzenhaus has put the point as follows: "[O]ne cannot, as Carl
Schmitt rightly argued, confine the exception. If it is introduced
into legal order and treated as such, it will spread."[116] Similarly,
Oren Gross has warned that "there is a strong probability that

---

[114] A search of CanLII identifies more than 300 Canadian cases where
Manitoba Language Rights has been cited.
[115] Bruce Ryder has observed that "a remedy initially designed to serve the rule
of law now risks promoting its violation." B. Ryder, "Suspending the Charter,"
(2003) 21 *S.C.L.R. (2d)* 267 at p. 288
[116] D. Dyzenhaus, "Humpty Dumpty Rules or the Rule of Law: Legal Theory
and the Adjudication of National Security" (2003) 28 *Aust. J. Legl. Phil.* 1 at
p. 29

measures used by the government in emergencies will eventually seep into the legal system even after the crisis has ended."[117]

Thus, the Supreme Court's decision in *Manitoba Language Rights* has become the touchstone for a generation of judges and lawyers who want to be able to respond pragmatically to the inevitable messiness that flows from findings of unconstitutionality. This concession to pragmatism has come at a high price. A power that was intended to be exercised in exceptional circumstances of public crisis has become normalized to the point of routine. Even more seriously, the country's legal culture has been affected in ways that are both profound and pernicious.

A key precept of the rule of law is that the judicial branch serves the role of umpire, calling balls and strikes, but not creating or changing the rules of the game.[118] Acknowledgement of a power of a court to give force and effect to laws which the Constitution says are "of no force or effect" is a big deal. Inevitably, judges who are told that they possess this power will lose some of the reverence that they should feel for the supremacy of the law. They may or may not be conscious of it, but it cannot be conducive to judicial modesty and self-restraint to be told that one has the power to grant dispensation from compliance with the country's

---

[117] O. Gross, "Chaos and Rules: Should Responses to Violent Crises Always be Constitutional?" (2003) 112 *Yale L.J.* 1011 at p. 1097. See also, S. Mueller, "Turning Emergency Powers Inside Out: Are Extraordinary Powers Creeping into Ordinary Legislation?" (2016) 18 *Flinders L.J.* 295 at p. 309

[118] At his Senate confirmation hearing, Chief Justice Roberts famously compared the role of a judge to that of a baseball umpire:

> Judges and justices are servants of the law, not the other way around. Judges are like umpires. Umpires don't make the rules, they apply them. The role of an umpire and a judge is critical. They make sure everybody plays by the rules. But it is a limited role. Nobody ever went to a ball game to see the umpire.

Quoted in A. Dyevre & A. Jakab, "Foreward: Understanding Constitutional Reasoning" (2013) 14 *German L.J.* 983 at p. 1004.

supreme law. Once that genie is released, there is no easy way to return it to its bottle.

The Supreme Court of Ireland recognized the gravity of departing from Ireland's equivalent of Canada's s. 52; that is, by purporting to give its determinations of unconstitutionality prospective effect only:

> By doing so, we would be sanctioning something which the Constitution prohibits. We would, in my opinion, be arrogating to ourselves *a power to supersede the Constitution* if we did this.[119] (emphasis added)

7.1 A Power to Supersede the Constitution

The legacy of *Manitoba Language Rights* stretches beyond suspended declaration jurisprudence. This case represents one of the first forays of the Supreme Court into the area of unwritten constitutional principles. Thus began a judicial odyssey with bountiful possibilities for the discovery and creation of new constitutional rights and obligations. An examination of that subject is beyond the scope of this work. Harry Arthurs, with his signature irreverence, pretty much summed it all up in his depiction of "idealistic law professors, persuasive advocates, and ingenious judges" being often caught in the act of:

> ... manipulating texts, rewriting history, reinventing tradition, using forked twigs to divine constitutional meanings, and pulling frantically on their own bootstraps as they struggle heroically to think the unthinkable and do the undoable.[120]

One of the relatively few vocal critics of the *Manitoba Language Rights* decision, Dale Gibson, characterized it as judicial amendment of the Constitution:

---

[119] *Murphy v. Attorney General*, [1982] 1 I.R. 241 at p. 333
[120] H. Arthurs, "Constitutional Courage" (2003) 49 *McGill L. J.* 1 at p.12

> When the courts, however, fashion constitutional
> supplements, from whole cloth, as I believe the
> Supreme Court of Canada did in the *Manitoba
> Language Reference*, it seems fair to say that they have
> surpassed the role of constitutional interpreters and
> have become amenders.[121]

The Supreme Court's decisions on the protection of judicial
salaries and other benefits, purportedly on the basis of the rule of
law coupled with an unwritten constitutional principle of judicial
independence,[122] have provided particularly fertile ground for
both criticism and ridicule. Professor Hogg has been harsh in his
criticism:

> The jurisprudence interpreting judicial independence is
> not based on any ambiguity or uncertainty in the text of
> the Constitution of Canada. Rather, the judges have
> constructed an elaborate edifice of doctrine with little
> or no basis in the text in order to protect the power,
> influence, salaries and perquisites of themselves and
> their colleagues.[123]

Showing no restraint at all was Australia's Jeffrey Goldsworthy,
who described the Supreme Court's decisions in the judicial
remuneration cases as "mush in the service of an agenda."[124]
According to Goldsworthy, the Court's reliance on unwritten,
underlying principles "confers on judges an unbounded authority
to find whatever they like in a constitution."[125]

---

[121] D. Gibson, "Founding Fathers-in-Law: Judicial Amendment of the
Canadian Constitution" (1992) 55 *Law & Contemp. Probs.* 261 at p. 276

[122] See, for example: *Reference re Public Sector Pay Reduction Act (P.E.I.),*
[1997] 3 SCR 3

[123] P.W. Hogg, "Canada: From Privy Council to Supreme Court," in J.
Goldsworthy ed., *Interpreting Constitutions: A Comparative Study*, (Oxford:
Oxford Univ. Press, 2006), 55 at p. 74

[124] J. Goldsworthy, "The Preamble, Judicial Independence and Judicial
Integrity" (2000) 11 *Const. Forum* 60 at p. 64

[125] *ibid.* at p. 62. The idea that unwritten principles and values can result in the
invalidation of otherwise valid legislation (as happened in the judicial

Sujit Choudhry has also been critical of the Supreme Court for using constitutional interpretation as a disguised form of constitutional amendment. He wrote as follows with respect to the Court's creation in *Secession Reference*[126] of an obligation on the part of the federal government to negotiate the terms of Quebec's secession in the event of a favourable referendum vote by a clear majority of Quebecers in response to a clear question:

> Although the Court purported to do otherwise, it amended the Canadian Constitution under the guise of constitutional interpretation. Moreover, since the relevant rules confer the power of constitutional amendment only on the political institutions, the Court acted extralegally.[127]

Similarly, Peter Hogg contended that the Court "invented a constitutional duty to negotiate secession with a province ...".[128]

According to Robin Elliot, the Court's approach in the *Secession Reference* made it vulnerable to criticism for violating the rule of law:

> It is inconsistent with the rule of law because it allows what amount to amendments to be made to the Constitution of Canada otherwise than in accordance with section 52(2) of the *Constitution Act, 1982*, which stipulates that such amendments can only be made on

---

remuneration cases) is especially difficult to fathom given that s. 52(1) is, by its terms, engaged only where the impugned law "is inconsistent with the provisions of the Constitution." The reference is not to "the Constitution" at large (which *might* arguably include unwritten principles) but to "the *provisions* of the Constitution," i.e. its textual content.

[126] *Reference re Secession of Quebec*, [1998] 2 SCR 217

[127] S. Choudhry, "Ackerman's Higher Lawmaking in Comparative Constitutional Perspective: Constitutional Moments as Constitutional Failures?" (2008) 6 *Int'l J. Const. L.* 193 at p. 214

[128] P.W. Hogg, "The Law-Making Role of the Supreme Court of Canada: Rapporteur's Synthesis" (2001) 80 *Can. B. Rev.* 171 at p. 175

the basis of the rules prescribed in Part V of that same instrument.[129]

A sign of just how far the Court has gone in using unwritten principles to give itself powers that are nowhere found in the Constitution[130] clearly emerges from Chief Justice Lamer's explanation of *Manitoba Language Rights* in a 1997 decision on judicial remuneration:

> The preamble, by its reference to "a Constitution similar in Principle to that of the United Kingdom", points to the nature of the legal order that envelops and sustains Canadian society. That order, as this Court held in *Reference re Manitoba Language Rights,* 1985 CanLII 33 (SCC), [1985] 1 S.C.R. 721, at p. 749, is "an actual order of positive laws", an idea that is embraced by the notion of the rule of law. In that case, the Court explicitly relied on the preamble to the *Constitution Act, 1867*, as one basis for holding that the rule of law was a fundamental principle of the Canadian Constitution. The rule of law led the Court to confer temporary validity on the laws of Manitoba which were unconstitutional because they had been enacted only in English, in contravention of the *Manitoba Act, 1870.* The Court developed this remedial innovation notwithstanding the express terms of a s. 52(1) of the *Constitution Act, 1982*, that unconstitutional laws are

---

[129] R. Elliot, "References, Structural Argumentation and the Organizing Principles of Canada's Constitution" (2001) 80 *Can. B. Rev.* 67 at p. 97. Jamie Cameron also added her voice of criticism of the *Secession Reference* decision, describing the Court's analysis as "deeply troubling." J. Cameron, "The Written Word and the Constitution's Vital Unstated Assumptions," in *Essays in Honour of Gérald-A. Beaudoin: The Challenges of Constitutionalism*, P. Thibault et al., ed's (Cowansville, Que.: Yvon Blais/Societe Thomson, 2002) 89 at p. 108

[130] Dale Gibson referred to *Manitoba Language Rights* as a decision "in which the Court decreed that it had the authority, again nowhere to be found in the Constitution Acts, to grant temporary validity, in the interests of preserving civil order, to laws that it had found to be constitutionally invalid." D. Gibson, "Founding Fathers-in-Law: Judicial Amendment of the Canadian Constitution" (1992) 55 *Law & Contemp. Probs* 261 at p. 271

"of no force or effect", a provision that suggests that declarations of invalidity can only be given immediate effect. The Court did so in order to not "deprive Manitoba of its legal order and cause a transgression of the rule of law" (p. 753). *Reference re Manitoba Language Rights* therefore stands as another example of how the fundamental principles articulated by preamble have been given legal effect by this Court.[131]

Now to deconstruct this. We have a reference in the preamble to the *Constitution Act, 1867* to: "a Constitution similar in principle to that of the United Kingdom." This becomes the basis for a statement that "the rule of law [is] a fundamental principle of the Canadian Constitution." All good so far, but what follows is remarkable. An unwritten principle of the Constitution is said to have "led the Court to confer temporary validity on the laws of Manitoba which were unconstitutional ...". What was the legal basis – not the pragmatic basis, the legal basis – for concluding that an unwritten constitutional principle could confer on the Court the power to put legislation in place? Even more puzzling is the question of how such an unwritten principle could override the supremacy clause in s. 52(1), so as to allow force and effect to be given to Manitoba's unconstitutional English-only laws. Taking as correct the proposition that "no part of the Constitution can abrogate or diminish another part of the Constitution,"[132] it is difficult to understand how an unwritten constitutional principle could effectively trump an express constitutional stipulation that the laws to which the Court was purporting to give force and effect were, in fact, of no force or effect.

Although *Manitoba Language Rights* was likely not the sole source of the Supreme Court's discovery and use of unwritten constitutional principles, it may fairly be likened to a gateway drug. Modern liberalism's abiding belief in the sanctity of the rule

---

[131] *Reference re Rumeration of Judges of Prov. Court of P.E.I.,* [1997] 3 S.C.R. 3 at para. 99
[132] *Doucet-Boudreau v. Nova Scotia (Minister of Education),* [2003] 3 S.C.R. 3 at para. 42

of law means that it suffers great dissonance when confronted with the idea of courts acting outside the law. This is what Carl Schmitt taught us. Thus, from the very beginning there has been an irresistible urge to rationalize the decision in *Manitoba Language Rights* so as to make it fit within legal parameters. Over time, what the Court did in *Manitoba Language Rights* became accepted as a lawful exercise of judicial powers to the point that it is now viewed as the wellspring for the normal and routine practice of giving force and effect to unconstitutional laws through so-called suspended declarations of invalidity.[133]

In summary, *Manitoba Language Rights* was a jurisprudential aberration. However, Canadian law was made to contort itself to rationalize the Court's exceptional *and extra-legal* exercise of law-making powers in that case. As the exercise of extra-legal power does not sit well with contemporary liberal thought, the extra-legal nature of the *Manitoba Language Rights* decision has never really been owned up to.[134] To the contrary, and quite ironically, the decision has been presented as an exercise in saving the rule of law (by preserving a body of positive law without which chaos and anarchy would reign supreme). Once it was announced by the Court that the rule of law – a fundamental postulate of Canadian constitutionalism – authorizes courts to put

---

[133] Professor Gibson correctly framed the issue in terms, not of whether the Court was right or wrong in what it did, but rather whether it should have pretended that it was acting under the law, as opposed to under an overriding non-legal survival factor:

> My point is not that it was necessarily wrong to do so, but that by doing so in the name of "law", rather than forthrightly acknowledging the "supremacy" of the non-legal survival factor...the Court obfuscated the meaning of "law", and damaged the vital principle of the rule of law.

D. Gibson, "The Real Laws of the Constitution" (1990) 28 *Alta. L. Rev.* 358 at p. 373. However, liberalism does not easily admit that officials may sometimes "legitimately" (in the political sense) act outside the law.

[134] Interestingly, however, Chief Justice Antonio Lamer, writing extra-judicially in 1996, came close to acknowledging the extralegal nature of the Court's actions in *Manitoba Language Rights* as he referred to the supremacy of the Constitution having had "to yield to" the demands of legal order in that case. See above at p. 104.

in place and enforce unconstitutional laws, it was impossible to restrain the judiciary's natural appetite for more and more discretionary remedial power. And so came onto the constitutional scene the suspended declaration of invalidity, accompanied always by its nebulous but dutiful accomplice – the underlying and unwritten values and principles of the Constitution.

A look at four cases where suspended declarations gave rise to troubling results will be accompanied by a consideration of the broader systemic pathology that the *Manitoba Language Rights* decision has helped wrought.

7.2   *A Power to Exact Unlawful Taxes*

In *Re Eurig Estate*,[135] the Supreme Court determined that a regulation imposing probate fees in Ontario was invalid and of no force or effect because it was a tax which the Constitution required to be imposed by legislation rather than by regulation.[136] However, in response to concerns about the potential negative impact of Ontario being deprived of this source of revenue pending the Legislature's enactment of a valid law, the Court purported to suspend its declaration of invalidity for six months:

> An immediate declaration of invalidity would deprive the province of the revenue derived from probate fees, with no opportunity to remedy the legislation or find alternative sources of funding. Probate fees have a lengthy history in Ontario, and the revenue derived therefrom is substantial. For example, the evidence presented to this Court indicated that in 1993 and 1994, probate fees collected in Ontario totaled $51.8 and $52.6 million, respectively. This revenue is used to defray the costs of court administration in the province. An immediate deprivation of this source of revenue would likely have harmful consequences for the

---

[135] [1998] 2 S.C.R. 565
[136] To similar effect, see *Confederation des syndicates nationaux v. Canada*, [2008] 3 S.C.R. 511

administration of justice in the province. The
declaration of invalidity is therefore suspended for a
period of six months to enable the province to address
the issue.[137]

In summary, the Court decided that because the government
needed the money, the Court had the power to impose for six
months a tax which it had just decided only the Legislature had
the constitutional power to impose. It did so without referring to
any legal authority. The sum total of the Court's analysis of its
power to order that validity be given to a law which the
Constitution said *is*, present tense, *is* "of no force or effect" was
the paragraph quoted above.

The creeping effect of *Manitoba Language Rights*, from situation
of dire emergency to casual exercise in non-emergency
circumstances, was commented upon by the late W. H. Hurlburt,
a lawyer from Alberta:

> The importance of the end in the Manitoba case, given
> the prospect of legal and governmental chaos, may
> have justified the means, even though it is richly ironic
> that the rule of law was maintained by the device of
> imposing unlawful law. Given that the legal bomb had
> been dropped, I do not have the same difficulties
> adopting any available means to stop it from going off
> and destroying the whole legislative, legal, and
> governmental systems, as I do with the later and almost
> casual exercise of powers to override specific
> provisions of the Constitution where the consequences
> of applying constitutional logic would not be as
> extreme. I turn now to those cases.[138]

One of the cases that Hurlburt examines is *Eurig Estate,* which he
criticizes mercilessly:

---

[137] *Re Eurig Estate*, [1998] 2 S.C.R. 565 at para. 44
[138] W. H. Hurlburt, "Fairy Tales and Living Trees: Observations on Some
Recent Constitutional Decisions of the Supreme Court of Canada" (1998) 26
Man. L. J. 181 at p. 194

Whether there was any evidence before the Court that the Province would not fund the administration of justice properly without the probate fees money is not apparent from the judgment, but even the proper funding of the administration of justice is not, in my submission, an end which justifies the exaction of illegal taxes. Even if the Province or the administration of justice had greater need of the money than the widows, widowers, and orphans from whose pockets most of the illegal taxes would be extracted – about which the judgment does not cite any evidence other than the huge sums which the Province had been collecting illegally – that greater need did not, in my submission, justify authorising the continuation of the illegal exactions.

...

I cannot see any legal rule, inside or outside the Constitution, that permits the Supreme Court to exercise a public power to allow a Province to make illegal exactions with impunity, and, more particularly to allow it to do so simply to protect the fisc.[139]

In addition, while the Court purported to breathe life into the unconstitutional probate fees, it decided to award a refund of the fees paid by the particular appellant before it. Thus, by happening to be the first of the aggrieved parties to reach the Supreme Court, this appellant was permitted to enjoy the protection of the Constitution, while other similarly-situated parties were forced to pay a judicially-imposed unconstitutional levy. According to John Rawls: "The rule of law ... implies the precept that similar cases will be treated similarly."[140] As stated by the Supreme Court of Canada in 2009:

Divergent applications of legal rules undermine the integrity of the rule of law. Dating back to the time of

[139] *ibid.* at pp. 200-201
[140] J. Rawls, *A Theory of Justice*, (Cambridge, Mass: Harvard Univ. Press, 1971) at p. 237

Dicey's theory of British constitutionalism, almost all
rule of law theories include a requirement that each
person in the political community be subject to or
guided by the same general law.[141]

Others have criticized the practice of singling out particular
persons as beneficiaries of a constitutional ruling that is denied to
others:

Once a rule or practice has been declared bad law or
unconstitutional, it violates the central notion of
equality before the law if the new rule is applied to
benefit one individual but not another. [142]

...

The Court's explicit refusal to treat like cases alike is
perhaps the closest it has come to an open abdication
of the judicial role.[143]

Justice Harlan, in his dissenting but ultimately highly influential
opinion in *Mackey*, lambasted the practice of selectively applying
the correct interpretation of the law:

Simply fishing one case from the stream of appellate
review, using it as a vehicle for pronouncing new
constitutional standards, and then permitting a stream
of similar cases subsequently to flow by unaffected by
that new rule constitute an indefensible departure from
this model of judicial review.

---

[141] *Canada (Citizenship and Immigration) v. Khosa*, [2009] 1 S.C.R. 339 at
para. 90

[142] M. Faure, M. Goodwin and F. Weber, "The Regulator's Dilemma: Caught
Between the Need for Flexibility and the Demands of Foreseeability:
Reassessing the *Lex Certa* Principle" (2014) 24 *Albany Law J. of Sci. and Tech.*
283 at p. 353

[143] K. Roosevelt III, "A Retroactivity Retrospective, with Thoughts for the
Future: What the Supreme Court Learned from Paul Mishkin, and What it
Might" (2007) 95 *Calif. L. Rev.* 1677 at p. 1685

> If we do not resolve all cases before us on judicial
> review in light of our best understanding of governing
> constitutional principles, it is difficult to see why we
> should so adjudicate any case at all.[144]

The practice of selective prospectivity has also been described as
the height of inequality:

> And selective prospectivity, of course, represents the
> height of inequality, in that it calls for the application
> of different legal rules to persons distinguishable only
> on the basis who was first able to persuade a precedent-
> setting court of the need for change.[145]

The Supreme Court of Canada, however (although it has not
consistently adhered to the practice), has signalled its *approval* of
selective prospectivity:

> In the rare cases in which this Court makes a
> prospective ruling, it has always allowed the party
> bringing the case to take advantage of the finding of
> unconstitutionality: see, e.g. *R. v. Brydges,* 1990
> CanLII 123 (SCC) [1990] 1 S.C.R. 190; *R. v. Feeney,*
> 1997 CanLII 343 (SCC), [1997] 2 S.C.R. 117.[146]

It is instructive to contrast the assumption by the Supreme Court
in *Eurig Estate* of a power to impose an unlawful tax with the
High Court of Australia's reaction to a similar request that for
fiscal reasons the government should be allowed to continue
collecting an unconstitutional tax during a transition period: " [I]t
would be a perversion of judicial power to maintain in force that

---

[144] *Mackey v. U.S.,* 401 U.S. 667 (1971) at p. 679. See also, *Jones v. Warden
of Mission Institution,* 2002 BCSC 12 (CanLII) at para. 31: "Mr.Illes and Mr.
Jones were in exactly the same position and Mr. Jones should not be denied the
relief he seeks merely because Mr. Illes made the first application to the Court."
[145] B.S. Shannon, "The Retroactive and Prospective Application of Judicial
Decisions" (2003) 26 *Harv. J.L. & Pub. Policy* 811 at p. 866
[146] *Reference re Remuneration of Judges of Prov. Court of PEI,* [1998] 1 S.C.R.
3 at para. 20

which is acknowledged not to be the law."[147] Similarly, *Eurig Estate* stands in stark contrast with a New Zealand High Court's decision that maintaining in force a provision found to be invalid would involve "an exercise of judicial power irreconcilable with the rule of law."[148]

A sign of how deeply *Manitoba Language Rights* has been allowed to permeate Canadian law and legal culture is the uncritical acceptance by Canadian lawyers of the idea that courts actually have the power to make the unlawful lawful. For example, one commentator on *Eurig Estate*, although skeptical of the merits of the Court's decision to suspend its declaration of invalidity in the circumstances of that particular case, accepted without question the existence of the Court's power: "Although such a suspension is clearly within the powers of the judiciary, it must be viewed as an extraordinary remedy."[149] In fairness, of course, lawyers should not be criticized too harshly for believing the Supreme Court of Canada when it claims for itself a power to make the unlawful lawful. The Court, however, should explain, as it has never done, how it obtained such a power.

7.3 A Power to Prosecute and Convict for Offences under Unconstitutional Laws

One of the most fundamental of all legal principles is that no person "may be convicted or punished for an act or omission that is not clearly prohibited by a valid law."[150] This principle is "based on the ancient Latin maxim *nullum crimen sine lege nulla poena sine lege* – that there can be no crime or punishment unless it is in accordance with law that is certain, unambiguous and not

---

[147] *Ha v. State of New South Wales* (1997), 189 CLR 465 at pp. 503-504
[148] *Willowford Family Trust v. Christchurch City Council*, [2006] 1 NZLR 791 at para. 20
[149] P. LeBreux, "*Eurig Estate*: Another Day, Another Tax" (1999) 47 *Can. Tax J.* 1126 at p. 1155
[150] *R. v. Levkovic,* [2013] 2 S.C.R. 204 at para.1

retroactive."[151] It finds expression in *Magna Carta*,[152] the writings of Thomas Hobbes,[153] and the French Declaration of the Rights of Man of 1789.[154]

The Supreme Court of Canada has repeatedly stated the principle that no person can be convicted under an unconstitutional law.[155] However, incongruently, it has also given permission to prosecutors and trial courts to charge and convict persons under provisions which have been adjudged unconstitutional but made the subject of a suspended declaration. To justify this, the Court must be taken to believe not only that it can make law to substitute for the law that it has found to be invalid, but that this judicially-created substitute law must have a validity that transcends or overrides the Constitution. Unless the Court is paying mere lip service to the principle that no person shall be convicted under an unconstitutional law, it must believe that it has a power to enact law that is somehow lawfully deemed to be compliant with the Constitution even though it has already been adjudged not to be so compliant. Not surprisingly, the Supreme Court has never attempted to explain how this judicial sleight-of-hand actually works. Yet, it continues to tell prosecutors, trial courts, and the

---

[151] *Reference re ss. 193 and 195.1(1)(c) of the Criminal Code*, [1990] 1 S.C.R. 1123 at p. 1151

[152] Justice Kennedy wrote in *Boumediene v. Bush*, 553 U.S. 723 (2008) at p. 748: "Magna Carta decreed that no man would be imprisoned contrary to the law of the land…".

[153] "[H]arm inflicted for a fact before there was a law that forbade it is not punishment, but an act of hostility; for before the law, there was no transgression of the law." T. Hobbes, *Leviathan* (1651) (Oxford: Oxford Univ. Press, 1996) Ch. 28, p. 207

[154] Article 8 states: "The law must prescribe only punishments that are strictly and evidently necessary; and no one may be punished except by virtue of a Law drawn up and promulgated before the offence is committed, and legally applied."

[155] For example, it stated in *R. v. Big M Drug Mart Ltd.*, [1985] 1 S.C.R. 295 at para. 38: "…no one can be convicted of an offence under an unconstitutional law." This is a reiteration of the ancient principle encapsulated in the maxim *nullum crimen sine lege, nulla poena sine lege* – there must be no crime or punishment except in accordance with law which is fixed and certain. See *R. v. Kelly*, [1992] 2 S.C.R. 170 at p. 203

public that unconstitutional laws can be enforced during the period of their suspended invalidity.

In *Canada (Attorney General) v. Bedford*,[156] the Court determined that various provisions of the *Criminal Code* pertaining to the sexual services industry were inconsistent with the Constitution, and, to that extent, of no force or effect. In particular, it was determined that the prohibitions against living off the avails of prostitution were overbroad in that they unlawfully interfered with sex workers' ability to arrange adequate security for themselves. Instead of allowing its declaration of constitutional invalidity to come into effect immediately, the Court decided to suspend it for one year to give Parliament the opportunity to enact constitutionally-compliant legislation. This is what Chief Justice McLachlin wrote with respect to the issue of suspension:

> This raises the question of whether the declaration of invalidity should be suspended and if so, for how long.
>
> On the one hand, immediate invalidity would leave prostitution totally unregulated while Parliament grapples with the complex and sensitive problem of how to deal with it. How prostitution is regulated is a matter of great public concern, and few countries leave it entirely unregulated. Whether immediate invalidity would pose a danger to the public or imperil the rule of law (the factors for suspension referred to in *Schachter v. Canada*, 1992 CanLII 74 (SCC), [1992] 2 SCR 679) may be subject to debate. However, it is clear that moving abruptly from a situation where prostitution is regulated to a situation where it is entirely unregulated would be a matter of great concern to many Canadians.
>
> On the other hand, leaving prohibitions against bawdy-houses, living on the avails of prostitution and public communication for purposes of prostitution in place in their present form leaves prostitutes at increased risk

---

[156] [2013] 3 S.C.R. 1101

for the time of the suspension – risks which violate their constitutional right to security of the person.

The choice between suspending the declaration of invalidity and allowing it to take immediate effect is not an easy one. Neither alternative is without difficulty. However, considering all the interests at stake, I conclude that the declaration of invalidity should be suspended for one year.[157]

Hugo Cyr has commented in very critical terms on the Court's decision to delay its declaration of invalidity in *Bedford*.[158] He makes the point that the courts have allowed the exceptional circumstances of extreme necessity recognized in *Manitoba Language Rights* to become normalized to the extent that suspended declarations have now become customary. To accede any power to the courts to override the Constitution is a slippery slope, or, as Cyr has aptly put it: [Translation] "[O]nce the worm is in the apple it is difficult to save the fruit."[159] Moreover, he observes the irony that the reason for finding the provisions to be unconstitutional – to protect the life and safety of sex workers who require security arrangements – appears to have been lost in the Court's balancing of competing interests, with primacy being given to the fact that it would be a matter of great concern to many Canadians that prostitution might be unregulated pending Parliament's enactment of a constitutionally valid law. Thus, the law in Canada is that courts can bestow legal validity upon constitutionally invalid laws because many Canadians would be concerned that compliance with the Constitution – by allowing

---

[157] *ibid* at para's 166-169
[158] H. Cyr, "Quelques reflexions sur la normalisation de l'exceptionel", Paper delivered at Conference at University of Montreal Faculty of Law on October 15, 2015. See also, C.R. Mouland, "Remedying the Remedy: Bedford's Suspended Declaration of Invalidity" (2018) *Manitoba Law J.* (forthcoming)
[159] *ibid.*, H. Cyr, at p. 17

sex workers to better protect their lives and safety – could give rise to a situation where prostitution is temporarily unregulated.[160]

Of course, another implication of the Court granting a suspension was that it would be possible for persons to be prosecuted and convicted under an unconstitutional law during the suspension period. In fact, there have been several cases where this actually happened. In one case, *R. v. Moazami,* the British Columbia Supreme Court, during the *Bedford* suspension period, refused to quash charges under the very sections of the *Criminal Code* which the Supreme Court in *Bedford* had determined to be unconstitutional. The trial judge expressed the view that "the suspension of the declaration of invalidity 'breathes life' into the impugned provision during its term."[161] The notion that courts can breathe life into unconstitutional laws stirs memories of C-grade movies featuring zombies arising from the dead and wreaking great public havoc. No less preposterous is the concept of courts issuing zombie orders and thereby giving life to constitutionally cadaverous enactments, as would be depicted in the film *Dead Law Walking.*

Similarly, in another case, *R. v. Ackman,* the Manitoba Court of Appeal dismissed the appeal against conviction of a person who had been charged under these same unconstitutional *Criminal Code* provisions during the *Bedford* suspension period.[162] So much for the principle that a person cannot be convicted under an unconstitutional law. This is only true if one accepts the proposition that courts, acting on perceived public concerns about the consequences of enforcing the Constitution, have the power

---

[160] It has been argued that "judicial independence requires that judges decide cases without regard to the public's view about the subject matter involved." D. Hellman, "The Importance of Appearing Principled" (1995) 37 *Ariz. L. Rev.* 1107 at p. 1127

[161] *R. v Moazami*, 2014 BCSC 261 (CanLII) at para. 22. See also, *R. v. Al-Qaysi,* 2016 BCSC 937 (CanLII). *Contra* see, *R. v. Guo,* 2014 ONCA 206 (CanLII)

[162] *R. v. Ackman*, 2017 MBCA 78 (CanLII)

to override the Constitution and "breathe life" into unconstitutional laws.[163]

A more recent example of the willingness of courts to tolerate the conviction of persons under unconstitutional laws is found in the Ontario Superior Court of Justice's decision in *R. v. Stupak*.[164] The Federal Court of Canada in *Allard v. Canada*[165] had declared unconstitutional the regulatory regime (the "MMPR") put in place to allow access to marijuana by persons with established medical need for it. The defence in *Stupak* argued that on the basis of the Court of Appeal's decision in *R. v. Parker*,[166] the absence of a regime allowing for medically-necessary access to marijuana resulted in the constitutional invalidation of the general statutory prohibitions against marijuana possession under which Stupak had been charged. However, the Crown argued that because the Federal Court judge in *Allard* had suspended his declaration of invalidity for six months, there, in fact, was a valid regulatory regime in place at the time Stupak was charged.[167] The defence countered by referring to the principle in *R. v. Big M Drug Mart Ltd.*[168] that "no one can be convicted of an offence under an unconstitutional law."[169] The *Stupak* judge acknowledged the difficulty in reconciling the principle in *Big M Drug Mart* with the idea of convicting a person under an unconstitutional law, but she concluded on the basis of various authorities, including the

---

[163] Robert Leckey has written with respect to the dangers of suspending declarations of invalidity in the criminal law context: "The prospect of incarceration under a prohibition found unjustifiably to limit rights might intensify concerns for the rule of law and for justice generally." R. Leckey, *Bills of Rights in the Common Law*, (Cambridge: Cambridge Univ. Press, 2015) at p. 176

[164] 2018 ONSC 1867 (CanLII)

[165] 2016 FC 236 (CanLII)

[166] 2000 CanLII 5762 (ONCA)

[167] According to the Supreme Court of Canada's decisions in *R. v. Lloyd*, [2016] 1 S.C.R. 130, and *Windsor (City) v. Canadian Transit Co.*, [2016] 2 S.C.R. 717, the Federal Court of Canada, as a statutory court of limited jurisdiction, did not have the power to issue formal declarations of invalidity. This issue does not appear to have been considered in *Allard* or elsewhere.

[168] [1985] 1 S.C.R. 295

[169] *ibid.* at para. 38

Moazami and *Ackman* cases discussed above, that this was indeed possible where a suspended declaration of invalidity had been issued:

> I agree that it is somewhat difficult to reconcile *Big M Drug Mart* with the Crown submission that the applicant could be convicted, even if a court found that the offence under which he was charged was unconstitutional. Despite that difficulty, however a number of authorities support the Crown position.
>
> ...
>
> In *R. v. Moazami*, 2014 BCSC 261 (CanLII), the defendant was charged with, among other offences, living off the avails of prostitution contrary to s. 212(1)(j) of the *Criminal Code*. He brought an application to quash, on the basis that the section had been found to be unconstitutional and of no force or effect in *Canada v. Bedford*, 2013 SCC 72 (CanLII). Although the court had suspended the declaration of invalidity for 12 months, the defendant argued that the suspension was an ancillary order and not binding. Bruce J. rejected this argument, and held that the suspension of invalidity was binding. In refusing to quash the charge, he [sic: she] further noted at para. 22 that the defendant's submission was "inconsistent with the nature of a suspension of invalidity. While s. 52 of the *Constitution Act* precludes a conviction for an offence declared unconstitutional, the suspension of the declaration of invalidity breathes life into the impugned provision during its term." The defendant was ultimately convicted. (*R. v. Moazami*, 2014 BCSC 1727 (CanLII), at paras. 402-405)
>
> More recently, in *Ackman*, the Manitoba Court of Appeal upheld the appellant's conviction for living off the avails of prostitution contrary to s. 212(1)(j) of the *Criminal Code*, despite the finding in *Bedford* that the section was unconstitutional. The court noted at para. 60 that the Government had passed new legislation

before the expiry of the period of suspension and thus the declaration of invalidity never took effect. The court further held at para. 75 that the rule of law justified the continued prosecution of the appellant, in a "manner similar to *Bilodeau*."

Based on the above authorities, it seems clear both that the *MMPR* operated as a valid regulatory regime during the period of suspension, and that, despite *Big M. Drug Mart*, individuals charged with marihuana offences during this time frame can be (subject to any argument in support of a constitutional exemption or other personal remedy) prosecuted and convicted. That finding is sufficient to dispose of this application.[170]

The seeds for the practice of convicting people under unconstitutional laws were, in fact, planted by the *Manitoba Language Rights* decision. On June 13, 1984, the day argument in *Manitoba Language Rights* concluded, the same panel of the Court heard the appeal of Roger Bilodeau who had been convicted of speeding contrary to the Manitoba *Highway Traffic Act*. This was one of the unilingual statutes which the Supreme Court found to be and always to have been invalid and of no force or effect. How could Bilodeau's conviction under an invalid law be upheld? Even assuming that the Court had the power to make law prospectively by conferring deemed validity on Manitoba's unconstitutional unilingual laws, how could it justify the use of those powers to give retroactive effect to an invalid statute so as to support Bilodeau's conviction for conduct in the 1970's, long before *Manitoba Language Rights* was decided? In particular, how could the Court reconcile this retroactive penal law-making with the guarantee against conviction under retroactive laws provided by s. 11(g) of the *Charter*?[171] The Court obviously

---

[170] *R. v. Stupak*, 2018 ONSC 1867 (CanLII) at para's 21, 26-28. The other authorities referred to by the judge in *Stupak* included: *Bilodeau v. Manitoba*, [1986] 1 S.C.R. 449; *R. v. Clay*, 2000 CanLII 5760 (ONCA); and *R. v. McCrady*, 2011 ONCA 820 (CanLII).
[171] Section 11(g) provides that any person charged with an offence has the right "not to be found guilty on account of any act or omission unless, at the time of

struggled with this as it reserved its decision in *Bilodeau* for twenty-three months, not releasing it until almost a full year after release of its decision in *Manitoba Language Rights*.[172] In the result, the Court simply and circuitously concluded that Bilodeau's conviction under a legally non-existent statute should be upheld because the rule of law required Manitoba's invalid unilingual laws to be deemed valid.[173]

This is not to say that the result in *Bilodeau* was necessarily wrong. Perhaps the extraordinary circumstances of Manitoba's constitutional crisis justified the imposition, even retroactively, of constitutionally invalid laws. However, the problem is that the Court did not really acknowledge what it was doing. It attempted to fit a flagrantly unconstitutional square peg into the round hole of the Constitution. By trying to normalize a situation which Carl Schmitt called the exception – where the Constitution could not provide the solution – the Court contorted itself and the Constitution in ways that have left a legacy of disrespect for the concept of the rule of law in Canada.

Manitoba Language Rights should always have been treated as the crazy uncle of Canadian constitutional law. As such, it ought to be kept safely confined to the basement of Supreme Court of Canada jurisprudence. Instead, it has been put on proud display in the grand entrance hall to the castle of the Constitution.[174]

---

the act or omission, it constituted an offence under Canadian or international law or was criminal according to the general principles of law recognized by the community of nations."

[172] Peter Hogg suggests that the delay in releasing its decision in *Bilodeau* "was perhaps intended to signal the Court's discomfort." P.W. Hogg, "Necessity in a Constitutional Crisis" (1989) 15 *Monash Univ. L. Rev.* 253 at p. 258

[173] *Bilodeau v. A.G. (Man.)*, [1986] 1 S.C.R. 449 at para. 14.

[174] In *Reference re Remuneration of Judges of Prov. Court of P.E.I.*, [1997] 3 S.C.R. 3 at para. 109, Lamer CJC described the preamble to the *Constitution Act, 1867* as "the grand entrance hall to the castle of the Constitution."

7.4   A Power to Allow Police Officers to Unlawfully Participate in Criminal Court Bail Hearings

In an Alberta case, it was decided that police officers were not permitted under the *Criminal Code* to appear as prosecutors at bail hearings for indictable offences.[175] However, this had been a long-standing practice in Alberta, and the Attorney General therefore requested a suspension of the court's declaration for six months so that a smooth transition to a new system could be implemented. That is, the court was asked to confer temporary legal validity on a practice that it had just found to be contrary to law. This was not a constitutional case. It concerned interpretation of provisions of the *Criminal Code*. In granting the requested suspension, the court specifically held that "the ability to suspend a declaration is not confined to constitutional cases, nor does the *Constitution* or the *Charter* ground a court's jurisdiction to suspend a declaration."[176] The court found its jurisdiction in broad remedial language under the *Judicature Act* and *Rules of Court,* including a power to stay the effect of an order or judgment. In explaining its decision, the court relied heavily on and quoted extensively from *Manitoba Language Rights.*

This case illustrates how an idea, once it is allowed to enter the legal system, can take on a life of its own and find application in the most inapt circumstances. *Manitoba Language Rights* was interpreted as authority for a general judicial power to suspend the effects of declarations of invalidity, and the *Rules of Court,* which authorize stays of judgments and orders, were interpreted as the jurisdictional basis for the exercise of this power. What the court failed to do, however, was consider what were the legal effects of its declaration of invalidity. If it had done that, it would have understood that a declaration merely describes an existing legal state of affairs, and nothing more. A declaration cannot cause a provision or practice to be valid or invalid; nor can a purported suspension of such declaration have any substantive legal

---

[175] *Hearing Office Bail Hearings (Re),* 2017 ABQB 74 (CanLII)
[176] *ibid.* at para. 137

effect. The court, having identified the practice of police officer prosecution as illegal, could not change that reality. Thus, if the court had approached the matter from the perspective of legal principles, it would have understood that the purported suspension of its declaration was legally a non-event, an empty legal vessel.[177]

The corrosive effects of *Manitoba Language Rights* on the rule of law in Canada are evident from this case and others like it. Even outside the constitutional context, judges have come to believe that they have the power to dispense justice by ordering that illegal conduct shall be deemed to be legal. And no less concerning is the fact that lawyers and law professors in Canada almost never question this. Thus, in an Ontario case, a municipal by-law was held to be invalid as it conflicted with the provincial *Human Rights Code;* yet the court purported to suspend its declaration of invalidity for six months in order to allow the municipality to continue enforcing the illegal by-law while it made the amendments necessary to render it legal.[178] Likewise, in another case, the Federal Court of Appeal purported to suspend a declaration (that certain financial charges were invalid as they were not authorized by statute) in order to allow the government to retain money that it had illegally collected.[179]

The power to suspend declarations of invalidity has even been extended to division of power cases. Thus, relying on *Manitoba Language Rights*, an *ultra vires* provincial regulatory scheme that infringed upon an area of exclusive federal jurisdiction was allowed to continue to operate for twenty-four months after it had been found to be unlawful.[180] More recently, the Alberta Court of

---

[177] See Part 1 of this essay, "Some Misconceptions About Constitutional Invalidation" at pp. 69-71.

[178] *2211266 Ontario Inc. (cob Gentlemen's Club) v. Brantford*, 2012 ONSC 5830 (CanLII)

[179] *British Columbia Ferry Corporation v. Canada (Minister of National Revenue)*, 2001 FCA 146 (CanLII)

[180] *Morton v. British Columbia*, 2010 BCSC 100 (CanLII). Contrast this result with the following Supreme Court of Canada statement made in 1879: "[A] Provincial statute, passed on a matter over which the Legislature has no

Queen's Bench purported to suspend for six months its declaration that certain financial charges on craft beer manufactured outside Alberta were illegal restraints on interprovincial trade contrary to s. 121 of the *Constitution Act, 1867*.[181] Thus, the Alberta government was essentially given a six-month judicial hall pass allowing it to continue collecting unconstitutional levies with impunity.

7.5 A Power to Deny Access to Medically-Assisted Death to Persons Suffering from Terminal Illnesses

In *Carter v. Canada (Attorney General)*,[182] a unanimous Supreme Court of Canada decided that provisions of the *Criminal Code* relating to assisted suicide were inconsistent with the Constitution to the extent that they prohibited physician-assisted death for people who met certain prescribed criteria, which the Court set out as follows in its discussion of remedy:

> The appropriate remedy is therefore a declaration that s. 241(b) and s. 14 of the *Criminal Code* are void insofar as they prohibit physician-assisted death for a competent adult person who (1) clearly consents to the termination of life; and (2) has a grievous and irremediable condition (including an illness, disease or disability) that causes enduring suffering that is intolerable to the individual in the circumstances of his or her condition. "Irremediable", it should be added, does not require the patient to undertake treatments that are not acceptable to the individual. The scope of this declaration is intended to respond to the factual circumstances in this case. We make no

authority or control, under the *British North America Act*, is a complete nullity, a nullity of *non esse*. *Defectus potestatis, nullitas nullitatum*. No power can give it vitality." (*Lenoir v. Ritchie*, (1879) 3 S.C.R. 575 at pp. 624-625)
[181] *Steam Whistle Brewing Inc. v. Alberta Gaming and Liquor Commission*, 2018 ABQB 476 (CanLII)
[182] [2015] 1 S.C.R. 331

pronouncement on other situations where physician-assisted dying may be sought.[183]

The Court then added: "We would suspend the declaration of invalidity for 12 months."[184] There was no discussion about the appropriateness of suspending the declaration, nor reasons given for doing so. The Court did, however, specifically reject a request that provision be made for case-by-case exemptions from the subject *Criminal Code* provisions of people who could establish that they met the prescribed criteria.[185]

What the Court created, then, was a situation where people who satisfied the criteria set out by the Court for a constitutional right to physician-assisted death, were told that they would have to continue suffering for at least another twelve months, because any physician who gave them such assistance during that period would be subject to criminal prosecution. The Court thus purported to breathe life into a law which s. 52(1) of the Constitution, speaking as Canada's supreme law, had decreed, to the extent of its inconsistency with the Constitution, to be of no force or effect.

There is no nice or diplomatic way to put it. We should call it what it is. The Supreme Court of Canada has asserted a right to override the Constitution and to proclaim that its judgments and orders, and not the Constitution, is the supreme law of Canada.

---

[183] *ibid.* at para. 127

[184] *ibid.* at para. 128

[185] Due to a change of government the replacement legislation was not ready for enactment within the 12-month suspension period, and the government was therefore granted a further 4-month extension, but with provision for individual exemptions, see 2016 SCC 4 (CanLII).

PART 3 – TRYING TO RIGHT THE SHIP

SUMMARY

Incoherence, ambiguity, and contradiction pervade the subject of constitutional invalidation in Canada. The refusal of the courts to acknowledge the extra-legal nature of the Supreme Court's actions in the *Manitoba Language Rights* case, has led judges to believe that they actually possess the power to deem the unlawful to be lawful. This has resulted in an approach to constitutional adjudication where words in the Constitution do not mean what they say, where life can mysteriously be breathed into constitutionally cadaverous enactments, and where unconstitutional laws can be regarded, like Schrodinger's cat, as both valid and invalid at the same time. It is well past time to establish a principle-based order and structure in this embarrassingly muddled area of the law. Canada's legal academy especially needs to step up to the plate. The principles of constitutional supremacy and the rule of law are too important to leave solely in the hands of judges.

1. Introduction

It is not easy for a court to explain how it acquires the power to make law, even temporarily – especially law that is inconsistent with the supreme law of the Constitution. *Manitoba Language Rights* provides, at most, a narrow range for a court, acting extra-constitutionally, to impose unconstitutional law where the survival of the legal and political order depends on it. Beyond that, no authority has been provided to justify the law-making role that the Supreme Court of Canada has assumed under its suspended declaration jurisprudence. This conundrum seems to have led to a recent shift in the Supreme Court's thinking, or at least in the presentation of its thinking. Instead of trying to defend the indefensible – that courts can turn invalid law into valid law – the Court appears now to have embraced a different concept. It is now suggested that courts, like Zeus, actually strike down or invalidate laws that do not conform to the Constitution. Thus, according to its 2016 decision in *R. v. Lloyd*,[1] unconstitutional laws have legal force and effect unless and until a court of inherent jurisdiction issues a formal declaration of their invalidity.[2] However, this is not a tenable position. It is not supported by the case law and it is contrary to the text of the Constitution. It cannot be reconciled with Justice La Forest's recognition in a 1993 case that a "declaration by its nature merely states the law without changing anything."[3]

It is flat out wrong.

---

[1] [2016] 1 S.C.R. 130 at para. 19

[2] As noted in Part 1 of this essay, "Some Misconceptions About Constitutional Invalidation", this is a dramatic shift from the view asserted by a unanimous Supreme Court in a 2003 case: "The invalidity of a legislative provision inconsistent with the Charter does not arise from the fact of its being declared unconstitutional by a court, but from the operation of s. 52(1) [the Constitution's supremacy clause]." *Nova Scotia (Workers' Compensation Board) v. Martin*, [2003] 2 S.C.R. 504 at para. 28

[3] *Kourtessis v. M.N.R.*, [1993] 2 S.C.R. 53 at p. 86

2. From Hamlet to Schrodinger's Cat

Hamlet envisaged human existence as a dichotomy, a binary choice: "To be, or not to be." Theoretical physicist Erwin Schrodinger envisaged the possibility of the simultaneous existence and non-existence of different states. He described an experiment where a cat would be placed in a box with radioactive material which, upon decay, would cause the cat to die. However, as the rate of decay of radioactive material is not predictable, an observer could not know whether the cat was dead or alive without looking inside the box. Thus, according to quantum theory, which recognizes the existence of all possible states, the cat would simultaneously be both dead and alive. This is similar to the Supreme Court of Canada's description of the process of constitutional invalidation. Laws can both exist as a matter of law, and simultaneously not exist.

This seemingly impossible paradox is illustrated by contrasting s. 52(1) of the Constitution: "The Constitution of Canada is the supreme law of Canada, and any law that is inconsistent with the provisions of the Constitution is, to the extent of the inconsistency of no force or effect," with this statement by the Supreme Court in the 2016 *Lloyd* case:

> The effect of a finding by a provincial court judge that a law does not conform to the Constitution is to permit the judge to refuse to apply it in the case at bar. The finding does not render the law of no force or effect under s. 52(1) of the *Constitution Act, 1982*. It is open to provincial court judges in subsequent cases to decline to apply the law, for reasons already given or for their own; however, the law remains in full force or effect, absent a formal declaration of invalidity by a court of inherent jurisdiction.[4]

So here is the situation. Suppose that there has been no formal declaration of invalidity by a court of inherent jurisdiction. Thus,

---

[4] *R. v. Lloyd*, [2016] 1 S.C.R. 130 at para. 19

the Supreme Court says: "[T]he law remains in full force or effect." Yet, the Constitution says that the same law "is of no force or effect." What is the provincial court judge to do? Hamlet would force the judge to choose between the law's effectiveness or ineffectiveness. In turn, the judge, taking instruction from s. 52(1), would refuse to apply the law to the extent of its inconsistency with the Constitution. Schrodinger, on the other hand, would tell the judge that the law can simultaneously be both effective and ineffective; and so too, apparently, would the Supreme Court of Canada. A situation where a judge is left with an apparent option to either apply or not apply a law that does not conform to the Constitution is anathema to the concept of the rule of law. "Self-evidently, the rule of law must mean that there is a clear distinction between the lawful and the unlawful."[5]

When Chief Justice McLachlin wrote in *Lloyd* that the effect of a provincial court judge finding that a law does not conform to the Constitution is to *permit* the judge to refuse to apply the law in the case at bar, she must have been imprecise in her choice of words. The rule of law, a fundamental postulate of the Constitution, surely *requires* that judges who are empowered to decide cases must decide those cases in accordance with the law.[6] Following the dictates of the Constitution, Canada's supreme law, can never be a matter of choice for a court. This was recognized by the Court in *R. v. Big M Drug Mart Ltd.*:

> If a court or tribunal finds any statute to be inconsistent with the Constitution, the overriding effect of the

---

[5] C. Forsyth, "Metaphysic of Nullity: Invalidity, Conceptual Reasoning and the Rule of Law" in C. Forsyth and I. Hare, ed's, *The Golden Metwand and the Crooked Cord: Essays in Honour of Sir William Wade, Q.C.* (Oxford: Clarendon Press, 1998) 141-160 at p. 141

[6] Chief Justice McLachlin recognized this in a 1996 case where she referred to "the general rule that all decision-making tribunals, be they courts or administrative tribunals, are bound to apply the law of the land. In doing so, they apply all the law of the land, including the *Charter*." (*Cooper v. Canada (Human Rights Commission)*, [1996] 3 S.C.R. 854 at para. 78). While this was a dissenting judgment, it was substantially adopted by the Court in 2003 (*Nova Scotia Workers' Compensation Board v. Martin*, [2003] 2 S.C.R. 504)

> *Constitution Act, 1982, s. 52(1)*, is to give the Court not
> only the power, but the duty, to regard the inconsistent
> statute, to the extent of the inconsistency, as being no
> longer "of force or effect."[7]

To similar effect, Chief Justice McLachlin said this in a 2015
case:

> No one should be subjected to an unconstitutional law:
> *Big M*, at p. 313. This reflects the principle that the
> Constitution belongs to all citizens, who share a right
> to the constitutional application of the laws of Canada.[8]

Thus, the Chief Justice in *Lloyd* must have meant to say that the
effect of the finding of inconsistency is to *require* the judge to
refuse to apply the law. But if this is correct – that all courts *must*
decide cases in accordance with the law – then what are we to
make of the Chief Justice's ensuing statement: "[H]owever, the
law remains in full force or effect, absent a formal declaration of
invalidity by a court of inherent jurisdiction"? How can a court
refuse to apply a law that the Supreme Court of Canada says
"remains in full force or effect?" At the same time, how can it
apply a law that the Constitution says is of "no force or effect?"

There simply is no way of untying this Gordion knot. It must be
cut by laying bare the logical impossibility of a law being at the
same time both valid ("in full force or effect" as per *Lloyd*) and
invalid ("of no force or effect" as per s. 52(1)). The reason why
the provincial court judge is required – not just permitted, but
required – to refuse to apply the law that does not conform to the
Constitution is that the law is of no force and effect. Period. This
is what s. 52(1) tells us. The opposite proposition – that the law
is of full force and effect until formally declared invalid by a court

---

[7] *R. v. Big M Drug Mart Ltd.*, [1985] 1 S.C.R. 295 at para. 143
[8] *R. v. Nur*, [2015] 1 S.C.R. 773 at para. 51; "There can be no question that an
enactment that breaches the Constitution is invalid and cannot impose any
enforceable duties." *R. v. Nikal*, [1996] 1 S.C.R. 1013 at para. 116

of inherent jurisdiction – must be wrong.[9] It simply cannot be that an unconstitutional law is other than void. If this were not so, it

---

[9] It is important to distinguish between a law's legal versus factual existence. A provision may be invalid as a matter of law, but still be capable of legal consequences because it exists as a matter of fact, and people rely upon its existence and reasonably assume that it is valid. "The law did not have legal existence, but it nevertheless existed as a fact and the legal system cannot but give effect to that reality if chaos is to be avoided." (*Nielsen v. Canada*, [1997] 3 F.C. 920 at pp. 930-931 (FCA)). Thus, various saving doctrines – de facto doctrine, mistake of law, *res judicata* – may come into play to protect the reliance interests of parties. "There is a clear distinction between declaring an Act unconstitutional and determining the practical and legal consequences that flow from that determination." (*Air Canada v. British Columbia*, [1989] 1 S.C.R. 1161 at p. 1195). "People act in reliance on such laws, and until their unconstitutionality has been judicially declared, those so relying upon them should be protected." (O.P. Field, "The Effect of an Unconstitutional Statute, (Washington, D.C.: Beard Books (1999) reprint), 1935) at p. 118) This is how the U.S. Supreme Court described it in *Chicot County Drainage Dist. v. Baxter State Bank*, 308 U.S. 371 (1940) at p. 374:

> The actual existence of a statute, prior to such a determination [of unconstitutionality], is an operative fact, and may have consequence which cannot justly be ignored. The past cannot always be erased by a new judicial declaration. The effect of the subsequent ruling as to invalidity may have to be considered in various aspects – with respect to particular relations, individual and corporate, and particular conduct, private and official. Questions of rights claimed to have become vested, of status, of prior determinations deemed to have finality and acted upon accordingly, of public policy in the light of the nature both of the statute and of its previous application, demand examination. These questions are among the most difficult of those which have engaged the attention of courts, state and federal, and it is manifest from numerous decisions that an all-inclusive statement of principle of absolute retroactive invalidity cannot be justified.

However, the fact that an unconstitutional law might result in legal consequences is not due to the law having any legal validity, but rather due to the operation of legal doctrines developed to protect parties who mistakenly believe that the law has legal force or effect. Accordingly, to describe an unconstitutional provision as being or remaining in "full force or effect" prior to a formal declaration of invalidity being made erroneously puts that provision on the same plateau as a constitutionally valid provision. At its highest, the unconstitutional provision may be said to be capable of resulting in legal

would not be possible for criminal courts of limited jurisdiction (where most criminal prosecutions occur) to entertain collateral challenges to the validity of unconstitutional laws. They would be required to convict persons found to have violated such laws until they had been formally declared invalid by a court of inherent jurisdiction.

This has been explained by Professor Forsyth: "For unless the challenged act is void it cannot be raised collaterally before a court that lacks power to quash an unlawful act..."[10] Thus, it is necessary that the unconstitutional law be void:

> Where a matter is properly raised by collateral challenge, then, once the unlawfulness of the act has been established, the court has no discretion, and rightly so, but to uphold the law. Indeed, this underlines the necessity that the unlawful act should be void. When the matter is raised collaterally, the unlawful act is denied effect without it having been quashed by the court; how can this be unless the unlawful act is void? Collateral challenge and the voidness of unlawful acts stand or fall together.[11]

It is difficult, however, for a court to cut this Gordion knot if it wants to continue to assert a power to breathe life into invalid laws

---

consequences, not by virtue of its own force or effect, but through the operation of recognized saving doctrines. So, for example, in a criminal case, it cannot be said that an unconstitutional provision has any force or effect (much less full force or effect) even though it has not been formally declared invalid. In all such cases, the court must recognize it as having no force and effect and dismiss the charges against persons prosecuted under such a law. This helps explain why collateral attack against invalid provisions is permitted in criminal or regulatory enforcement proceedings. (*R. v. Consolidated Maybrun Mines Ltd.,* [1998] 1 S.C.R. 706 at para. 25; *R. v. Sharma,* [1993] 1 S.C.R. 650)

[10] C. Forsyth, "The Legal Effect of Unlawful Administrative Acts: The Theory of the Second Actor Explained and Developed" (June/July 2001) 35 *Amicus Curiae* 20 at p. 20

[11] C. Forsyth, "Metaphysic of Nullity: Invalidity, Conceptual Reasoning and the Rule of Law" in C. Forsyth and I. Hare, ed's, *The Golden Metwand and the Crooked Cord: Essays in Honour of Sir William Wade, QC,* (Oxford: Clarendon Press, 1998) pp. 141-160 at p. 157.

by issuing suspended declarations of invalidity. If forced to give up the pretense that unconstitutional laws are of full force and effect until formally declared invalid by a particular kind of court, the court must then undertake the Sisyphean task of explaining the basis in law for its power to create and put temporarily in place laws that are inconsistent with the Constitution. Mere reference to the Supreme Court's extraordinary, extra-constitutional, non-binding, advisory opinion in *Manitoba Language Rights* will not do the trick. Not even close.

3. Is Means Is -- No Means No

Words and their meaning should matter to lawyers and judges. This is so notwithstanding one author's warning that: "Attention to text earns only professional scorn in constitutional law."[12] Although there may be room to argue about the place of unwritten constitutional principles and gap-filling interpretative approaches, the rule of law surely demands at a minimum, that the words of constitutional instruments, especially where those words admit of no ambiguity, must be respected and followed. Thus, when s. 52(1) of the Constitution stipulates that any inconsistent law *is*, to the extent of the inconsistency, of *no* force or effect, the words do not permit a court to decide that such inconsistent law *will*, for a temporary period, be of *full* force or effect. Yet, this is what the courts do when they purport to issue suspended declarations of invalidity.

What is it about the words *is* and *no* that these courts do not understand?[13] In the absence of another explanation, we are left to

---

[12] H.A. Linde, "'Clear and Present Danger' Reexamined: Dissonance in the *Brandenburg* Concerto" (1970) 22 *Stan. L. Rev.* 1163 at p. 1175, quoted in J. Harrison, "Power, Duty and Facial Invalidity" (2013) 16 *U. Pa. J. Const. L.* 501 at p. 501

[13] President Bill Clinton once infamously called into question the meaning of the word "is": "It depends on what the meaning of 'is' is." K. Starr, The Starr Report: The Official Report of the Independent Counsel's Investigation of the President (Forum, An Imprint of Prima Publishing, Edition, 1998) at footnote 1,128), quoted in S.B. Presser, *Law Professors: Three Centuries of Shaping American Law*, (St. Paul: West Academic Publishing, 2017) at p. 445

conclude that the courts do not consider themselves bound to observe the Constitution as the supreme law of Canada, as s. 52(1) directs, but rather that they possess a higher and overriding power to give legal life and vitality to laws which the Constitution deems to be of no force or effect.

This calls again to mind Chief Justice Lamer's attempt in a 1997 decision to explain what the Court did in *Manitoba Language Rights*:

> The rule of law led the Court to confer temporary validity on the laws of Manitoba which were unconstitutional because they had been enacted only in English, in contravention of the *Manitoba Act, 1870*. The Court developed this remedial innovation notwithstanding the express terms of a s. 52(1) of the *Constitution Act, 1982*, that unconstitutional laws are "of no force or effect", *a provision that suggests* that declarations of invalidity can only be given immediate effect. The Court did so in order to not "deprive Manitoba of its legal order and cause a transgression of the rule of law" (p. 753). *Reference re Manitoba Language Rights* therefore stands as another example of how the fundamental principles articulated by preamble have been given legal effect by this Court.[14] (emphasis added)

However, the word "is" in s. 52(1) does more than just *suggest* that a law that is inconsistent with the Constitution is, to the extent of the inconsistency, of no force or effect. It states it as a legal fact in the present tense. Subsection 52(1), on its face, is automatic and self-executing. The point could not be made more clearly.

Justice Southin, in the early days of *Charter* interpretation, demonstrated a clear understanding of what words s. 52(1) did and did not contain. In a 1988 decision, she rejected the notion:

---

[14] *Reference re Rumeration of Judges of Prov. Court of P.E.I.*, [1997] 3 S.C.R. 3 at para. 99

> ...that s. 52(1) can be read as if it had added to it the
> words "and if a statute or regulation is inconsistent with
> this Charter, the Court may amend it in such manner as
> the court thinks appropriate and just."[15]

The existence of s. 52(1), and its unbending directive that
inconsistent laws *are* of *no* force or effect, also means that courts
do not have flexibility to allow Canadian common law to develop
in ways that would permit unconstitutional laws to be given legal
force and effect by judicial fiat. In Part 2 of this essay, there is a
review of a number of cases from other common law jurisdictions
– New Zealand, Hong Kong, Australia and the UK – in which the
courts, applying long-standing common law principles, refused to
recognize as legal that which had been determined not to be
legal.[16] To the extent that this was the result of judge-made law,
one might argue that it would be open to Canadian courts to go in
another direction, and to develop and apply different principles.
In theory, this might be true as a matter of the common law, but
s. 52(1) precludes the possibility of Canadian constitutional law
developing in that direction, in the absence of a constitutional
amendment.

This point was recognized by Justice Bastarache in his concurring
opinion in *Canada (Attorney General v. Hislop)*.[17] In response to
the majority's suggestion that the retroactivity or prospectivity of
a judicial decision depends on whether the court is operating
inside or outside of the Blackstonian paradigm (that is,
Blackstone's traditional declaratory/retroactive theory of the
law), Justice Bastarache explained that the Constitution itself, and
not Blackstone's declaratory theory (a judge-made concept),
requires that unconstitutional laws are invalidated from the
moment the law came into effect:

> The basis for general retroactivity is not Blackstone's
> declaratory theory, but the Constitution itself. Section

---

[15] *R. v. Van Vliet*, 1988 CanLII 3281 (BCCA) at para. 103
[16] "Fidelity to the Law: The Good, the Bad, and the Ugly" at pp. 76-91.
[17] [2007] 1 S.C.R. 429

> 52(1) of the *Constitution Act, 1982* establishes that any
> law which is inconsistent with the Constitution "is, to
> the extent of the inconsistency, of no force or effect."
> The Constitution exists independently of judicial
> decisions and, as such, any law which is inconsistent
> with it is invalidated from the moment the law came
> into effect.[18]

If s. 52(1) means what it says, a law which is inconsistent with the Constitution cannot, even temporarily, be endowed by a court with legal force or effect.

The apparent ease with which the Supreme Court is able to depart from the text of s. 52(1) in ordering that unconstitutional laws should be given force and effect, stands in stark contrast to the stringency that it has applied in interpreting statutes in other contexts. In 2014, the federal government appointed Justice Marc Nadon of the Federal Court of Appeal to fill a vacancy on the Supreme Court of Canada. Nadon was actually sworn in as a Supreme Court justice, but before he assumed his duties, questions were raised about his eligibility to fill this vacancy as it was earmarked for a representative from Quebec. Given Quebec's unique civil law system, the *Supreme Court Act* stipulates that at least three of the nine justices must come from the Quebec courts or "from among the advocates of [Quebec]." Nadon had spent his entire career as a member of the Quebec bar (that is, as an advocate of Quebec), but was required to resign his membership in the Quebec bar when he took his Federal Court appointment. The issue was whether the words "from among the advocates of [Quebec]" required current membership in the Quebec bar, or whether long-term previous membership would suffice.

When questions as to the proper interpretation of these words were raised, Parliament responded by enacting clarifying legislation which deemed the section to include both current and past membership in the Quebec bar. However, on a statutory

---

[18] *ibid.* at para. 138. To be precise, of course, such a law would actually never have come into effect.

reference, the Supreme Court, by a majority, rejected this interpretation and held that Parliament's clarifying legislation was, in fact, an unauthorized attempt to amend a constitutional requirement as to the composition of the Supreme Court. Thus, Nadon, not being a current member of the Quebec bar, was held not eligible to sit on the Supreme Court.[19]

Reasonable people might disagree about whether reference to a particular status or qualification necessarily requires incumbency. For example, would reference to "Nobel prize winners" mean only current or incumbent winners or also past winners? Accordingly, it must be asked whether the issue in Nadon's case was so clear cut that the Court, exercising its best efforts, had no alternative but to prevent the government from appointing the person it considered to be the best available candidate? More to the point, was there not something a bit off about the Court applying such rigour in its interpretation of the ambiguous statutory language in the Nadon case, whereas, just three months earlier in the *Bedford* case, it had read s. 52(1) as sufficiently pliant to allow the prosecution and conviction of people under sections of the *Criminal Code* which the Court had just found to be unconstitutional?[20] Words and their meaning do matter and, as the Supreme Court has itself said, courts must avoid the Humpty Dumpty approach to interpretation, where words mean whatever the interpreter chooses them to mean.[21]

4. Suspended Declarations and the Rule of Law

Like world peace and white tigers: "Everyone, it seems, is for the rule of law."[22] No one, however, can provide a universally-accepted definition of this amorphous concept. "Advocates tend

---

[19] *Reference re Supreme Court Act, ss. 5 and 6*, [2014] 1 S.C.R. 433

[20] *Canada (Attorney General) v. Bedford*, [2013] 3 S.C.R. 1101 (See Part 2 of this essay, "Fidelity to the Law: The Good, the Bad, and the Ugly" at pp. 65-72

[21] *2747-3174 Quebec Inc. v. Quebec*, [1996] 3 S.C.R. 919 at para's 170-171

[22] B. Z. Tamanaha, "The History and Elements of the Rule of Law," (2012) *Sing. J. Legal Stud.* 232 at p. 232

to read into the principle of the rule of law anything which supports their particular view of what the law should be."²³ The Supreme Court of Canada certainly professes devotion to the rule of law, having made some mention of it in more than two hundred decisions since its incorporation into the Charter's preamble in 1982.²⁴ Among the Supreme Court's many encapsulations of the concept are these: "the root of our system of government;"²⁵ "a principle of profound constitutional and political significance;"²⁶ "clearly implicit in the very nature of a Constitution;"²⁷ a "corner stone of our democratic form of government;"²⁸ "the very foundation of the *Charter*;"²⁹ and, a "fundamental postulate of our constitutional structure."³⁰

At a minimum, the rule of law must consist of the two elements identified by Professor Joseph Raz which the Supreme Court approved of in *Manitoba Language Rights*: "(1) that people should be ruled by the law and obey it, and (2) that the law should be such that people will be able to be guided by it."³¹ Thus, the Court reasoned, the rule of law cannot be fulfilled unless there exists a body of positive law for the people to follow.

That much may be true, but it tells only part of the story. It says nothing about the legitimacy of the source of those laws. It says nothing about whether those laws conform to the requirements of a higher constitutional instrument. In the most brutal totalitarian

---

²³ *Singh v. Canada*, [2000] 3 FC 185 at para. 33 (FCA)

²⁴ A. Heard, "Constitutional Conventions and Written Constitutions: The Rule of Law Implications in Canada" (2015) 38 *Dublin Univ. L.J.* 331 at p. 332

²⁵ *Reference re Secession of Quebec*, [1998] 2 S.C.R. 217 at para. 70

²⁶ *ibid.* at para. 71

²⁷ *Reference re Manitoba Language Rights*, [1985] 1 S.C.R. 721 at para. 64

²⁸ *Canadian Council of Churches v. Canada*, [1992] 1 S.C.R. 236 at p. 250

²⁹ *British Columbia Government Employees' Union v. British Columbia (Attorney General)*, [1988] 2 S.C.R. 214 at p. 229

³⁰ *Roncarelli v. Duplessis*, [1959] S.C.R. 121 at p. 142. See also, *British Columbia v. Imperial Tobacco Canada Ltd.*, [2005] 2 S.C.R. 473 at para's 57-63.

³¹ [1985] 1 SCR 721 at para. 62, quoting J. Raz, *The Authority of Law,* (Oxford: Oxford Univ. Press, 1979) at pp. 212-213

state there could exist a clear body of positive law, but one would not conclude from that that the concept of the rule of law had been achieved. A chocolate cake consists of a number of essential ingredients. Yet, one would not grab hold of just one those ingredients and proclaim the creation of a chocolate cake. So, too, with the rule of law. The existence of a body of positive law may be a necessary, but certainly not a sufficient, condition for it to be said that rule of law exists.

Herein lies the fallacy of *Manitoba Language Rights*. A body of positive law that is put in place by extra-legal means amounts not to a realization of the rule of law, but rather to rule *by* law or the rule of *order*. Professor Dale Gibson argued that the Court's decision was actually based on the doctrine of state necessity which allows the state to act *contrary* to the law in emergency situations: "Far from being a part of the rule of law, the doctrine of state necessity is its antithesis."[32] Gibson goes on to state that it is "obvious that the Court was giving priority to order over law."[33] Essentially the same point was made by Hugo Cyr and Monica Popescu, who referred to the "intellectual contortion" which allowed the Court to claim that it was not suspending the Constitution:

> In other words, the meaning given by the Court to the rule of law entails that the existence of a concrete order could, in certain exceptional circumstances, trump the respect for actual legal rules. This sounds more like a simple "principle of order" than "the rule of law". At any rate, this intellectual contortion allowed the Court to claim that it was not suspending the Constitution in itself – it was not the same thing as a Schmittian case of "exception" – but that the protection of the rule of law required that the Court suspend temporarily the applicability of their judgment declaring the invalidity of the quasi-totality of Manitoba statutes during the

---

[32] D. Gibson, "The Real Laws of the Constitution" (1990) 28 *Alta. L. Rev.* 358 at p. 372
[33] *ibid.* at p. 373

minimum period necessary for correcting the situation.[34]

This is not to say that a body of positive law should not have been imposed in Manitoba in 1985. Clearly, it was necessary that that be done by someone. It should not, however, have been done by a court, but rather by a body which under a democratic system of government has the authority to prescribe laws:

> The *rule of law*, accordingly requires state coercion to be limited and regulated by published or promulgated and determinate rules, issued or enacted according to settled public procedures for making law.[35]

The idea that a court can give legal force and effect to a law that the Constitution says is of no force or effect is perplexing.[36] However, with relatively few exceptions, it has not been questioned to a great extent by either judges or academics in Canada. Doubts have been voiced tepidly. One judge from British Columbia diplomatically described it as a legal paradox: "A suspension of a declaration of invalidity is a legal paradox, in that a law which is invalid from its start is nonetheless considered alive for a brief period...".[37] Even more understated was Justice Marceau of the Federal Court of Appeal who described the

---

[34] H. Cyr and M. Popescu, "The Supreme Court of Canada" in A. Jakab, A. Dyevre and G. Itzcovich, ed's, *Comparative Constitutional Reasoning*, (Cambridge: Cambridge Univ. Press, 2017) pp. 154-198 at pp. 174-175

[35] T.R.S. Allan, "The Rule of Law" in D. Dyzehaus and M. Thorburn, ed's , *Philosophical Foundations of Constitutional Law*, (Oxford: Oxford Univ. Press, 2016) at p. 201

[36] It is especially ironic that *Manitoba Language Rights* has become the wellspring of justification for the imposition of unconstitutional laws by way of suspended declarations given that the Court in that decision described the Constitution as "unsuffering of laws inconsistent with it." (*Manitoba Language Rights*, [1985] 1 SCR 721 at para. 48) This is not how things have worked out for the Constitution. It has often been made to suffer the existence of unconstitutional laws put in place by judicial decree under colour of suspended declarations of invalidity.

[37] *British Columbia Teachers' Federation v. British Columbia*, 2014 BCSC 121 (CanLII) at para. 560

concept as "difficult to understand": "It may be difficult to understand that the judiciary may give temporary effect to a provision of law that the legislature had no power to enact...".[38]

Professor Leckey has noted that suspended declarations are contrary to the text of the Constitution:

> [T]he practice of delaying a declaration of invalidity has no textual foundation in Canada. The supremacy clause in section 52(1) of the *Constitution Act, 1982* states, in the present tense, that any law inconsistent with the Constitution is, to the extent of that inconsistency, "of no force or effect".[39]

Thomas Cromwell, eventually of the Supreme Court of Canada, writing prior to his appointment to the bench, acknowledged that "allowing unconstitutional laws to operate is subversive of the principle of legality."[40] Professor Grant Huscroft, prior to his appointment to the Ontario Court of Appeal, went further than most academic commentators in describing suspended declarations as "arguably extra-constitutional."[41] Some of the strongest resistance to suspended declarations of invalidity, however, has come from outside of Canada, with Canadian practices being described by some observers as "counterintuitive and unpalatable."[42] As well, as outlined in Part 2 of this essay, courts in New Zealand, Hong Kong, and the United Kingdom

---

[38] *Nielsen v. Canada (Employment and Immigration Commission),* [1997] 3 F.C. 920 at p. 931

[39] R. Leckey, "Realizing Rights Here and Now" (available online, forthcoming in of *Australian J. of Human Rights*) at p. 4

[40] T.A. Cromwell, "Aspects of Judicial Review in Canada" (1995) 46 *So. C. L. Rev.* 1027 at p. 1040

[41] G. Huscroft, "Rationalizing Judicial Power: The Mischief of Dialogue Theory" in J.B. Kelly and C.P. Manfredi, ed's, *Contested Constitutionalism : Reflections on the Canadian Charter of Rights and Freedoms*, (Vancouver: UBC Press, 2009) 50-65 at p. 56

[42] A. O'Neill, "Invalidity and Retrospectivity under the Irish and Canadian Constitutions" (2006) 15 *Constitutional Forum* 147 at p. 153. Professor O'Neill, however, does not fully agree with the criticisms of Canadian practices.

have considered and declined to follow Canadian suspended declaration jurisprudence.

These relatively isolated voices of criticism, however, pale in comparison to the overall chorus of approval. To the extent that concerns are expressed, they tend to focus on specific instances where the power to suspend was or was not exercised, or they consist of the general observation that what originated as an emergency power has become routinely exercised. Rarely has it been asked if the courts have *in any circumstance* the legal authority to ignore or override the Constitution.[43] For the most part, the practice has been enthusiastically embraced by those described by Robert Leckey as the judiciary's "cheerleaders on

---

[43] Bruce Ryder understands, at least partly, the problem with allowing courts to override the Constitution:

> The nub of the problem with suspended declarations is that they sanction continuing violations of Charter rights and freedoms by unjustifiable laws.

However, he accepts that there may be circumstances where governments can justify their use. He does not dig deep into the fundamental question of the source of this judicial power:

> In any case, I suggest below, suspended declarations should only be issued when governments ask for them and demonstrate the need for them. If they do, intrusion into the legislative field is not likely to be a serious concern.

B. Ryder, "Suspending the Charter," (2003) 21 *S.C.L.R. (2d)* 267 at p. 280. Similarly, Grant Hoole is critical of indiscriminate overuse of suspended declarations, but he concedes that the courts' exercise of a power to ignore the dictates of s. 52(1) may be justified in certain circumstances:

> As section 52 states, "the Constitution is the supreme law of Canada." The suppression of its dictates, even temporarily, for reasons that are inadequate, ill-conceived or simply unprincipled, is inimical to the Constitution's primary character.

G.R. Hoole, "Proportionality as a Remedial Principle: A Framework for Suspended Declarations of Invalidity in Canadian Constitutional Law" (2011) 49 *Alta. L. Rev.* 107 at p. 136. While both Hoole and Ryder are skeptical of suspended declarations (and propose that their use be made subject to justification by analogy to s. 1 of the *Charter* and the *Oakes* tests) neither them questions the right of courts *in any circumstance* to defy the dictates of s. 52(1).

the sidelines."[44] As noted earlier, members of the Canadian legal academy have described suspended declarations as important, novel, ingenious, remarkable, powerful and innovative.[45] Leckey, on the other hand, has refused to join in the celebration:

> If, all things considered, delayed remedies are appropriate in some cases, they are not something to celebrate. A sociological or psychological inquiry may lurk beyond these legal matters: Why should distinguished scholars of dialogue and remedies anthropomorphize impersonal institutions – depicting them as gently and patiently speaking or nudging – while attending so little to the actual humans whose rights are at stake?[46]

What accounts for this lack of critical scrutiny of a practice which strikes at the heart of the rule of law? Various explanations may be proffered, including that suspended declarations are favoured, particularly within legal academia, because they are conducive judicial activism.[47] They advance the prevailing liberal view that constitutional litigation is a good way to bring about political and

---

[44] R. Leckey, "The Harms of Remedial Discretion" (2016) 14 *Int'l J. Const. L.* 584 at p. 603.

[45] See Part 1 of this essay, "Some Misconceptions About Constitutional Invalidation" at p. 15.

[46] R. Leckey, "The Harms of Remedial Discretion" (2016) 14 *Int'l J. Const. L.* 584 at p. 607.

[47] The issuance of suspended declarations is typically presented as an exercise in judicial restraint, but this is not necessarily so. By arrogating to itself a power to override the Constitution, the Court is able to find laws unconstitutional without having to contend with the inevitable messiness that would normally flow from such determinations. This makes it easier for the Court to adjudge laws unconstitutional. What is passively packaged as judicial deference to the legislatures may, in fact, be a gateway to more aggressive judicial review of legislation. It is therefore no coincidence that the U.S. Supreme Court's daliance with prospective overruling in the 1960's corresponded with the Warren Court's activist period. Thus, Justice Scalia described prospective decsionmaking as "the handmaid of judicial activism, and the born enemy of *stare decisis*." (*Harper v. Virginia Dep't of Taxation*, 509 U.S. 86 (1993) at p. 105)

social change.[48] It is also possible that the legal community has passively accepted suspended declarations because the Supreme Court has the final and authoritative say on what the Constitution means and so there is really no point in questioning their legality. What is the point in howling at the moon?[49]

The most likely explanation, however, is that pragmatism has been allowed to hold sway over considerations of the law. Suspended declarations of invalidity are considered to be good because they provide courts with flexibility to modulate and control the consequences of determinations of unconstitutionality. In fact, Chief Justice Lamer in the seminal *Schachter* case made express reference to "good pragmatic reasons" for allowing an unconstitutional law to persist for a time.[50] And Chief Justice McLachlin, writing extra-judicially in 2002, referred to the inductive and pragmatic nature of the remedial techniques of the Court under s. 52(1): "They are inductive and pragmatic, rather than deductive and logical."[51]

Pragmatism involves a search for what works; a search for a practical solution to the particular problem at hand. There is, of course, nothing wrong with looking for practical solutions to problems, but difficulties may arise if this results in *ad hoc* decision-making unmoored from a set of underlying principles.

---

[48] However, proponents' enthusiasm for judicial activism wanes somewhat when courts act less liberally, for example, by striking down laws limiting hours of work, *Lochner v. New York*, 198 U.S. 45 (1905); by nullifying laws which decriminalized abortion in Germany and Spain; or by invalidating a nationalization law in France on grounds that it did not adequately compensate stockholders (see A. Stone Sweet, *Governing with Judges: Constitutional Politics in Europe*, (Oxford: Oxford Univ. Press, 2000) at p. 66.

[49] Harry Arthurs has mused about the futility of challenging the explanations of judges as to the nature and extent of their powers: "All of these explanations are circular and solipsistic; however, since they are found in judicial rulings, there is not much that anyone can do to challenge them." H. Arthurs, "Constitutional Courage" (2003) 49 *McGill L. J.* 1 at p. 17

[50] *Schachter v. Canada*, [1992] 2 S.C.R. 679 at p. 716

[51] B.M. McLachlin, "Bill of Rights in Common Law Countries" (2002) 51 *Int'l & Comp. L. Q.* 197 at p. 203

The problem with legal pragmatism – in the sense that courts should find the solution that will work in the particular case whether or not it fits with underlying principles – is that it gnaws away at and ultimately will devour the fundamental precepts of the rule of law.

The fact that adherence to the law may give rise to hardship is not an adequate reason for ignoring it:

> All arguments on the hardships of a case must be rejected when we are pronouncing what the law is, for such arguments are only quicksands in the law and, if indulged, will soon swallow up every principle of it.[52]

Chief Justice O'Higgins of the Supreme Court of Ireland (dissenting on another point) said this in rejecting the suggestion that courts have discretion to make their rulings of unconstitutionality retroactive or prospective depending upon the practical needs and circumstances of particular cases:

> A declaration, once made, has the effect and operates in accordance with what the Constitution, correctly interpreted, ordains and not in accordance with what may be thought desirable, feasible or convenient by the court making the declaration.[53]

The problem with suspended declarations of invalidity does not relate to their practical utility or lack thereof. The problem is that they are not authorized by law. They are illegal. And allowing courts to make illegal orders, even if they bring about wonderful results in the particular case at hand, is corrosive of the rule of law.[54] "It goes to the heart of rule of law that the judges, like everyone else, should be ruled by *law*, i.e. rules fixed and

---

[52] *Yates v. Hall* (1785), 1 T.R. 73 at p. 80, *per* Buller J.

[53] *Murphy v. Attorney General*, [1982] 1 I.R. 241 at p. 296

[54] Justice Brennan, dissenting in *U.S. v. Calandra*, 414 U.S. 338 (1974) at p. 357, warned that judges should "avoid the taint of partnership in official lawlesness."

announced beforehand."[55] Once armed with the power to ignore or overlook the law in certain types of cases, it becomes tempting to expand the reach of this power to every situation where judges believe that they know what the answer should be. That is the road to authoritarianism. It does not require malevolence. To the contrary, what makes it pernicious is that honest and good people, believing that they can and will do the right thing, naturally seek out more and more discretionary power.

Lord Shaw eloquently articulated the danger of allowing constitutional rights to become matters of discretion: "To remit the maintenance of constitutional right to the region of judicial discretion is to shift the foundations of freedom from the rock to the sand."[56] Harry Arthurs has described this phenomenon in damning terms:

> Judges believe in their own omniscience, neutrality, and capacity to do good. This belief – benignly and strongly held, if quite mistaken – prompts judges to seek out ways to expand their own mandate, powers , and prerogatives.[57]

Christopher Forsyth has also warned of the dangers of arming judges with broad remedial discretion:

> Judges often wield remedial discretion as if they had a free hand to do what was necessary to achieve justice. These judges are the heirs to Coke confident that they have ample Kingly power to do justice and this extends even to vivifying an invalid act.[58]

---

[55] C. Forsyth, "The Metaphysic of Nullity: Invalidity, Conceptual Reasoning and the Rule of Law," in C. Forsyth and I. Hare, ed's, *The Golden Metwand and the Crooked Cord: Essays in Honour of Sir William Wade QC,* (Oxford: Clarendon Press, 1998) 141-160 at pp. 145-146

[56] *Scott v. Scott,* [1913] AC 417 at p. 477

[57] H. Arthurs, "Constitutional Courage" (2003) 49 *McGill L.J.* 1 at p. 16

[58] C. Forsyth, "The Rock and the Sand: Jurisdiction and Remedial Discretion" University of Cambridge, Legal Studies Research Paper Series, Paper No. 31/2013, retrievable at www.law.com.ac.uk/ssrn at p. 13

In 1878, Chief Justice Cockburn had this to say about the role and power of the judge: "He cannot set himself above the law which he has to administer, or make or mould it to suit the exigencies of the particular occasion."[59] As Justice Peter Lauwers of the Ontario Court of Appeal recently put it: "We are not roving dispensers of law or justice."[60] And Chief Justice Gleeson of New South Wales has similarly rejected the idea that judges can determine cases according to their own views of what would be the appropriate outcome: "[Judges] have no mandate to act as ad hoc legislators who, by decree, determine an appropriate outcome on a case-by-case basis."[61] It can safely be assumed that a judge who does the right thing for the wrong reasons, will eventually do the wrong thing.

If judges truly are guardians of the Constitution, as the Supreme Court of Canada has proclaimed on numerous occasions, they must assiduously confine themselves to lawful exercises of power.[62] The rule of law cannot become rule by judges.[63] "Governmental power cannot be lawfully exercised, unless it conforms to the Constitution."[64] Along with the guarantee of the judiciary's independence from interference by the other branches of government comes a solemn duty for judges to conduct

---

[59] *Martin v. Mackonochie* (1878), 3 QBD 730 at p. 775

[60] P. Lauwers, speech delivered to the Runnymede Society in Toronto on January 12, 2018.

[61] A.M. Gleeson, "Individualized Justice – The Holy Grail" (1995) 69 *ALJ* 421 at p. 432

[62] Professor Tremblay has written that:

> Judicial authority may be accepted as legitimate if, and only if, it acts in accordance with the law. This condition entails not only that the composition of the courts and the judicial process must be "according to law", but that judicial decisions must be based on reasons that are, in a certain sense, "legal".

L.B. Tremblay, "The Legitimacy of Judicial Review: The Limits of Dialogue Between Courts and Legislatures" (2005) 3 *Int'l J. Const. L.* 617 at pp. 638-639

[63] B.Z. Tamanaha, "The History and Elements of the Rule of Law" (2012) *Singapore J. of Legal Stud.* 232 at p. 245

[64] *Reference re Senate Reform*, [2014] 1 S.C.R. 704 at para. 23

themselves in accordance with the rule of law and other constitutional norms and limitations. As Richard Fallon has said: "Rule of Law implies that officials, including judges, must be ruled by law."[65] In fact, the judiciary, which Bickel described as the "least dangerous branch,"[66] has the capacity to become very dangerous, indeed, if it oversteps itself. Alexander Hamilton noted this when he wrote: "But the errors and usurpations of the Supreme Court of the United States will be uncontrollable and remediless."[67] Similarly, Justice Harlan Stone of the U.S Supreme Court acknowledged the great responsibility for judges to stay within their lawful powers: "[T]he only check on our own exercise of power is our own sense of self-restraint."[68]

An especially harsh critic of the Supreme Court of Canada and its judicial independence jurisprudence, Jeffrey Goldsworthy of Monash University in Australia, has written:

> They [judges] should reflect on the fact that they too are subject to the rule of law and that, ultimately, the only practical mechanism for ensuring that they abide by it is their own scrupulous intellectual honesty. If that cannot be trusted, the rule of law is in peril.[69]

As Oxford Professor Timothy Endicott has observed, our system of government depends upon the judiciary, especially courts of final appeal, respecting and observing the rule of law:

---

[65] R.H. Fallon, "The Rule of Law as a Concept in Constitutional Discourse" (1997) 97 *Columbia L. Rev.* 1 at p. 10

[66] A.M. Bickel, *The Least Dangerous Branch: The Supreme Court at the Bar of Politics,* (New Haven: Yale Univ. Press, 1962)

[67] Quoted in A.R. Brewer-Carias, *Constitutional Courts as Positive Legislators: A Comparative Law Study*, (Cambridge: Cambridge Univ. Press, 2011) at p. 39

[68] *U.S. v. Butler,* 297 U.S. 1 (1936) at p. 79, quoted in J. Agresto, *The Supreme Court and Constitutional Democracy*, (Ithaca: Cornell Univ. Press, 1984) at pp. 103-104

[69] J. Goldsworthy, "The Preamble, Judicial Independence and Judicial Integrity" (2000) 11 *Const. Forum* 60 at p. 64

> [B]cause there is no legal recourse from its decisions, it [the House of Lords] has opportunities that lower courts do not have, to ignore the law and to get away with it. To the extent that it ignores the law, Britain is ruled not by law, but by judges.[70]

Indeed, written constitutions are next to useless if courts can just ignore them: "And if judges are free to create constitutional law out of thin air, why do we bother having a written and popularly ratified Constitution at all?"[71] The rule of law insists that all exercises of governmental power, including judicial power, comply with the law.[72]

There is no reason to believe that the Supreme Court developed its suspended declaration jurisprudence otherwise than with the honest and good faith belief that it would be beneficial to Canada in dealing with the disruptive effects of findings of unconstitutionality. Strong arguments can be made as to the virtue and utility of suspended declarations in many situations, although their indiscriminate use without regard for justifying principles is discomfiting. However, that is not the point. Either they are legal, or they are not – and the case for their legality, resting as it ultimately does on *Manitoba Language Rights*, is very tenuous.

As discussed in the next section, the constitutions of many countries expressly endow their constitutional courts with the power to control the effective dates of their findings of unconstitutionality. Some of these provisions have existed for

---

[70] T.A.O. Endicott, "The Impossibility of Rule of Law" (1999) 19 *Oxford J. of Legal Stud.* 1 at p. 10

[71] D.A. Farber, "Legal Pragmatism and the Constitution" (1988) 72 *Minn. L. Rev.* 1331 at p. 1339

[72] "The rule of law principle requires that all government action must comply with the law, including the Constitution." *Reference Re Secession of Quebec*, [1998] 2 S.C.R. 217 at para. 72; "Another social goal served by judicial independence is the maintenance of the rule of law, one aspect of which is the constitutional principle that the exercise of all public power must find its ultimate source in a legal rule." *Reference re Remuneration of the Prov. Court of P.E.I.*, [1997] 3 S.C.R. 3 at para. 10

almost a century and they would have been known to the people involved in the preparation of Canada's modern Constitution in the early 1980's. However, they were not included in Canada's Constitution. Moreover, not all countries believe that it is a good thing for courts to have these powers. In fact, in Ireland, a government-appointed Constitution Review Group considered in 1996 and recommended against a proposal to amend Ireland's Constitution so that "the courts should have jurisdiction to declare invalid, otherwise than *ab initio*, a statutory provision which at the date of its passing was repugnant to the Constitution."[73]

And in any event, even assuming that an overwhelmingly persuasive case could be made that courts should have the power to make suspended declarations, that does not make it so.[74] As Alberta lawyer, W. H. Hurlburt, noted: "I think that a court, when interpreting a Constitution, should refrain from finding that something is there merely because it would be a good thing if it were, no matter how admirable the reasons."[75] Similarly, Robert Leckey has observed, with reference to South Africa's Constitution which does contain provisions permitting suspended declarations: "Significantly, the Canadian judges have asserted discretion for themselves as if they enjoyed the power granted by the Constitution of South Africa."[76]

5. When in Vienna

The constitutions of a number of countries expressly authorize courts to control the temporal effects of their determinations of unconstitutionality. The model for this approach comes from Austria where the constitutional theorist, Hans Kelsen, heavily

---

[73] Report of the Constitution Review Group, Dublin, Stationary Office, 1996
[74] In a different context, the Supreme Court wrote in 1988: "It is a deeply ingrained value in our democratic system that the ends do not justify the means." *R. v. Mack,* [1988] 2 S.C.R. 903 at para. 74
[75] W.H. Hurlburt, "Fairy Tales and Living Trees: Observations on Some Recent Decisions of the Supreme Court of Canada" (1998) 26 *Man. L.J.* 181 at p. 201
[76] R. Leckey, *Bills of Rights in the Common Law,* (Cambridge: Cambridge Univ. Press, 2015) at p. 144

influenced the drafting of the Austrian Constitution of 1920. It provides, as a general rule, that a determination of unconstitutionality is given only prospective (*ex nunc*) effect, except for the particular case in which the determination is made, which is given the benefit of the determination of unconstitutionality. The court may decide also to give the decision wholly or partial retrospective (*ex tunc*) effect, but the presumption is in favour of prospective effect only. In addition, the Austrian Constitution provides that the unconstitutional statute does not become nullified until the nullifying decision is published, and the constitutional court is expressly permitted to order the effective date of the nullification to be delayed for up to eighteen months from the date of publication.

Thus, it can be seen that the Austrian constitutional model is in many respects the opposite of the approach taken in most common law jurisdictions. In particular, prospectivity is the rule in Austria, rather than common law retroactivity. In addition, the ability of the Austrian Constitutional Court to delay the effective date of its nullification for up to eighteen months represents a constitutionally authorized means of achieving essentially the same result as the unauthorized Canadian practice of suspending declarations of invalidity.[77] Also of particular note is that the Austrian Constitution contemplates that the court's determination has the effect of nullifying or rescinding the unconstitutional law. This is unlike in most common law jurisdictions where the constitutionally infirm provision is void, i.e., invalid and of no force or effect from the time of enactment by reason of the self-executing force of the constitution, independently of any court order.

---

[77] See, M. Stelzer, "*Pro Futuro* and Retroactive Effects of Rescissory Judgments in Austria" in P. Popelier, S.A. Verstraelen, D. Vanheule and B. Vanlerberghe, ed's., *The Effects of Judicial Decisions in Time*, (Cambridge: Intersentia Publishing, 2014) 63-75 at p. 64; A.R. Brewer-Carias, *Constitutional Courts as Positive Legislators: A Comparative Law Study*, (Cambridge: Cambridge Univ. Press, 2011) at pp. 5-12

The process in Austria works as follows:

> If a law (or the contested part of it) is found to be
> unconstitutional, the Constitutional Court rescinds it.
> Rescission is published in the designated form (for
> instance, in the Federal Law Gazette). As a rule,
> rescission becomes effective at the close of the day of
> publication. The Constitutional Court may, however,
> set a time limit for rescission, which in the case of a
> parliamentary statute may not exceed 18 months. If a
> time limit is set, rescission comes into force only after
> expiry of the specified period.[78]

This is consistent with Hans Kelsen's conception of constitutional
invalidity as involving voidability rather than nullification *ab
initio*:

> For example, he [Kelsen] posits that legislation or legal
> regulation that is constitutionally defective is not void
> ab initio but only voidable in the sense that it is valid
> law and, thus an act of state, until it has been annulled
> by a legal competent organ."[79]

In constitutional systems modelled on the Austrian approach, "a
judicial body performing constitutional review can cause an
enacted statute to cease to be legally operative after it has gone
into force, in effect repealing it."[80] Similarly, in Italy, laws that
conflict with constitutional principles *must* be enforced by the

---

[78] M. Stelzer, *The Constitution of the Republic of Austria: A Contextual
Analysis*, (Oxford and Portland: Hart Publishing, 2001) at pp. 201-202

[79] F. Tanguay-Renaud, "The Intelligibility of Extra-Legal State Action: A
General Lesson For Debates on Public Emergencies and Legality" (2010) 16
Legal Theory 161 at pp. 169-170, citing H. Kelsen, *General Theory of Law and
State* (1945) at pp. 157-58

[80] J. Harrison, "The Relations Between the Courts and the Law" (2016) 35 *U.
Queensland L.J.* 99 at p. 109

ordinary Courts until they are formally nullified by the Constitutional Court which has sole jurisdiction to nullify laws.[81]

This is diametrically opposed to the common law's conception of invalid acts as void *ab initio*.[82] Accordingly, the Supreme Court of Canada has recognized an unconstitutional law as "invalid from the moment it is enacted."[83] Professor Hogg has put it this way: "A judicial decision that a law is unconstitutional is retrospective in the sense that it involves the nullification of the law from the outset."[84] Again according to the Supreme Court of Canada: an unconstitutional statutory restriction is "null and void;"[85] and "the effect of s. 52(1) is to render the law null and void"[86] In summary, the idea of an unconstitutional law being merely voidable is utterly foreign to the common law's conception of constitutional invalidation.

It has been noted that the constitutions of many countries have adopted the Austrian model by expressly allowing courts to establish a future date on which a determination of unconstitutionality shall become effective, "such as France (see

---

[81] G. Scaccia, "Constitutional Values and Judge-Made Law" (2017) 3 *Italian L.J.* 177 at p. 189

[82] Professor Leckey describes it as follows:

> On the understanding of nullity prevailing in the Commonwealth tradition, a law declared invalid should cease to have effect *immediately*. Moreover, the theory of nullity implies that legislative invalidity reaches back to the law's purported enactment or the entry into force of the superior norm rendering it invalid, such as a bill of rights. That is, the nullity is *retrospective*, running back to the incident undermining the purportedly invalid law.

R. Leckey, "The Harms of Remedial Discretion" (2016) 14 *Int. J. of Const. L.* 584 at p. 586

[83] *Nova Scotia (Workers' Compensation Board) v. Martin*, [2003] 2 S.C.R. 504 at para. 28

[84] P.W. Hogg, *Constitutional Law of Canada*, looseleaf (Toronto: Thomson Reuters, 2007) at para. 58.1

[85] *R. v. Smith*, [2015] 2 S.C.R. 602 at para. 30; "[T]he Charter deems it void." B. McLachlin, "Bill of Rights in Common Law Countries," (2002) 51 *Int. & Comp. Law Quarterly* 197 at p. 200

[86] *R. v. Ferguson*, [2008] 1 S.C.R. 96 at para. 35

article 62 of the French Constitution), Belgium (see article 8 of the *Loi special du 6 janvier 1989 sur la Cour d'arbitrage*), Hungary (see article 43.4 of the *Act XXXII of 1989 on the Constitutional Court*), Poland (see article 190.3 of the Polish Constitution), Albania (see article 132.2 of the Albanian Constitution), Estonia (see article 58.3 of the *Constitutional Review Court Procedure Act*, March 13, 2002), and South Africa (see article 172.1.b of the South African Constitution)."[87] Another author adds Greece, the Czech Republic, Croatia, Peru and Brazil to the list of countries with constitutions which allow courts to postpone the effects of their decisions so as to extend the operation of an invalidated statute.[88] Interestingly, Brazilian law requires that at least two-thirds of the members of the Federal Supreme Court agree to the exercise of this exceptional power.[89] Two other jurisdictions with provisions which effectively permit suspended declarations of invalidity are Scotland[90] and Northern Ireland.[91] Significantly however, this is not a power that exists under the common law, as was observed by Lord Hope in the 2000 *Brockhill Prison* case: "No such power [to remove or limit the retroactivity of decisions] is currently recognised by the common law."[92]

Certain European countries go even further in providing courts with flexibility in the nullification of unconstitutional laws. For example, Italy and Germany allow for the issuance of admonitory judgments where it is declared that the impugned law is not yet

---

[87] V.F. Comella, *Constitutional Courts & Democratic Values*, (New Haven and London: Yale Univ. Press, 2009) at pp. 176-177, note 23

[88] A.R. Brewer-Carias, *Constitutional Courts as Positive Legislators: A Comparataive Law Study*, (Cambridge: Cambridge Univ. Press, 2011), at p. 903

[89] H.D.B. de Pinho, "Judicial Rulings with Prospective Effect in Brazilian Law", in E. Steiner, ed., *Comparing the Prospective Effect of Judicial Rulings Across Jurisdictions*, (Switzerland: Springer, 2015) 285 at p. 297

[90] section 102 of *Scotland Act 1998*

[91] section 81 of *Northern Ireland Act 1998*

[92] *R. v. Governor of Brockhill Prison, ex p. Evans (No. 2)*, [2000] 4 All ER 15 at p. 28 (H.L.). However, the House of Lords, in *obiter,* said "never say never" to prospective overruling in *Re Spectrum Plus*, [2005] 2 AC 680 at para. 41.

unconstitutional, but that it will become so in the future.[93] This warning of impending nullification is intended to prompt the legislature to amend the law to bring it into compliance with constitutional requirements. This is very similar, in effect, to Canadian suspended declarations of invalidity, but it differs in that continental European countries generally subscribe to a voidable as opposed to void *ab initio* approach to constitutional invalidation. Thus, it is possible for their courts to allow an unconstitutional law to continue to operate without having to engage in the absurdity of purporting to "breathe life" into constitutionally comatose laws.

The fact that the constitutions of a number of other countries expressly authorize suspended declarations of invalidity, or similar remedies, provides no basis for courts' assertion of such powers in the Canadian context. To the contrary, they must deal with Canada's actual Constitution, not an imaginary, idealized or invented one. And Canada's actual Constitution not only makes no provision for such orders, it actually negatives them by expressly providing that laws inconsistent with the Constitution *are* to the extent of the inconsistency of no force or effect. Only by creating constitutional law out of thin air – law that contradicts the constitutional text – can it be contended that a court order can be given supremacy over the provisions of the Constitution.

6. A Judicial Hall Pass for Ongoing Rights Violations

In addition to the fundamental illegality of suspended declarations, they are also objectionable because they result in the denial of claims for remedies by persons whose constitutional rights and freedoms have been infringed or denied. Not only is this contrary to the Constitution, it is also contrary to Canada's international treaty obligations.

Subsection 24(1) of the *Charter* provides as follows:

---

[93] M. de Visser, *Constitutional Review in Europe: A Comparative Analysis*, (Oxford and Portland, Oregon: Hart Publishing, 2015) at pp. 310-324

> (1) Anyone whose rights or freedoms, as guaranteed by this Charter, have been infringed or denied may apply to a court of competent jurisdiction to obtain such remedy as the court considers appropriate and just in the circumstances.

This (together with s. 24(2) which provides for the exclusion of illegally obtained evidence) is the only section of the Constitution which deals with remedies for violations of the Constitution. As argued earlier, although s. 52(1) is commonly described as a remedial provision, it is actually a substantive interpretation provision which gives overriding effect to the Constitution to the extent that other laws conflict with it. Subsection 52(1) does not give jurisdiction to the courts to make any orders or grant any relief which they could not make or grant in its absence.

What is the remedy of a person who believes that a law is inconsistent with the Constitution? First, it must be recognized that s. 24(1) provides no remedy directly with respect to an unconstitutional enactment. Subsection 24(1) is engaged only where a person's rights or freedoms under the *Charter* have been infringed or denied. Enactment of a constitutionally invalid statute, by itself, is not a legally recognized wrong.[94] By itself, it causes no infringement or denial of anyone's rights or freedoms. However, a government official, in acting in accordance with the unconstitutional enactment, may infringe or deny a person's *Charter* right or freedom. It is the government official's action, rather than the enactment itself, which potentially supports a request for a remedy under s. 24(1). But if the enactment has not previously been adjudged unconstitutional, the general rule in Canada is that a damages remedy will not be available under s.

---

[94] Justice Scalia explained this point as follows:

> A court does not – in the nature of things *can* not – give a "remedy" for an unconstitutional statute, since an unconstitutional statute is not in itself a cognizable "wrong". (If it were, every citizen would have standing to challenge every law). In fact, what a court does with regard to an unconstitutional law is simply to *ignore* it.

Reynoldsville Casket Co. v. Hyde, 514 U.S. 749 (1995) at pp. 759-760

24(1).[95] The rationale is that if the government official acted on the good faith belief that the impugned law was valid, it would not be appropriate to impose liability for a remedy under s. 24(1). Thus, it is often said that s. 52(1) remedies generally cannot be combined with s. 24(1) remedies.[96] In other words, government officials who rely on invalid laws (which appear to be valid) have limited or qualified immunity and will not be held liable for resulting infringements or denials of *Charter* rights. It actually has nothing to do with s. 52(1) since, contrary to conventional thought and practice, there is no such thing as a remedy under that section. The important point is that, as a matter of policy, the courts have decided that it will usually not be appropriate and just to award remedies for breaches of *Charter* rights which occur as a result of a government actor relying upon apparently constitutional, though actually unconstitutional, enactments.

Another context in which the constitutional validity of a provision may arise is where a person is charged with an offence under such provision. The accused is entitled to argue that the charge must be dismissed since it is based on a provision which is inconsistent with the Constitution and, to the extent of such inconsistency, of no force or effect. No remedy need be sought under s. 24(1).[97] The prosecution simply collapses because it is not based on a valid and enforceable law. Although the accused sometimes also requests a formal declaration of invalidity, that is not necessary. Indeed, formal declaratory relief can generally be granted only by superior courts of inherent jurisdiction, but that is obviously no impediment to another court deciding the case in accordance with the law and dismissing the charge accordingly.[98] It is often said that such formal declarations of invalidity are made under s. 52(1), but this is wrong. The jurisdictional basis for such orders is either the superior court's inherent jurisdiction or general statutory provisions or rules allowing for actions or applications

---

[95] See, *Guimond v. Quebec,* [1996] 3 S.C.R. 347; *Mackin v. New Brunswick (Min. of Fin.),* [2002] 1 S.C.R. 405

[96] *Schachter v. Canada,* [1992] 2 S.C.R. 679

[97] *R. v. Big M Drug Mart Ltd.,* [1985] 1 S.C.R. 295 at para. 37

[98] *ibid.* at para. 47

for declaratory relief. The court's power to declare the existence or non-existence of a legal state of affairs, including in constitutional matters, does not depend on s. 52(1) and existed long before the enactment of that provision in 1982.

When a court identifies a constitutionally invalid enactment but decides that the impugned provision should be granted temporary validity while the government decides what to do about it, a so-called suspended declaration of invalidity is made. If the government elects to do nothing, the declaration of invalidity will take effect at the end of the suspension period with both prospective and retroactive effect. In that scenario, it would make sense that rights violations which occur during the suspension period should be the subject of a s. 24(1) remedy, although the point seems never to have been determined. The more difficult question is with respect to rights violations which occur during the suspension period where the legislature *does* enact replacement legislation before the suspension expires. There seems to be a disturbing trend in such situations towards deference on the part of courts to legislative formulation of remedies. Professor Leckey explains it as follows:

> The notion that delay is necessary to avoid legal discontinuities has given way to the view that the legislature is often better suited than the court to formulate remedies. The primary purpose of a suspended decalaration of invalidity is now "to facilitate the legislature's function in crafting a remedy".[99]

Elsewhere, Leckey has expressed the view that suspended declarations of invalidity involve "in essence, delegating remedial action to the other branches of government ...".[100] Thus it appears that the courts are simply leaving it to the legislatures to decide

[99] R. Leckey, *Bills of Rights in the Common Law*, (Cambridge: Cambridge Univ. Press, 2015 at p. 139, quoting D.F. Guttman, "*Hislop v. Canada* – A Retroactive Look" (2008) 42 *S.C.L.R. (2d)* 547 at p. 551
[100] R. Leckey, "The Harms of Remedial Discretion" (2016) 14 *Int. J. of Const. Law* 584 at p. 591

whether any relief should be given for rights violations which occurred prior to enactment of the new legislation. As Professor Roach has observed, "Even at the remedial stage, however, the Court has bent over backward to let the legislature have its say."[101] In theory, the legislature's remedial response is itself subject to further judicial *Charter* scrutiny,[102] but given the strong tendency of courts to defer to legislatures in this area, the reality seems to be one of passive acceptance by courts of legislative judgments.

This punting by the courts of the question of remedy to the legislators has been described as legislative remand.[103] It is a suspect practice in terms of constitutional theory and the rule of law. It involves an abdication by the courts of their mandate to grant appropriate and just remedies to victims of rights violations. Although it is packaged in sunny-sounding terms as part of a process of constitutional dialogue between the judicial and legislative branches, the reality is that it is an abandonment of judicial responsibility.

The very governmental body which enacted the unconstitutional legislation is entrusted with the task of deciding what remedy, *if any*, should be afforded to persons who suffered rights violations as a result of that unconstitutional legislation. This has prompted questions as to whether litigants' "rights are being protected by an independent judiciary or sacrificed by a cooperative partner of government in an ongoing process of metaphysical confabulation."[104]

Not surprisingly, the new legislation crafted by the legislators almost invariably provides no relief to victims of historical rights

---

[101] K. Roach, *The Supreme Court on Trial: Judicial Activism or Democratic Dialogue*, (Toronto: Irwin Law, rev'd ed., 2016) at p. 226

[102] *Canada (Attorney General) v. Hislop*, [2007] 1 S.C.R. 429 at para. 39

[103] A. Sathanapally, *Beyond Disagreement: Open Remedies in Human Rights Adjudication*, (Oxford: Oxford Univ. Press, 2012), at p. 3

[104] R. Haigh and M. Sobkin, "Does the Observer Have an Effect? An Analysis of the Use of the Dialogue Metaphor in Canada's Courts" (2007) 45 *Osgoode Hall L.J.* 67 at p. 71

violations.[105] Entrusting the job of determining governmental liability for constitutional remedies to the very governmental body that caused the underlying rights violations is akin to putting Colonel Saunders in charge of guarding one's chicken coop. In a different context, the idea that governments should be allowed to set the rules for their own liability for *Charter* breaches was rejected as follows by the Ontario Court of Appeal:

> The purpose of the *Charter*, in so far as it controls excesses by governments, is not at all served by permitting those same governments to decide when they would like to be free of those controls and put their houses in order without further threat of complaint.[106]

This calls to mind the principle: *Nemo judex in sua causa*: No one should be a judge in their own cause. This is itself an important part of the principle of the rule of law.

Even assuming that it is appropriate for courts to adopt the position that there should be no remedies under s. 24(1) for rights violations which occur before the constitutional infirmity of the impugned enactment has been identified, once the courts have determined that the enactment is unconstitutional, it is difficult to justify giving the government what amounts to a judicial hall pass allowing it with impunity to continue violating citizens' rights

---

[105] It has been noted that only rarely have legislators responded to legislative remands with legislation that provides any kind of retroactive remedies. See K. Roach, "Remedies for Laws that Violate Human Rights" in J. Bell, M. Elliott, J.N.E. Varuhas and P. Murray, ed's., *Public Law Adjudication in Common Law Systems: Process and Substance*, (Oxford and Portland, Oregon: Hart Publishing, 2016) 269-299 at pp. 272, 295. Choudhry and Roach have explained that this may largely be due to the fact that legislatures are accustomed to making laws prospectively and may reflexively look at the issues from that perspective and not consider whether retroactive remedies are appropriate. See S. Choudhry and K. Roach, "Putting the Past Behind Us? Prospective Judicial and Legislative Constitutional Remedies," (2003) 21 *S.C.L.R. (2d)* 205 at p. 242

[106] *Prete v. Ontario (Attorney General)* (1993), 110 DLR (4th) 94 at p. 101 (Ont. C.A.)

throughout a suspension period.[107] Unless one buys into the dubious notion that no rights violations occur during the suspension period because the court has given validity to what the Constitution says is invalid, we are left with a situation of rights violations which are purportedly shielded from the remedial reach of s. 24(1) by reason of a court's so-called suspended declaration of invalidity. This means that all courts of competent jurisdiction are effectively stripped of their power and responsibility under s. 24(1) to grant such remedies as *they* consider appropriate and just in respect of rights violations brought before them. It amounts to one court purporting to enjoin other courts from performing their constitutional obligations. Not only is this profoundly disrespectful of the independence of the courts enjoined, it is also itself inconsistent with the provisions of the Constitution which empower and require courts to grant appropriate and just remedies under s.24(1). As Professor Roach has said: "The remedial discretion of independent judges is an important part of Canada's constitutional structure."[108]

Accordingly, any attempt by a higher court to tie the remedial hands of lower courts for rights violations occurring prior to or during the suspension period should itself be deemed of no force or effect under the Constitution's supremacy clause, s. 52(1). It deserves to be ignored. Moreover, and for the same reasons, any attempt by government authorities to enforce unconstitutional laws by way of prosecution during a suspension period deserves to be ignored. This, of course, would require courage and independence on the part of our judges. It would require them to

---

[107] Sometimes courts will relieve against the apparent injustice of subjecting people to unconstitutional laws by granting so-called constitutional exemptions which effectively suspends the suspension of invalidity vis-à-vis specific individual applicants. See, for example, *Wakeling v. U.S.A.*, [2014] 3 S.C.R. 549 at para. 149. The idea of citizens being required to come cap in hand asking the court to exempt them from enforcement of unconstitutional laws seems rather Kafkaesque.

[108] K. Roach, "Enforcement of the Charter – Subsections 24(1) and 52(1)" (2013) 62 *S.C.L.R. (2d)* 473 at p. 477

act as faithful servants of the Constitution. It would require judicial backbone.

The time-honoured maxim – where there's a right, there must be a remedy – is deeply ingrained in Western legal thought and culture. It finds expression in the writing of Blackstone,[109] in the seminal U.S. case on judicial review, *Marbury v. Madison,*[110] and in numerous decisions of the Supreme Court of Canada.[111] Writing extra-judicially in 1991, then Justice McLachlin eloquently made the point that rights must be accompanied by effective remedies, lest they become meaningless things written only on paper:

> Without effective remedies, the law becomes an empty symbol; full of sound and fury but signifying nothing. One need only look to the elaborate guarantees of rights found in the constitutions of many non-democratic countries for evidence of the importance of effective remedies. The paper reads magnificently, but the reality is otherwise.[112]

While there is no absolute rule,[113] and there will be situations where countervailing considerations of the public interest can

---

[109] "[I]t is a settled and invariable principle in the laws of England, that every right when withheld must have a remedy, and every injury its proper redress." W. Blackstone, *Commentaries*, 14th ed. (London: A. Strahan, 1803), Book 3, ch. 7 at 109

[110] "The Government of the United States has been emphatically termed a government of laws, and not of men. It will certainly cease to deserve this high appellation if the laws furnish no remedy for the violation of a vested legal right." *Marbury v. Madison*, 5 U.S. 137 (1803) at p. 163

[111] "[A] right, no matter how expansive in theory, is only as meaningful as the remedy provided for its breach." *R. v. 974649 Ontario Inc.*, [2001] 3 S.C.R. 575 at para. 20; "To deny a remedy in tort is, quite literally, to deny justice." *Hill v. Hamilton-Wentworth Regional Police Serves Board*, [2007] 3 S.C.R. 129 at para. 35; and see *infra* footnotes 121-124 and accompanying text.

[112] B.M. McLachlin, "The Charter: A New Role for the Judiciary" (1991) 29 *Alta. L. Rev.* 540 at p. 548

[113] In *Kazemi v. Islamic Republic of Iran*, [2014] 3 S.C.R. 176 at para's 164-165, the Court held that the maxim "where there is a right there must be a

justify the denial of a remedy,[114] there should be a strong operative presumption in favour of the provision of remedies. A heavy onus should be placed upon those who would seek to deny relief to victims of rights violations. At a minimum, it should be subject to scrutiny according to the principles for the application of s.1 of the *Charter* as enunciated in *R. v. Oakes*.[115] The Canadian judicial practice of deferentially remanding questions of remedy to the government – the rights violator – pushes in precisely the opposite direction and is fundamentally wrong.

In still another respect there is something conceptually odd about courts remanding questions of remedy to the government. The Supreme Court held in *Ford v. Quebec (Attorney General)*[116] that it is not possible for the government to invoke the s. 33 override of the *Charter* retroactively.[117] Most *Charter* rights can be suspended for up to five years at a time, but s. 33 cannot be used to wash away rights violations which have already occurred. Yet, the courts, in remanding questions of remedy for historical rights violations to the legislatures through issuance of suspended declarations of invalidity, are effectively authorizing the very sort of retroactive white-washing which the Court declared to be impermissible in *Ford*. It is irrational that courts, through suspended declarations of invalidity, can effectively authorize the

---

remedy" was not sufficiently manageable or concrete to constitute a principle of fundamental justice under s.7 of the *Charter*.

[114] "As a fundamental right, however, the right to a remedy can still be denied if that denial is necessary to a compelling state interest." T.A. Thomas, "Ubi Jus, Ibi Remedium: The Fundamental Right to a Remedy Under Due Process" (2004) 41 *San Diego L. Rev.* 1633 at p. 1643. *Canada (Prime Minister) v. Khadr,* [2010] 1 S.C.R. 44, is an example of a case where for reasons of overriding state interest, the Court decided that no remedy (other than a largely symbolic declaration) was warranted in respect of various admitted rights violations by the Government of Canada. However, Khadr was ultimately successful in negotiating a significant financial settlement with the Government.

[115] [1986] 1 S.C.R. 103

[116] [1988] 2 S.C.R. 712 at para. 36

[117] For the text of s. 33, see *infra*, p. 207, footnote 156.

retroactive override of *Charter* rights, whereas legislatures cannot themselves do so.

There is a logical conundrum in courts, especially statutory courts like the Supreme Court of Canada, purporting to exercise powers which the legislatures could not themselves exercise. As Peter Hogg has explained, if Parliament cannot effectively enact a law that is inconsistent with the Charter (at least not without invoking the s. 33 override), it also cannot authorize another body (including a judicial body) to put such a law in place:

> Action taken under statutory authority is valid only if it is within the scope of that authority. Since neither Parliament nor a Legislature can itself pass a law in breach of the Charter, neither body can authorize action which would be in breach of the Charter. Thus, the limitations on statutory authority which are imposed by the Charter will flow down the chain of statutory authority and apply to regulations, by-laws, orders, decisions and all other action (whether legislative, administrative *or judicial*) which depends for its validity on statutory authority.[118] (emphasis added)

Where is the statutory authority for judges of the Supreme Court of Canada, whose powers derive solely from statute, to put in place, even temporarily, laws which are inconsistent with the Constitution? Of course, no such authority exists. Furthermore, as Professor Hogg explains, it would be constitutionally impossible for Parliament to give the Court such authority. From whence then did these powers arise? The answer is both obvious and unsettling. The Supreme Court of Canada decided that it would be a good thing if it had such powers and so it decided to create them. It acted without any support in the common law, and without any textual support in the Constitution. In fact, it acted in the face of language to the contrary in s. 52(1).

---

[118] P.W. Hogg, *Constitutional Law of Canada*, looseleaf (Toronto: Thomson Reuters, 2007) at para. 37.2(c)

Suspended declarations of invalidity are also inconsistent with Canada's international treaty obligations to the extent that such orders allow *legislatures* to establish what remedy, if any, persons should receive in respect of rights violations. Consider, for example, Article 8 of *The Universal Declaration of Human Rights (1948)* which states:

> Everyone has the right to an effective remedy by the competent national *tribunals* for acts violating the fundamental rights granted him by the constitution or by law. (emphasis added)

Similarly, Article 18 of the *American Declaration of the Rights and Duties of Man* of 1948, to which Canada, as a member of the Organization of American States, is subject as a matter of international law, provides as follows:

> Every person may resort to the *courts* to ensure respect for his legal rights. There should likewise be available to him a simple, brief procedure whereby the *courts* will protect him from acts of authority that, to his prejudice, violate any fundamental constitutional rights. (emphasis added)

The Supreme Court of Canada has recognized in a number of cases that Canada's international human rights obligations can properly guide the interpretation and application of the *Charter*. It has been declared that the *Charter* is presumed to grant protection at least equal to that provided by international treaties ratified by Canada.[119]

We have, however, a situation where Canadian courts, in issuing suspended declarations of invalidity: (1) authorize during the

---

[119] *Henry v. British Columbia (Attorney General)*, [2015] 2 S.C.R. 214 at para. 136; *Loyola High School v. Quebec (Attorney General)*, [2015] 1 S.C.R. 613 at para. 97; *Saskatchewan Federation of Labour v. Saskatchewan*, [2015] 1 S.C.R. 245 at para. 64; 157; *Divito v. Canada*, [2013] 3 SCR 157 at para. 23. See also, M.-F. Major, "Reporting to the Human Rights Committee: The Canadian Experience" (2000) 38 *Can. Y.B. Int'l Law* 261

suspension period state conduct that is clearly unconstitutional (or at least would clearly be unconstitutional but for the judicial hall pass given to the government); and, (2) delegate to the rights violator the task of enacting legislation which will determine whether victims of rights abuses can obtain a remedy for previous violations. It is simply impossible to reconcile this result with Canada's international human rights obligations.[120]

It is also irreconcilable with numerous pronouncements of the Supreme Court with respect to the importance of remedies for constitutional violations:

> To create a right without a remedy is antithetical to one of the purposes of the *Charter* which surely is to allow courts to fashion remedies when constitutional infringements occur.[121]
>
> ...
>
> Section 24(1) establishes the right to a remedy as the foundation stone for the effective enforcement of *Charter* rights ... I am of the view that a person whose Canadian *Charter* rights have been infringed or denied has the right to obtain the appropriate and just remedy under the circumstances. A corollary which flows from this is the fundamental principle that there must always be a court available to grant, not only a remedy, but the

---

[120] Canada's behaviour on the human rights front does not always match its exceedingly positive self-image. Louise Arbour, former Supreme Court of Canada justice and U.N. High Commissioner for Human Rights, has commented as follows on the Canadian penchant for self-admiration in this area:

> There is little room for progress while indulging in self-righteousness and self-congratulation, an endearing tendency Canadians seem to have when nurturing their national self-image as humanitarian, pro-human rights, and internationalist.

L. Arbour and F. Lafontaine, "Beyond Self-Congratulations: The Charter at 25 in an International Perspective" (2007) 45 *Osgoode Hall L. J.* 239 at p. 240.
[121] *Nelles v. Ontario*, [1989] 2 S.C.R. 170 at p. 196

remedy which is the *appropriate* and *just* one under the circumstances.[122]

...

A purposive approach to remedies in a *Charter* context gives modern vitality to the ancient maxim *ubi jus, ibi remedium*: where there is a right, there must be a remedy. More specifically, a purposive approach to remedies requires at least two things. First, the purpose of the right being protected must be promoted: courts must craft *responsive* remedies. Second, the purpose of the remedies provision must be promoted: courts must craft *effective* remedies.[123] (emphasis in original)

...

A court which has found a violation of a *Charter* right has a duty to provide an effective remedy.[124]

What courts say and what they do, however, are sometimes quite different things.

7. Lost at Sea

Sivia v. British Columbia (Superintendent of Motor Vehicles)[125] is a case which illustrates just how far off course the Canadian judicial fleet has been allowed to drift. The issue was whether a person who had successfully challenged the constitutionality of a law should be made to suffer penalties under that very unconstitutional law. Most thoughtful people would readily agree that this should not happen. The courts of Canada would not agree with them.

---

[122] *R. v. Mills*, [1986] 1 S.C.R. 863 at paras. 27, 30
[123] *Doucet-Boudreau v. Nova Scotia (Minister of Education)*, [2003] 3 S.C.R. 3 at para. 25
[124] *R. v. Ferguson*, [2008] 1 S.C.R. 96 at para. 34
[125] 2012 BCSC 1030 (CanLII)

In an earlier decision,[126] it had been determined that provisions of British Columbia's *Motor Vehicle Act*, which allowed for the immediate suspension of licences and seizures of vehicles of persons who registered excessive blood-alcohol readings at roadside testings, were unconstitutional in that they involved unreasonable seizures of breath samples contrary to s. 8 of the *Charter*.[127] The court suspended its declaration of invalidity for six months and deferred to a later proceeding the question of what remedies, if any, should be available to the parties who had successfully challenged the subject legislation.[128]

In the 2012 *Sivia* remedies proceeding, the court saw the threshold issue to be whether its earlier declaration of invalidity had been both prospective and retroactive. Following the Supreme Court's majority decision in *Canada (Attorney General) v. Hislop*,[129] the court posited that if its declaration was prospective only, then no remedy would be called for because the impugned provisions would have been valid at the time they were applied to the petitioners. Therefore, no rights violations would have occurred.[130]

In the result, the court concluded that its earlier declaration of invalidity had been prospective only. Thus, no rights were violated. This meant not only that the petitioners could obtain no

---

[126] *Sivia v. British Columbia (Superintendent of Motor Vehicles)*, 2011 BCSC 1639 (CanLII)

[127] Section 8 of the *Charter* provides as follows: "Everyone has the right to be secure against unreasonable search or seizure."

[128] *Sivia v. British Columbia (Superintendent of Motor Vehicles)*, 2011 BCSC 1783 (CanLII)

[129] [2007] 1 S.C.R. 429. See critique of *Hislop* in Part 1 of this essay, "Some Misconceptions About Constitutional Invalidation" at pp. 49-54.

[130] This involved confusion and conflation of the issues of rights and remedies. The court's declaration of invalidity did not render the impugned law invalid, but rather identified its inconsistency with the Constitution, at which point the automatic operation of s. 52(1) deemed it to be of no force or effect. There is nothing remedial about the constitutional invalidation of laws. Only after the substantive law has been determined – after it has been decided if rights were violated – does the question of remedy arise.

relief for what had happened prior to the legislation being adjudged unconstitutional, but they could actually be subjected to further penalties under the impugned legislation even after its unconstitutionality had been established.[131] Accordingly, the petitioners whose licence suspensions had not yet been fully served, or whose fines had not yet been paid, were still subject to enforcement of this unconstitutional law:

> ... the result of my conclusion that the declaration of invalidity does not have retroactive effect is that the law was not invalid when the petitioners were subject to it.
>
> ...
>
> Finally, I have found that as a result of the prospective only application of the declaration of invalidity, any petitioner with any outstanding fees, penalties or suspensions is still subject to paying/serving such fees, penalties and/or suspensions.[132]

What we have, therefore, is a law enacted in 2010, which, upon enactment, was inconsistent with the *Charter* and, as such, of no force or effect according to s. 52(1). Yet, it was held in 2012 that people were required to pay still outstanding fines and to serve still outstanding licence suspensions imposed under a law which the Constitution deemed to be of no force or effect from the moment of its enactment. This decision was subsequently affirmed by the British Columbia Court of Appeal,[133] and the

---

[131] The unconstitutionality of the impugned provisions was affirmed by the British Columbia Court of Appeal (*Sivia v. British Columbia (Superindendent of Motor Vehicles)*, (2014), 55 BCLR (5th) 1), and further affirmed by the Supreme Court of Canada (*Goodwin v. British Columbia (Superintendent of Motor Vehicles)*, [2015] 3 S.C.R. 250).

[132] *Sivia v. British Columbia (Superintendent of Motor Vehicles)*, 2012 BCSC 1030 (CanLII) at para's 112, 119

[133] *sub nom., Jaswal v. British Columbia (Superintendent of Motor Vehicles)*, 2016 BCCA 245 (CanLII)

Supreme Court of Canada denied leave to appeal from the Court of Appeal decision.[134]

It is important to differentiate this case from cases such as *R. v. Sarson*[135] where the doctrine of *res judicata* came into play. In *Sarson*, a person who had been convicted and sentenced under a law which was subsequently adjudged unconstitutional in another case was held unable to challenge his conviction and continued imprisonment based on that conviction. Sarson's case had been finally and conclusively decided by the time the relevant law was adjudged invalid. Thus, the *res judicata* doctrine precluded opening up his case for reconsideration. In *Sivia*, on the other hand, the parties against whom the unconstitutional law was being enforced had not been the subject of any final adjudication. It was within the very case in which the impugned law was determined to be unconstitutional that the court imposed upon the parties penalties provided for under that unconstitutional law. The term "Orwellian" comes to mind.

Another illustration of how lost Canadian courts have become with respect to the temporal effects of determinations of unconstitutionality is found in *R. v. Lorincz*.[136]

In an earlier case, *R. v. Cobham*,[137] the Supreme Court of Canada had decided that the accused's *Charter* rights had been denied as a result of the police not informing him of the availability of free duty counsel advice prior to making a breathalyzer demand. He was originally convicted at trial of refusing to provide a breath sample. It was determined on summary conviction appeal that Cobham's rights under s. 10(b) of the *Charter* "to retain and instruct counsel without delay and to be informed of that right" had been denied. Thus, the summary conviction appeal court, acting under s. 24(2) of the *Charter*, excluded the evidence of his refusal to provide a breath sample and, therefore, an acquittal was

---

[134] December 1, 2016, SCC Case Information 37128
[135] *R. v. Sarson*, [1996] 2 S.C.R. 223
[136] 1995 ABCA 35 (CanLII)
[137] [1994] 3 S.C.R. 360

entered.[138] On further appeal, the Alberta Court of Appeal concluded that Cobham's *Charter* rights *had not* been denied, and restored his conviction. On final appeal to the Supreme Court of Canada, it was decided that Cobham's *Charter* rights *had* been denied and that the appropriate remedy was exclusion under s. 24(2) of the evidence of refusal. Accordingly, the appeal was allowed and an acquittal was entered in place of the conviction.

Out of concern for the possible disruptive effects of this decision on other cases, the government returned to the Supreme Court a few days later and requested that it stay its judgment in *Cobham* in order to provide a transition period. On October 20, 1994, the Supreme Court issued a further order "that the operation of the judgment herein is stayed for a period of 21 days from the date such judgment was issued, namely September 29, 1994."[139] It is not clear what the Supreme Court intended to accomplish by this 21-day stay order, as it provided no further reasons or explanation. Presumably, it intended at a minimum that during this stay period, failure by the police to provide the required information as to the availability of free duty counsel advice would not result in the exclusion of evidence. Perhaps it intended something more – that any failures to provide such advice, even prior to the Court's judgment in *Cobham,* should not result in the exclusion of evidence. How the Court would have the power to make either type of order is a mystery. The *Charter* means what the *Charter* means, and if Mr. Cobham's *Charter* rights were denied, then so too would be denied the *Charter* rights of all similarly-situated persons. The Court could not, by purporting to

---

[138] Subsection 24(2) reads as follows:

> (2) Where, in proceedings under subsection (1), a court concludes that evidence was obtained in a manner that infringed or denied any rights or freedoms guaranteed by this Charter, the evidence shall be excluded if it is established that, having regard to all the circumstances, the admission of it in the proceedings would bring the administration of justice into disrepute.

[139] Supreme Court of Canada Case Information – Docket # 23585. A similar case where the Court ordered a 30-day transition period is *R. v. Brydges,* [1990] 1 S.C.R. 190.

stay its judgment in *Cobham*, change the law as it had been explained in its reasons for judgment in that case. This simple point, which seems to be a matter of inescapable logical deduction, has been recognized by other courts.[140] It was simply and elegantly expressed by P.Y. Lo of the University of Hong Kong:

> Like an arrow shot from a bow, once a provision has been declared unconstitutional, the declaration has operated and arguably cannot be put back.[141]

This then takes us to the Alberta Court of Appeal's subsequent decision in the *Lorincz* case. In upholding the accused's conviction, the Court held that his rights under the *Charter* had not been infringed because, in its view, the Supreme Court's decision in *Cobham* did not apply retrospectively:

> The Crown concedes that the advice given here falls short of the requirements to inform an accused of how to access free and immediate legal advice as set out in *R. v. Cobham*. The Supreme Court of Canada, on application by the Attorney General of Alberta, granted an order staying the operation of *Cobham* for 21 days from the 29th of September, 1994. The facts giving rise to this prosecution occurred quite some time before September, 1994, that is in February, 1993. By reason of the stay of the *Cobham* and related decisions, the

---

[140] The New Zealand Court of Appeal recognized this in *A.G. on behalf of Ministry of Health v. Spencer*, [2015] NZCA 143 at para. 36: "… a declaration is merely a formal order encapsulating the consequences of the legal reasoning set out in the preceding reasons for decision. The existence of the remedy makes no difference to the law as found in the judgment. While the formal order may be notionally suspended, its substance – the reasoning process and its results – remains unchanged." See further discussion of this case in Part 2 of this essay, "Fidelity to the Law: The Good, the Bad, and the Ugly" at pp. 78-80. See also, the Hong Kong Court of Appeal's decision in *A. v. Director of Immigration*, [2008] HKCA 330 at para. 8, as discussed further in Part 2 of this essay, *ibid.* at p. 83.

[141] P.Y. Lo, "Levitating Unconstitutional Law" (2006) 36 *Hong Kong L.J.* 433 at p. 438

> advice given to this appellant was not deficient. The
> law in *Cobham* does not apply retrospectively.
> Accordingly the appeal is dismissed.[142]

On the face of the matter, to say that the law in *Cobham* did not
apply retrospectively is demonstrably incorrect. The Supreme
Court allowed Mr. Cobham's appeal and ordered that he be
acquitted based on conduct of the police that had occurred in the
past. Clearly, the Supreme Court did apply its decision in
Cobham retrospectively. Even if the Supreme Court had intended
that its judgment in *Cobham* would operate prospectively only
(except, of course, for Mr. Cobham),[143] what would be the source
of the power of the Supreme Court to make such an order? The
Charter means what it means, and once the Supreme Court had
decided in *Cobham* that people have the right to be told about the
availability of free duty counsel advice, there was no undoing that.
The arrow had been shot from the bow. Subsection 52(1) declares
that the Constitution is the supreme law of Canada, and no other
law – including an order of the Supreme Court of Canada
purporting to deem the law to be different than it actually is – can
override the Constitution. Referring again to what Justice Black
of the U.S. Supreme Court wrote many years ago, a court cannot

---

[142] *R. v. Lorincz*, 1995 ABCA 35 (CanLII) at para. 5

[143] See Part 2 of this essay, "Fidelity to the Law: The Good, the Bad, and the
Ugly" at pp. 137-139, for a critique of the practice of selectively giving only
certain parties the benefit of a constitutional right, including Justice John
Harlan's blistering attack in *Mackey v. U.S.*, 401 U.S. 667 (1970) at p.679:

> Simply fishing one case from the stream of appellate review,
> using it as a vehicle for pronouncing new constitutional
> standards, and then permitting a stream of similar cases
> subsequently to flow by unaffected by that new rule
> constitute an indefensible departure from this model of
> judicial review.
>
> If we do not resolve all cases before us on judicial review in
> light of our best understanding of governing constitutional
> principles, it is difficult to see why we should so adjudicate
> in any case at all.

establish a timetable for when the Constitution shall be permitted
to operate:

> Once the Court determines what the Constitution says,
> I do not believe it has the power, by weighing
> "countervailing interests" to legislate a timetable by
> which the Constitution's provisions shall become
> effective.[144]

The law as recognized by the Court in its reasons in *Cobham* was
the law as dictated by the Constitution. No judicial power existed
that could retroactively change that law by deeming the
Constitution not to be operable for some period of time.

However, this does not mean that the courts were as a result of the
Supreme Court's decision in *Cobham* required to acquit every
person who had not been notified of free duty counsel availability.
As explained earlier, there is a significant difference between the
existence or non-existence of substantive rights, and the question
of what remedy, if any, should be given for a violation of a right
so found. The fact that people in the position of the accused in
Lorincz suffered rights violations did not necessarily entitle them
to any particular remedy, or to any remedy at all. Under s. 24(2)
of the *Charter*, evidence does not have to be excluded unless the
court concludes that "having regard to all the circumstances, the
admission of it would bring the administration of justice into
disrepute." Given that the law as found in *Cobham* might have
represented a shift from prior understanding of what the *Charter*
required, it would have been open to trial courts in other cases,
such as *Lorincz,* to refuse to exclude evidence obtained following
a denial of this *Charter* protection. However, it was wrong to
conflate rights and remedies so as to conclude that no rights were
violated, or, as stated by the Court of Appeal in *Lorincz*, to
conclude that "the advice given to this appellant was not
deficient."

---

[144] *Stovall v. Denno,* 388 U.S. 293 (1967) at p. 304

An appropriate, principled-based analysis of the issues is important because conflation of rights and remedies can lead to courts coming to believe, as Canadian courts apparently do, that they have a discretion to deem the law to be different than it actually is, even to the point of deeming ordinary law to be superior to the Constitution. This is what we see when courts assume the power to breathe life into unconstitutional laws.

To be fair, responsibility for the unsoundness of decisions, such as in the *Sivia* and *Lorincz* cases, cannot properly be placed at the feet of the lower court judges. They must sing from the garbled hymn book composed and handed to them by the Supreme Court of Canada. For the same reason, the Supreme Court must take responsibility for the preposterous notion that a suspended declaration of invalidity "breathes life" into unconstitutional *Criminal Code* provisions so as to allow people to be convicted under them.[145] Where in the Constitution, where in the common law, where in any recognized legal principle, are courts given the power to breathe life into unconstitutional criminal law provisions?

Whither the rule of law?

8. Putting an End to Suspended Declarations

What would the situation be if courts stopped issuing suspended declarations of invalidity? The most significant consequence would be that the rule of law would be upheld, and a message sent that pragmatic reasons, however good they may be, cannot justify overriding the Constitution. The integrity of the rule of law is degraded when unconstitutional actions are given a veneer of legality. As Hugo Cyr has put it [translation]: "It is not appropriate to confer on actions that contravene the Constitution the

---

[145] *R. v. Moazami*, 2014 BCSC 261 (CanLII). See Part 2 of this essay, "Fidelity to the Law: The Good, the Bad, and the Ugly" at p. 144.

legitimacy that comes with a declaration of conformity with the law.[146]

A message would also be sent to legislators that greater care should be taken to ensure that only constitutionally-compliant legislation is enacted, since the courts will not be able to issue a judicial hall pass allowing the unconstitutional law to continue to operate while a constitutional replacement law is being prepared. A downside of suspended declarations is that they encourage a lack of care by legislators at the stage of original enactment. This point was made by an English court in response to a proposal that the disruptive effects of a finding of illegality could be alleviated by applying the doctrine of prospective overruling:

> To do otherwise [than to give retroactive effect to the court's decision] will in effect legalize the illegal and the courts are not in business to do that. Moreover, once the courts start to give some effect to illegal legislation, there will be less incentive for the legislator to refrain from such illegality.[147]

Professor Leckey similarly warns that:

> Judicial willingness to delay declarations – and one may add to rule prospectively – may lessen the consequences for lawmakers of enacting laws that violate the bill of rights. That, in turn, reduces the incentives for complying with rights when making law.[148]

---

[146] H. Cyr, "Quelques reflexions sur la normalisation de l'exceptionel" Paper delivered at Conference of University of Montreal Faculty of Law on October, 15, 2015 at pp. 26-27

[147] *Percy v. Hall*, [1997] QB 924 at p. 951 (C.A.)

[148] R. Leckey, "Realizing Rights Here and Now" (available online, forthcoming in the *Australian J. of Human Rights*) at p. 17; See also, B. Ryder, "Suspending the Charter" (2003) 21 *S.C.L.R. (2d)* 267 at p. 288:

> Lawmakers might be getting the message that they take no significant risks if they pass laws without serious regard for Charter rights and freedoms. Even if legislation is found to violate the Charter, the courts

Another consequence of ending the use of suspended declarations might be to shift the focus away from rights denial, to issues of remedy where it more properly belongs. A major problem with suspended declarations is that they involve a court deeming an unconstitutional law to be valid with the resulting appearance that no constitutional rights are infringed or denied during the suspension period. Of course, this appearance is a fiction, a mirage. There is an important distinction between a situation where rights are not violated, and a situation where the state is temporarily given a licence to violate rights with impunity. A court that actually buys into the fiction that rights violations are not occurring because the law's invalidity has been suspended, may be more sanguine about the situation than would be the case if it were forced to acknowledge that it is being asked to excuse the state from knowingly and deliberately engaging in violations of constitutional rights.

As protectors of the constitutional rights of persons, courts should be vigilant in demanding that the state minimize rights violations during suspension periods and that the state only be excused from liability where it can provide compelling justification for that result. Thus, unlike under the suspended declaration regime where the court participates in a charade that rights violations either are not occurring or are not legally wrong, a more candid regime would openly acknowledge the reality of rights violations and put the onus on the rights violator to explain why the victim deserves no remedy.[149]

---

appear increasingly likely to issue a suspended declaration of invalidity, or find some other means of avoiding an immediate declaration of invalidity, especially if the political or policy stakes are high. The consequences of drafting laws that may violate the Charter, from a government's point of view, may be nothing worse than litigation and a second chance at drafting Charter-compliant legislation a few years down the road. In this way, a remedy initially designed to serve the rule of law now risks promoting its violation.

[149] See, H. Lau, "Comparative Perspectives on Strategic Remedial Delays" (2016) 91 *Tulane L. Rev.* 259, where the author draws a distinction between delaying the recognition of rights and delaying the provision of remedies, and

Ending current practices regarding suspended declarations would also force the courts to be more candid and forthright. The euphemistic term "suspended declaration" would disappear from the lexicon. It is dangerous to speak in terms of suspension or delay of a declaration of invalidity because this creates the impression that during the period of suspension or delay, no violations of constitutional rights will occur. This, of course, is an incorrect impression. In truth, the court's suspension of its declaration does not change the law, just as issuance of the declaration does not do so. The reality is that the constitutional violations do continue to occur during the period of suspension – but the court, presumably for what it considers valid and justifiable reasons, chooses to turn a blind eye to these violations. It effectively announces, when it suspends its declaration of invalidity, that it will grant no remedies for violations during the suspension period. It further purports to enjoin other courts from granting such remedies.

This is not just linguistic nicety. Judicial candor matters. It is important that judges understand – and the public understands – that the Constitution is being violated and that the courts, perhaps for good reasons, have decided not to do anything about it. Courts should be straight about it. If they do not think it is appropriate to grant a remedy for a rights violation, they should say so directly. They should not pretend that the law is different than it actually is and, thus, that no rights have been violated. The reality of the situation should not be clouded by metaphysical discussions of the Blackstonian paradigm.[150]

In other jurisdictions with constitutions similar to Canada's, the problems associated with the effects of findings of unconstitutionality have been managed without resort to the suspended declaration contrivance. For example, in the United

---

argues that it is generally better to delay remedy. To similar effect, see J.M. Greabe, "Remedial Discretion in Constitutional Adjudication" (2014) 62 *Buff. L. Rev.* 881 at p. 886

[150] See, *Canada (Attorney General) v. Hislop*, [2007] 1 S.C.R. 429 at para's 86-93

States, with its much larger population and 250 years of constitutional experience, there are only a handful of cases in which courts have granted relief similar to the Canadian-style suspended declaration of invalidity.[151] In large part, this is due to the U.S. courts' more conservative and less intrusive "as applied" approach to constitutional adjudication:

> The American approach to constitutional remedies is markedly different from recent Canadian developments. When faced with constitutional violations, American courts have preferred an "invalid as applied" remedy as opposed to "facial invalidity".[152]

Thus, as a general rule in the U.S., laws are not invalidated in their entirety unless they are incapable of any constitutional applications.[153] They simply are not applied in situations where application would violate constitutional rights; but otherwise they are left alone for application in constitutionally permissible situations. This is the opposite of the Canadian facial challenge approach where provisions are ignored entirely if their application in a reasonably foreseeable hypothetical situation could violate constitutionally-protected rights.[154] This results in many more

---

[151] For a review of cases in which U.S. courts have made orders allowing unconstitutional statutes to continue in operation temporarily, see the following: C.S. Kovacic, "Remedying Underinclusive Statutes" (1986) 33 *Wayne L. Rev.* 39 at p. 89, fn. 382; R.M. Levin, "'Vacation' at Sea: Judicial Remedies and Equitable Discretion in Administrative Law'" (2003) 53 *Duke L. J.* 291 at pp. 327-329; B.J. Gorod, "The Collateral Consequences of Ex Post Judicial Review" (2013) 88 *Wash. L. Rev.* 903 at pp. 948-951; S. Mariella, "Levelling Up Plenary Power: Remedying an Impermissible Gender Classification in the Immigration and Nationality Act" (2016) 96 *Bost. Univ. L. Rev.* 219 at pp. 253-256

[152] G.W. Adams, "Remedial and Procedural Issues Arising from the Charter of Rights and Freedoms" (1988) 13 *Queen's L.J.* 301 at p. 305

[153] *United States v. Salerno*, 481 U.S. 739 (1987)

[154] *R. v. Smith*, [1987] 1 S.C.R. 1045; *R. v. Nur*, [2015] 1 SCR 773; and see Part 1 of this essay, "Some Misconceptions About Constitutional Invalidation" at p. 47, footnote 120.

situations arising in Canada where the disruptive effects of constitutional invalidation need to be addressed.

U.S. courts have also been able to handle the disruptive effects of invalidation through the use of existing saving doctrines. Such doctrines could, as necessary, be further developed by Canadian courts to deal, in a *lawful* manner, with the consequences of findings of constitutional invalidity.

As well, the availability of the suspended declaration device, and its first cousin, prospective overruling, has probably emboldened Canadian courts to more readily find laws to be constitutionally invalid. As noted earlier,[155] by sidestepping the normal consequences of constitutional invalidation, Canadian courts have allowed themselves the opportunity to play a more activist role than they might otherwise have played.

However, most germane to the Canadian experience is that there already exists a unique tool which could *lawfully* be used to address the vast majority of situations where suspended declarations might be considered appropriate. Section 33 of the *Constitution Act, 1982,* gives legislators the power to stipulate that a law will, for up to five years, operate notwithstanding inconsistency with most *Charter* rights.[156] Professor Burningham

---

[155] See *supra* footnote 47 at p. 170

[156] Section 33 reads as follows:

> 33(1) Parliament or the legislature of a province may expressly declare in an Act of Parliament or of the legislature, as the case may be, that the Act or a provision thereof shall operate notwithstanding a provision included in section 2 or sections 7 to 15 of this Charter.
>
> (2) An Act or a provision of an Act in respect of which a declaration made under this section is in effect shall have such operation as it would have but for the provision of this Charter referred to in the declaration.
>
> (3) A declaration made under subsection (1) shall cease to have effect five years after it comes into force or on such earlier date as may be specified in the declaration.
>
> (4) Parliament or the legislature of a province may re-enact a declaration made under subsection (1).

has argued that it may be appropriate to require legislators to do the work of conferring temporary validity on laws that have been adjudged invalid:

> Override legislation could be enacted rapidly following an immediate declaration of invalidity and would allow the unconstitutional law to operate while the government develops new legislation. Requiring the government to use s. 33 would have the added benefit of making the reality of the situation explicit: both s. 33 and suspended invalidity declarations sanction and permit continuing rights violations. Though the suspension is the judicial equivalent of s. 33, it is not thought of in this manner, leading to its unrestrained and unprincipled use. Requiring a government to resuscitate the unconstitutional law through s. 33 would clearly demonstrate the competing social, political and rights interests at play, rather than obscuring the ongoing rights breach through the use of the suspension.[157]

There is much to be said for this approach. Most importantly, it would be legal, unlike current judicial suspensions. It would also place responsibility for fixing the problem where it belongs – with the legislators who enacted the unconstitutional law.[158]

There is little reason to believe that legislators could not enact the necessary temporary override provisions in a timely manner. Judicial declarations of invalidity do not often arise suddenly and

---

(5) Subsection (3) applies in respect of a re-enactment made under subsection (4).

[157] S. Burningham, "A Comment on the Court's Decision to Suspend the Declaration of Invalidity in *Carter v. Canada*" (2015) 78 *Sask. L. Rev.* 201 at pp. 204-205

[158] Interestingly, when the federal government sought an extension of the original 12 month suspension in *Carter* (the assisted death case), Justice Brown specifically queried government counsel as to why Parliament itself, which was then in session, could not use s. 33 to provide itself with an extension. This apparently shocked some observers at the hearing. R. Knopff, R. Evans, D. Baker and D. Snow, "Dialogue: Clarified and Reconsidered" (2017) 54 *Osgoode Hall L.J.* 609 at p. 625

without warning. Protective legislation could be enacted whenever it is thought that a law might be vulnerable to attack, perhaps even in advance of the court's decision, with power being delegated to the executive to proclaim it in force if it should become necessary. It may also be useful to consider the provisions of the U.K. *Human Rights Act* which enable a Minister to put in place temporary corrective legislation for up to 120 days pending Parliamentary action.[159] This sort of delegation of s. 33 powers might well be held to not pass constitutional muster in Canadian courts.[160] However, the irony of such a scenario would be rich. The courts, having asserted for themselves an essentially legislative power to impose unconstitutional laws without any

---

[159] Section 10 of the UK *Human Rights Act 1998* allows a Minister, in situations of urgency, to put temporary corrective legislation in place where incompatibility with the European Human Rights Convention is found by a court. Such temporary legislation can be effective for up to 120 days, which affords Parliament the opportunity to decide on whether more permanent legislative changes should be enacted.

[160] Professor Weinrib has expressed the view that the power to enact a s. 33 override could not be delegated to the executive, and she is probably correct. (L. Weinrib, "Learning to Live with the Override" (1990) 35 *McGill L.J.* 541 at p. 561. However, the executive could be given power to proclaim into force an override provision enacted by the legislature. In theory, Parliament and the provincial Legislatures could lawfully take care of the problem by passing an omnibus statute which would insert a five-year s. 33 override into every section of every enactment under its jurisdiction, and give the executive power to proclaim such override into force with respect to any given provision when and as may be required in consequence of actual or anticipated judicial decisions. At least every five years such omnibus s. 33 override statute would have to be re-enacted. Thus, governments would no longer need to ask courts to unlawfully purport to suspend the operation of the Constitution. This would cover almost all situations where suspended declarations are granted, but not violations of those rights which s. 33 cannot be used to override. As well, given the Supreme Court's decision in *Ford v. Quebec (Attorney General)*, [1988] 2 S.C.R. 712 at para. 36, that s. 33 cannot be used retroactively, the ability of legislators to retroactively white-wash rights violations would be circumscribed. Of course, as noted at pp. 190-191 above, courts authorize this sort of retroactive white-washing through their use of suspended declarations. Accordingly, it would not be a departure for courts to allow the continuation of this situation through legislative use of s. 33, although this would presumably require reversal of *Ford* (which was probably wrongly decided in any event).

authority under the Constitution or the common law, would be objecting to the executive doing essentially the same thing under colour, at least, of s. 33 authority.

The political reality, of course, is that use of s. 33 override powers is considered dangerous territory given the public popularity of the *Charter*.[161] Indeed, it may be that the politicians would prefer that courts continue to do the dirty work of overriding constitutional rights. As well, there might be concern among *Charter* enthusiasts that once legislators get a taste for the use of s. 33, the current political taboo against its use might begin to dissipate. However, where the alternative is to continue allowing courts to *unlawfully* override the Constitution, it is hard to accept that, for political reasons, legislators should be excused from having to decide on the use of a *lawful* power that the Constitution has given to them.

9. Conclusion: Howling at the Moon?

It is fair to ask if the fundamental point of this essay – that suspended declarations of invalidity illegally purport to authorize unlawful conduct – is belied by the fact that the Supreme Court of Canada believes that it can make these orders and has been doing so for more than twenty-five years. To paraphrase Richard Nixon: "When the Supreme Court of Canada does it, that means that it is not illegal." There are a number of responses to this.

The Supreme Court of Canada is not infallible, and has never made a claim to infallibility.[162] It can render opinions as to what the Constitution means, but its opinions, as subordinate law, are

---

[161] Chief Justice McLachlin commented as follows on the political realties: "Section 33 has not often been used. Perhaps legislators are reluctant to be seen by the voters as suspending constitutional rights, given the general popularity of the *Charter*." B.M. McLachlin, "Charter Myths" (1999) 33 *U.B.C. Law Rev.* 23 at p. 29

[162] As Justice Jackson of the U.S. Supreme Court once famously observed: "[R]eversal by a higher court is not proof that justice is thereby better done ... We are not final because we are infallible, but we are infallible only because we are final." *Brown v. Allen*, 344 U.S. 443 (1953) at p. 540

of no force and effect to the extent that they are inconsistent with the Constitution.[163] Even the venerable doctrine of *stare decisis* cannot give incorrect interpretations of the Constitution supremacy over the Constitution itself.[164] As it was put by Australia's highest court:

> To refuse to decide in a constitutional case what one is convinced is right because there is a [contrary] recent decision of the Court is, to my mind, to deny the claims of the Constitution itself and to substitute for it a decision of the Court.[165]

It is open to any citizen, and indeed any judge, to question the correctness of Supreme Court decisions about the Constitution, and it is not sufficient to dismiss such questions with *ipse dixit,* circular, or self-serving reasons.[166]

Justice Felix Frankfurter recognized the importance of the public's right to criticize the judiciary:

---

[163] Prior to his appointment to the Ontario Court of Appeal, Grant Huscroft wrote: "The executive and the legislature are duty bound to act in accordance with the constitution, and the constitution is not simply whatever the Court says it is." G. Huscroft, "Constitutionalism from the Top Down" (2007) 45 *Osgoode Hall L. J.* 91 at p. 101

[164] *Canada (Attorney General) v. Bedford*, [2013] 3 S.C.R. 1101 at para's 43-44; Justice Felix Frankfurter recognized that "the ultimate touchstone of constitutionality is the Constitution itself and not what we [judges] have said about it." *Graves v. New York*, 306 U.S. 466 (1939) at pp. 491-92; G. Lawson, "The Constitutional Case Against Precedent" (1994) 17 *Harvard J.L. & Pub. Pol'y* 23; G. Lawson, "Mostly Unconstitutional: The Case Against Precedent Revisited" (2007) 5 *Ava Maria L. Rev.* 1; "[C]onstitutional law and the Constitution are not the same." E. Meese III, "The Law of the Constitution" (1987) 61 *Tulane L. Rev.* 979 at p. 983

[165] *Queensland v. The Commonwealth*, [1977] HCA 60 at para. 8

[166] "The famous parental reason for last resort, 'Because I say so', does not render the parental command reasonable to the child or to anyone else." M. Shapiro, "The Giving of Reasons Requirement" (1992) *U. Chi. Legal Forum* 179 at pp. 192-193. This has been described as "it is so because we say so" jurisprudence. See *Webster v. Reprod. Health Services*, 492 U.S. 490 (1989) at p. 552, *per* Scalia J.

> Judges as persons, or courts as institutions, are entitled to no greater immunity from criticism than other persons or institutions…[J]udges must be kept mindful of their limitations and of ultimate public responsibility by a vigorous stream of criticism expressed with candor however blunt.[167]

It was fifteen years ago that the Supreme Court's rulings with respect to suspended declarations were said to have resulted in "an embarrassing amount of confusion."[168] The situation is even worse today – much worse. The current state of Canadian law relating to the consequences and effects of findings of unconstitutionality is a quagmire of incoherence, ambiguity, and contradiction. Lower court judges have been assigned the unenviable task of trying to understand and apply the Supreme Court's embarrassingly muddled constitutional invalidation jurisprudence. Regardless of how the issues are ultimately resolved, it is important that a principle-based order and structure be established in this area of the law. A great deal of work needs to be done.

The legal academy especially needs to step up to the plate. It must challenge circular and self-serving reasoning. It must resist the allure of pragmatism over principle. It must assume a more robust role in the process of judicial oversight.

Supremacy of the Constitution and the rule of law are principles that are too important to leave solely in the hands of judges.[169] It is all fine and good for judges to declare themselves the guardians of the Constitution, but care must be taken to ensure that they do

---

[167] F. Frankfurter, "Foreword" (1962), 3 The Supreme Court Review, ii, quoted in E.J.M. McBride, "Judging and Equality: *Quis Custodies Ipsos Custodes*" (1986) 10 *Dalhousie L.J.* 1 at p. 6

[168] S. Choudhry and K. Roach, "Putting the Past Behind us? Prospective Judicial and Legislative Constitutional Remedies" (2003), 21 *S.C.L.R. (2d)* 205 at p. 209

[169] The Chief Justice of New Zealand has stated that "the constitution is too important to be the preserve of judges or indeed lawyers." S. Elias, "Judgery and the Rule of Law" (2015) 14 *Otago L. Rev.* 49 at p. 50.

not regard themselves as entitled to do anything more than express opinions as to what the Constitution means and to decide cases on the basis of those opinions. Even more than as guardians, judges should regard themselves as dutiful *servants* of the Constitution:

> Judges, if not lawyers more generally, must be imbued
> with the sense that their special task and obligation is
> fidelity to the law.[170]

As the court of final resort in Canada, the Supreme Court of Canada should be especially careful to remain within the limits of its judicial role.

And finally, regardless of what the Supreme Court of Canada decides with respect to cases on its own docket, its stature within international legal circles will be greatly diminished if it does not provide legally coherent justifications for its actions. Courts in other jurisdictions will for good reason resist calls to follow the lead of Canadian jurisprudence if it is shown to rest on foundations of sand. Canadian courts must do more than refer to *Manitoba Language Rights* and its troubled progeny as justification for their asserted power to breathe life into invalid law and to give force and effect to laws which the Constitution says are of no force or effect.

---

[170] B. Z. Tamanaha, *On the Rule of Law: History, Politics and Theory*, (Cambridge: Cambridge Univ. Press, 2004) at p. 59

BIBLIOGRAPHY

ARTICLES

G.W. Adams, "Remedial Procedural Issues Arising for the Charter of Rights and Freedoms" (1988) 13 *Queen's L. J.* 301

T. Adams, "The Standard Theory of Administrative Unlawfulness" (2017) 76 *Cambridge L. J.* 289

T.R.S. Allan, "The Rule of Law" in D. Dyzenhaus and M. Thorburn, ed's, *Philosophical Foundations of Constitutional Law*, (Oxford: Oxford Univ. Press, 2016) pp. 201-220

L. Arbour and F. Lafontaine, "Beyond Self-Congratulations: The Charter at 25 in an International Perspective" (2007) 45 *Osgoode Hall L. J.* 239

H. Arthurs, "Constitutional Courage" (2003) 49 *McGill L. J.* 1

J. Birch, "Staying Declaratory Relief" in K. Dharmananda and A. Papamatheos, ed's, *Perspectives on Declaratory Relief*, (Sydney: The Federation Press, 2009) pp. 163-178

B. Bird, "The Unbroken Supremacy of the Canadian Constitution" (2018) 55 *Alta. L. Rev.* 755

E.M. Borchard, "The Declaratory Judgment – A Needed Procedural Reform" (1918) 28 *Yale L. J.* 1

L.B. Boudin, "The Problem of *Stare Decisis* in Our Constitutional Theory" (1931) 8 *N.Y.U.L.Q. Rev.* 589

S. Burningham, "A Comment on the Court's Decision to Suspend the Declaration of Invalidity in *Carter v. Canada*" (2015) 78 *Sask. L. Rev.* 201

J. Cameron, "The Written Word and the Constitution's Vital Unstated Assumptions" in P. Thibault et al., ed's, *Essays in Honour of Gerald-A. Beaudoin: The Challenges of Constitutionalism*, (Cowansville, Que.: Yvon Blais/Societe Thomson, 2002) at p. 89

E. Campbell, "Relitigation in Government Cases: A Study of Estoppel Principles in Public Law Litigation" (1994) 20 *Monash Univ. L. Rev.* 21

S. Choudhry, "Ackerman's Higher Lawmaking in Comparative Constitutional Perspective: Constitutional Moments as Constitutional Failures?" (2008) 6 *Int'l J. Const. L.* 193

S. Choudhry and K. Roach, "Putting the Past Behind Us? Prospective Judicial and Legislative Constitutional Remedies" (2003) *21 S.C.L.R. (2d)* 205

P.-A. Cote, "La Preseance de la Charte Canadienne des Droits et Libertes" (1984) 18 *R.J.T. n.s.* 105

T.A. Cromwell, "Aspects of Judicial Review in Canada" (1995) 46 *So. C. L. Rev.* 1027

H. Cyr and M. Popescu, "The Supreme Court of Canada" in A. Jakab, A. Dyevre and G. Itzcovich, ed's, *Comparative Constitutional Reasoning*, (Cambridge: Cambridge Univ. Press, 2017) pp.154-198

M. Dawson, "From the Backroom to the Front Line: Making Constitutional History or Encounters with the Constitution: Patriation, Meech Lake and Charlottetown" (2012) 57 *McGill L. J.* 955

H.D.B. de Pinho. "Judicial Rulings With Prospective Effect in Brazilian Law" in E. Steiner, ed., *Comparing the Prospective Effect of Judicial Rulings Across Jurisdictions*, (Switzerland: Springer, 2015) at p. 285

S.A. de Smith, "Constitutional Lawyers in Revolutionary Situations" (1968) 7 *W. Ontario L. Rev.* 93

P. Devlin, "Judges and Lawmakers" (1976) 39 *Mod. L. Rev.* 1

R. Dixon and S. Issacharoff, "Living to Fight Another Day: Judicial Deferral in Defence of Democracy" (2016) *Wis. L. Rev.* 683

A.J. Duggan and K. Roach, "A Further Note on *Final Note*: The Scope and Limits of Judicial Law Making" (2002) 36 *Can. Bus. L. J.* 115

A. Dyevre and A. Jakab, "Foreward: Understanding Constitutional Reasoning" (2013) 14 *German L. J.* 983

D. Dyzenhaus, "Humpty Dumpty Rules or the Rule of Law: Legal Theory and the Adjudication of National Security" (2003) 1 *Austl. J. Leg. Phil.* 1

D. Dyzenhaus, "*Schmitt v. Dicey*: Are States of Emergency Inside or Outside the Legal Order?" (2006) 27 *Cardoza L. Rev.* 2005

S. Elias, "Judgery and the Rule of Law" (2015) 14 *Otago L. Rev.* 49

M. Elliott, "The Legal Status of Unlawful Legislation" [2013] Public Law for Everyone, online

R. Elliot, "References, Structural Argumentation and the Organizing Principles of Canada's Constitution" (2001) 80 *Can. B. Rev.* 67

T.A.O. Endicott, "The Impossibility of the Rule of Law" (1999) 19 *Oxford J. of Legal Stud.* 1

R.H. Fallon, "The Rule of Law as a Concept in Constitutional Discourse"(1997) 97 *Columbia L. Rev.* 1

D.A. Farber, "Legal Pragmatism and the Constitution" (1988) 72 *Minn. L. Rev.* 1331

M. Faure, M. Goodwin and F. Weber, "The Regulator's Dilemma: Caught Between the Need for Flexibility and the Demands of Foreseeability: Reassessing the Lex Certa Principle" (2014) 24 *Albany L. J. Of Sci. & Tech.* 283

S. Fine, Supreme Court of Canada to Keep Records of Deliberations Secret for at Least 50 Years" *The Globe and Mail*, Toronto, May 14, 2018

S. Fine, "Retired Top Court Judges Object to 50-year Embargo" *The Globe and Mail*, Toronto, May 15, 2018

E. Fish, "Choosing Constitutional Remedies" (2016) 63 *U.C.L.A. Law Rev.* 322

O.M. Fiss. "Dombrowski" (1977) 88 *Yale L. J.* 1103

C. Forsyth, "Metaphysic of Nullity: Invalidity, Conceptual Reasoning and the Rule of Law" in C. Forsyth and I. Hare, ed's, *The Golden Metwand and the Crooked Cord: Essays in Honour of Sir William Wade QC*, (Oxford: Clarendon Press, 1998) pp. 141-160

C. Forsyth, "The Legal Effect of Unlawful Administrative Acts: The Theory of the Second Actor Explained and Developed" (2001) 35 *Amicus Curiae* 20

C. Forsyth, The Rock and the Sand: Jurisdiction and Remedial Discretion" Paper No. 31/2013 of the University of Cambridge Faculty of Law Research Paper Series, retrievable at www.law.cam.ac.uk/ssrn

C. Forsyth, "'Blasphemy Against Basics: Doctrine, Conceptual Reasoning and Certain Decisions of the UK Supreme Court" in J. Bell. M. Elliott, J. Varuhas and P. Murray, ed's, *Public Law Adjudication in Common Law Systems*, (Oxford and Portland, Oregon: Hart Publishing, 2016) pp. 145-163

F. Frankfurter, "Foreword" (1962) 3 *Supreme Court Law Review* (ii)

J. Fremont, "The Dickson Court, the Courts, and the Constitutional Balance of Powers in the Canadian System of Government" (1991) 20 *Man. L. J.* 451

A. Gautron, "French/English Discrepancies in the Canadian Charter of Rights & Freedoms" (1982) 12 *Man. L.J.* 220

J. Gerards, "The European Court of Human Rights" in A. Jakab, A. Dyevre and G. Itzcovich, ed's, *Comparative Constitutional Reasoning*, (Cambridge: Cambridge Univ. Press, 2017) 237-276

D. Gibson, "The Real Laws of the Constitution" (1990) 28 *Alta. L. Rev.* 358

D. Gibson, "Founding Fathers-in-Law: Judicial Amendment of the Canadian Constitution" (1992) 55 *Law & Contemp. Probs.* 261

M. Gleeson, "Individualized Justice—The Holy Grail" (1995) 69 *ALJ* 421

J. Goldsworthy. "The Preamble, Judicial Independence and Judicial Integrity" (2000) 11 *Const. Forum* 60

B.J. Gorod, "The Collateral Consequences of Ex Post Judicial Review" (2013) 88 Wash. L. Rev. 903

J.A.C. Grant, "The Legal Effect of a Ruling that a Statute is Unconstitutional" (1978) *Det. Coll. of Law Rev.* 201

J. M. Greabe, "Remedial Discretion in Constitutional Adjudication" (2014) 62 *Buff. L. Rev.* 881

O. Gross, "The Normless and Exceptionless Exception: Carl Schmitt's Theory of Emergency Powers and the 'Norm-Exception' Dichotomy" (2000) 21 *Cardoza L. Rev.* 1825

O. Gross, "Chaos and Rules: Should Responses to Violent Crises Always be Constitutional?" (2003) 112 *Yale L. J.* 1011

D. Guttman, "*Hislop v. Canada* – A Retroactive Look" (2008) 42 *S.C.L.R. (2d)* 547

R. Haigh and M. Sobkin, "Does the Observer Have an Effect? An Analysis of the Use of the Dialogue Metaphor in Canada's Courts" (2007) 45 *Osgoode Hall L. J.* 67

G.R. Hall. "Panel: Discussion of the Supreme Court's *Final Note* Decision" (2002) 36 *Can. Bus. L. J.* 89

J. Harrison, "Power, Duty and Facial Invalidity" (2013) 16 *Univ. Pa. J. Const. L.* 501

J. Harrison, "Severability, Remedies, and Constitutional Adjudication" (2014) 83 *Geo. Wash. L. Rev.* 56

J. Harrison, "The Relations Between the Courts and the Law" (2016) 35 *Univ. of Queensland L. J.* 99

A. Heard, "Constitutional Conventions and Written Constitutions: The Rule of Law Implications in Canada" (2015) 38 *Dublin Univ. L. J.* 331

D. Hellman, "The Importance of Appearing Principled" (1995) 37 *Ariz. L. Rev.* 1107

P.W. Hogg, "Necessity in a Constitutional Crisis" (1989) 15 *Monash Univ. L. Rev.* 253

P.W. Hogg, "Judicial Amendment of Statutes to Conform to the Charter of Rights" (1994) 28 *R.J.T. n.s.* 533

P.W. Hogg, The Law-Making Role of the Supreme Court of Canada: Rapporteur's Synthesis" (2001) 80 *Can. B. Rev.* 171

P.W. Hogg, "Canada: From Privy Council to Supreme Court" in J. Goldsworthy, ed., *Interpreting Constitutions: A Comparative Study,* (Oxford: Oxford Univ. Press, 2006) pp. 55-105

P.W. Hogg and A.A. Bushell, "The *Charter* Dialogue Between Courts and Legislatures (Or Perhaps *The Charter of Rights* Isn't Such A Bad Thing After All)" (1997) 35 *Osgoode Hall L. J.* 75

P.W. Hogg, A.A. Bushell Thornton and W.K. Wright, "Charter Dialogue Revisited – Or 'Much Ado About Metaphors'" (2007) 45 *Osgoode Hall L.J.* 1

P.W. Hogg and C.F. Zwibel, "The Rule of Law in the Supreme Court of Canada" (2005) 55 *Univ. of Toronto L.J.* 715

G.R. Hoole, "Proportionality as a Remedial Principle: A Framework for Suspended Declarations of Invalidity in Canadian Constitutional Law" (2011) 49 *Alta. L. Rev.* 107

W.H. Hurlburt, "Fairy Tales and Living Trees: Observations on Some Recent Constitutional Decisions of the Supreme Court of Canada" (1998) 26 *Man. L. J.* 181

G. Huscroft, "Constitutionalism for the Top Down" (2007) 45 *Osgoode Hall L. J.* 91

G. Huscroft, "Rationalizing Judicial Power: The Mischief of Dialogue Theory" in J.B. Kelly and C.P. Manfredi, ed's, *Contested Constitutionalism: Reflections on the Canadian Charter of Rights and Freedoms*, (Vancouver: UBC Press, 2009) pp. 50-65

V. Iyer, "Courts and Constitutional Usurpers: Some Lessons from Fiji" (2005) 28 *Dalhousie L. J.* 27

B. Juratowitch, "Questioning Prospective Overruling" (2007) *N.Z.L. Rev.* 393

B. Juratowitch, "The Temporal Effects of Judgments in the United Kingdom", in P. Popelier, S. Verstraelen, D. Vanheule and B. Vanlerberghe, ed's, *The Effects of Judicial Decisions in Time*, (Cambridge: Intersential Publishing, 2014) pp. 159-179

R.S. Kay, "Retroactivity and Prospectivity of Judgments in American Law" (2014) 62 *Am. J. of Comp. Law Supp.* 37

R.W. Kerr, "The Remedial Power of the Courts after the Manitoba Language Rights Case" (1986) 6 *Windsor Yearbook of Access to Justice* 252

R. Knopff, R. Evans, D. Baker and D. Snow, "Dialogue: Clarified and Reconsidered" (2017) 54 *Osgoode Hall L. J.* 609

T. Koopmans, "Retroactivity Reconsidered" (1980) 39 *Cambridge L.J.* 287

C.S. Kovacic, "Remedying Underinclusive Statutes" (1986) 33 *Wayne L. Rev.* 39

G.V. La Forest, "The Canadian Charter of Rights and Freedoms: An Overview" (1983) 61 *Can. B. Rev.* 19

A. Lamer, "The Rule of Law and Judicial Independence: Protecting Core Values in Times of Change" (1996) 45 *U.N.B.L.J.* 3

K. Lane Scheppele, "Law in a Time of Emergency: States of Exception and the Temptations of 9/11" (2004) 6 *U. Pa. J. Const. L.* 1001

R. Lardner, "The Young Immigrunts", (1920), in *The Ring Lardner Reader* (Maxwell Geismar, ed., 1963) 411

H. Lau, "Comparative Perspectives on Strategic Remedial Delays" (2016) 91 *Tulane L. Rev.* 259

G. Lawson, "The Constitutional Case Against Precedent" (1994) 17 *Harvard J. L. & Pub. Policy* 23

G. Lawson, "Mostly Unconstitutional: The Case Against Precedent Revisited" (2007) 5 *Ava Maria L. Rev.* 1

B.C. Lea, "Situational Severability" (2017) 103 *Va. L. Rev.* 735

P. LeBreux "*Eurig Estate*: Another Day, Another Tax" (1999) 47 *Can. Tax J.* 1126

R. Leckey, "The Harms of Remedial Discretion" (2016) 14 *Int'l J. Const. L.* 584

R. Leckey, "Remedial Practice Beyond Constitutional Text" (2016) 64 *Am. J. of Comp. L.* 1

R. Leckey, "Realizing Rights Here and Now" (available online, forthcoming in the *Australian J. of Human Rights*)

J. Leclair, "Canada's Unfathomable Unwritten Constitutional Principles" (2002) *27 Queen's L. J.* 389

G. LeDain, "Jean Beetz as Judge and Colleague" (1994) 28 *R.J.T. n.s.* 721

S. Letourneau, "L' Autorite d'Un Jugement Pronancant l'Inconstitutionnalite d'Une Loi" (1989) 23 *R.J.T. n.s.* 173

R.M. Levin, "'Vacation' at Sea: Judicial Remedies and Equitable Discretion in Administrative Law" (2003) 53 *Duke L. J.* 291

C.L. L'Heureux-Dube, "Bijuralism: A Supreme Court of Canada Justice's Perspective" (2002) 62 *La. L. Rev.* 449

H.A. Linde, "'Clear and Present Danger' Reexamined: Dissonance in the *Brandenburg* Concerto" (1970) 22 *Stan. L. Rev.* 1163

N.O. Littlefield, "Stare Decisis, Prospective Overruling and Judicial Legislation in the Context of Sovereign Immunity" (1964) 9 *St. Louis Univ. L. J.* 56

J. Lovell, "From Now On: Temporal Issues in Constitutional Adjudication" (2005) 18 *Nat'l J. Const. L.* 17

P.Y. Lo, "Levitating Unconstitutional Law" (2006) 36 *Hong Kong L. J.* 433

P.Y. Lo, "Impact of Jurisprudence Beyond Hong Kong" in S.N.M. Young and Y. Ghai, ed's, *Hong Kong's Court of Final Appeal*, (Cambridge: Cambridge Univ. Press, 2014) pp. 579-607

K. Low Fatt Kin, K. Loi Chit Fai and S. Wee Ai Yin, "Towards a Maintenance of Equality (Part I): A Study of the Constitutionality of Maintenance Provisions that Sexually Discriminate" (1998) 19 *Sing. L. Rev.* 45

G.H.A. Mackintosh, "Heading off Bilodeau: Attempting Constitutional Amendment" (1985) 15 *Man. L. J.* 271

J.P.H. MacKay, "Can Judges Change the Law?" (1987) 73 *Proceedings of the British Academy* 285

M.-F. Major, "Reporting to the Human Rights Committee: The Canadian Experience" (2000) 38 *Can. Y. B. Int'l L.* 261

S. Mariella, "Leveling Up Plenary Power: Remedying an Impermissible Gender Classification in the Immigration and Nationality Act" (2016) 96 *Bost. Univ. L. Rev.* 219

R. Martin, "Notes on Emergency Powers in Canada" (2005) 54 *U.N.B.L.J.* 161

A. Mason, "The Common Law" in S.N.M. Young and Y. Ghai, ed., *Hong Kong's Court of Final Appeal*, (Cambridge: Cambridge Univ. Press, 2014) pp. 327-351

E.J.M. McBride, "Judging and Equality: *Quis Custodies Ipsos Custodes*" (1986) 10 *Dalhousie L. J.* 1

F.G. McKean, "Border Lines of Judicial Power" (1943) 48 *Dick. L. Rev.* 1

B.M. McLachlin, "The Charter: A New Role for the Judiciary" (1991) 29 *Alta. L. Rev.* 540

B.M. McLachlin, "Charter Myths" (1999) 33 *U.B.C. Law Rev.* 23

B.M. McLachlin, "Bill of Rights in Common Law Countries" (2002) 51 *Int'l & Comp. Law Q.* 197

E. Meese III, "The Law of the Constitution" (1987) 61 *Tulane L. Rev.* 979

P.J. Mishkin, "The High Court, the Great Writ and the Due Process of Time and Law" (1965) 79 *Harvard L. Rev.* 56

C. Morey,"A Matter of Integrity: Rule of Law, the *Remuneration Reference*, and Access to Justice" (2016) 49 *U.B.C. Law Rev.* 275

C.R. Mouland, "Remedying the Remedy: Bedford's Suspended Declaration of Invalidity" (2018, *Man. L.J.*, forthcoming)

S. Mueller, "Turning Emergency Powers Inside Out: Are Extraordinary Powers Creeping into Ordinary Legislation?" (2016) 18 *Flinders L. J.* 295

T. Nardin, "Emergency Logic: Prudence, Morality and the Rule of Law" in V.V. Ramraj, ed., *Emergencies and the Limits of Legality*, (Cambridge: Cambridge Univ. Press, 2008) 97-117

Note, "What is the Effect of a Court's Declaring a Legislative Act Unconstitutional?" (1926) 39 *Harvard L. Rev.* 373

A. O'Neill, "Invalidity and Retrospectivity under the Irish and Canadian Constitutions" (2006) 15 *Const. Forum* 147

J.W. Penny and R.J. Danay, "The Embarrassing Preamble? Understanding the 'Supremacy of God' and the *Charter*" (2006) 39 *U.B.C.L. Rev.* 287

P. Perell, "Changing the Common Law Why The Supreme Court of Canada's Incremental Change Test Does Not Work" (2003) 26 *Advoc. Q.* 345

V.V. Ramraj, "Emergency Powers and Constitutional Theory" (2011) 41 *Hong Kong L. J.* 165

G.J. Reynolds, "Reconsidering Copyright's Constitutionality" (2016) 53 *Osgoode Hall L. J.* 898

J.D. Richard, "Separation of Powers: The Canadian Experience" (2009) 47 *Duq. L. Rev.* 731

K. Roach, "Remedial Consensus and Dialogue Under the *Charter*: General Declarations and Delayed Declarations of Invalidity" (2002) 35 *U.B.C. Law Rev.* 211

K. Roach, "Dialogic Judicial Review and its Critics" (2004) 23 *S.C.L.R. (2d)* 49

K. Roach, "Principled Remedial Discretion Under the Charter" (2004) 25 *S.C.L.R. (2d)* 101

K. Roach, "Enforcement of the Charter – Subsections 24(1) and 52(1)" (2013) 62 *S.C.L.R. (2d)* 473

K. Roach, "Remedies for Laws that Violate Human Rights" in J. Bell, M. Elliott, J. Varuhas and P. Murray, ed's, *Public Law Adjudication in Common Law Systems*, (Oxford and Portland, Oregon: Hart Publishing, 2016) pp. 269-299

K. Roach, "The Judicial, Legislative and Executive Roles in Enforcing the Constitution: Three Manitoba Stories" in R. Albert and D.R. Cameron, ed's, *Canada in the World: Comparative Perspectives on the Canadian Constitution* (Cambridge: Cambridge Univ. Press, 2018) pp. 264-302

K. Roach and G. Bunlender, "Mandatory Relief and Supervisory Jurisdiction: When is it Appropriate, Just and Equitable" (2005) 122 *S. African L.J.* 325

K. Roosevelt III, "A Retroactivity Retrospective, With Thoughts for the Future: What the Supreme Court Learned from Paul Mishkin, and What it Might" (2007) 95 *Calif. L. Rev.* 1677

T. Ross, "Metaphors and Paradox" (1989) 23 *Ga. L. Rev.* 1053

W. Rupp-v. Brunneck, "Admonitory Functions of Constitutional Courts – Germany" (1972) 20 *Am. J. of Comp. L.* 387

B. Ryder, "Suspending the Charter" (2003) *21 S.C.L.R. (2d)* 267

M. St. Hilaire, "The Codification of Human Rights in Canada" (2012) 42 *R.D.U.S.* 506

G. Scaccia, "Constitutional Values and Judge-Made Law" (2017) 3 *Italian L. J.* 177

B.S. Shannon, "The Retroactive and Prospective Application of Judicial Decisions" (2003) 26 Harv. J. L. & Pub. Policy 811

M. Shapiro, "The Giving of Reasons Requirement" (1992) *Univ. of Chicago Leg. Forum* 179

M. Shapiro, "Judges As Liars" (1994) 17 *Harvard J. L. & Pub. Policy* 155

R. Slovenko, "Euphemisms" (2005) 33 *J. Psychiatry & Law* 533

M.R. Smith, "Levels of Metaphor in Persuasive Legal Writing" (2007) 58 *Mercer L. Rev.* 919

M.M. Stavsky, "The Doctrine of State Necessity in Pakistan" (1983) 16 *Cornell Int'l L. J.* 341

E. Steiner, "Judicial Rulings with Prospective Effect – From Comparison to Systemization" in E. Steiner, ed., *Comparing the Prospective Effect of Judicial Rulings Across Jurisdictions*, (Switzerland: Springer, 2015) pp. 1-23

M. Stelzer, "*Pro Futuro* and Retroactive Effects of Rescissory Judgments in Austria" in P. Popelier, S.A. Verstralen, D. Vanheule and B. Vanlerberghe, ed's, *The Effects of Judicial Decisions in Time*, (Cambridge: Intersential Publishing, 2014) pp. 63-75

B.Z. Tamanaha, "The History and Elements of the Rule of Law" (2012) *Sing. J. Leg. Stud.* 232

F. Tanguay-Renaud, "The Intelligibility of Extra-Legal State Action: A General Lesson for Debates on Public Emergencies and Legality" (2010) 16 *Legal Theory* 161

T.A. Thomas, Ubi Jus, Ibi Remedium: The Fundamental Right to a Remedy Under Due Process" (2004) 41 *San Diego L. Rev.* 1633

L.B. Tremblay, The Legitimacy of Judicial Review: The Limits of Dialogue Between Courts and Legislatures" (2005) 3 *Int'l J. Const. L.* 617

R.L. Tsai, "Fire, Metaphor, and Constitutional Myth-Making" (2004) *93 Geo. L. J.* 181

M. Tushnet, "Shut Up He Explained" (2001) 95 *Nw. Univ. L. Rev.* 907

M. Tushnet, "Defending Korematsu: Reflections on Civil Liberties in Wartime" (2003) *Wis. L. Rev.* 273

R. Von Moschzisker, "Stare Decisis in Courts of Last Resort" (1924) 37 *Harvard L. Rev.* 409

K.C. Walsh, "Partial Unconstitutionality" (2010) 85 *N.Y.U.L. Rev.* 738

L.E. Weinrib, "Learning to Live with the Override" (1990) 35 *McGill L. J.* 541

W. Zeidler, "The Federal Constitutional Court of the Federal Republic of Germany: Decisions on the Constitutionality of Legal Norms" (1986) 62 *Notre Dame L. Rev.* 504

CONFERENCE PAPERS

H. Cyr, "Quelques reflexions sur la normalisation de l'exceptionel" Paper delivered at Conference at University of Montreal Faculty of Law on October 15, 2015

B.M. McLachlin, "Rights and Remedies – Remarks" Conference of the Canadian Institute for the Administration of Justice, Ottawa, October 2, 2009

J.C. Tait, "Charter Remedies and Democracy" Canadian Institute for the Administration of Justice Conference Papers, *Human Rights in the 21st Century: Prospects, Institutions and Processes*, Halifax, October 16-19, 1996, at p. 288

BOOKS

J. Agresto, *The Supreme Court and Constitutional Democracy*, (Ithaca: Cornell Univ. Press, 1984)

R. Albert and D.R. Cameron, ed's, *Canada in the World: Comparative Perspectives on the Canadian Constitution*, (Cambridge: Cambridge Univ. Press, 2018)

M.C. Beardsley, *Thinking Straight*, 2nd ed. (Englewood Cliffs, N.J.: 1950)

J. Bell, M. Elliott, J. Varuhas and P. Murray, *Public Law Adjudication in Common Law Systems*, (Oxford and Portland, Oregon: Hart Publishing, 2016)

A.M. Bickel, *The Least Dangerous Branch: The Supreme Court at the Bar of Politics*, (New Haven: Yale Univ. Press, 1962)

W. Blackstone, *Commentaries*, 14th ed. (London: A. Strahan, 1803)

H. Bosmajian, *Metaphor and Reason in Judicial Opinions*, (Carbondale and Edwardsville: So. Ill. Univ. Press, 1992)

A.R. Brewer-Carias, *Constitutional Courts as Positive Legislators: A Comparative Study*, (Cambridge: Cambridge Univ. Press, 2011)

G. Calabresi, *A Common Law for the Age of Statutes*, (Cambridge, Mass.: Harvard Univ. Press, 1982)

V.F. Comella, *Constitutional Courts & Democratic Values*, (New Haven and London: Yale Univ. Press, 2009)

M. de Visser, *Constitutional Review in Europe: A Comparative Analysis*, (Oxford and Portland, Oregon: Hart Publishing, 2015)

K. Dharmananda and A. Papamatheos, ed's, *Perspectives on Declaratory Relief*, (Sydney: The Federation Press, 2009)

D. Dyzenhaus, ed., *Law as Politics: Carl Schmitt's Critique of Liberalism*, (Durham and London: Duke Univ. Press, 1998)

D. Dyzenhaus, *The Constitution of Law: Legality in a Time of Emergency*, (Cambridge: Cambridge Univ. Press, 2006)

D. Dyzenhaus and M. Thorburn, ed's, *Philosophical Foundations of Constitutional Law*, (Oxford, Oxford Univ. Press, 2016)

C. Fatovic, *Outside the Law: Emergency and Executive Power*, (Baltimore: John Hopkins Univ. Press, 2009)

P.F. Ford, ed., *The Writings of Thomas Jefferson*, (New York: G.B. Putman's Sons, 1893)

C. Forsyth and I. Hare, ed's, *The Golden Metwand and the Crooked Cord: Essays in Honour of Sir William Wade QC*, (Oxford: Clarendon Press, 1998)

J. Goldsworthy, ed., *Interpreting Constitutions: A Comparative Study*, (Oxford: Oxford Univ. Press, 2006)

R. Hirschl, *Towards Juristocracy: The Origins and Consequences of the New Constitutionalism*, (Cambridge, Mass.: Harvard Univ. Press, 2004)

T. Hobbes, *Leviathan*, (1651), (Oxford: Oxford Univ. Press. 1996)

P.W. Hogg, *Constitutional Law of Canada*, looseleaf (Toronto: Thomson Reuters, 2007)

P.W. Hogg, P.J. Monahan and W.K Wright, *Liability of the Crown*, 4th ed., (Toronto: Carswell, 2011)

A. Jakab, A. Dyevre and G. Itzcovich, ed's, *Comparative Constitutional Reasoning*, (Cambridge: Cambridge Univ. Press, 2017)

B Juratowitch, *Retroactivity and the Common Law*, (Oxford and Portland, Oregon: Hart Publishing, 2008)

J.B. Kelly and C.P. Manfredi, ed's, *Contested Constitutionalism: Reflections of the Canadian Charter of Rights and Freedoms*, (Vancouver: UBC Press, 2009)

H. Kelsen, *General Theory of Law and State* , trans. by A. Wedberg (Cambridge, Mass.: Harvard Univ. Press, 1945)

I. Kramnick, ed., *A. Hamilton, Madison and J. Jay, The Federalist Papers*, (London: Penguin, 1987)

D. Lange, *The Doctrine of Res Judicata in Canada*, (Toronto: LexisNexis, 4th ed., 2015)

R. Leckey, *Bills of Rights in the Common Law*, (Cambridge: Cambridge Univ. Press, 2015)

J. Locke, *Two Treatises of Government*, P. Laslett, ed., (Cambridge: Cambridge Univ. Press, 1988)

C. H. Mendes, *Constitutional Courts and Deliberative Democracy*, (Oxford: Oxford Univ. Press, 2013)

A. Petter, *The Politics of the Charter: The Illusive Promise of Constitutional Rights*, (Toronto: Univ. of Toronto Press, 2010)

P. Popelier, S. Verstraelen, D. Vanheule and B. Vanlerberghe, ed's, *The Effects of Judicial Decisions in Time*, (Cambridge: Intersential Publishing, 2014)

R.A. Posner, *Not a Suicide Pact: The Constitution in Times of National Emergency*, (New York and Oxford: Oxford Univ. Press, 2006)

S.B. Presser, *Law Professors: Three Centuries of Shaping American Law*, (St. Paul: West Publishing, 2017)

V.V. Ramraj, ed., *Emergencies and the Limits of Legality*, (Cambridge: Cambridge Univ. Press, 2008)

J. Rawls, *A Theory of Justice*, (Cambridge, Mass.: Harvard Univ. Press, 1971)

J. Raz, *The Authority of Law*, 2nd ed. (Oxford: Oxford Univ. Press, 2009)

K. Roach, *Constitutional Remedies in Canada*, (Toronto: Thomson Reuter, 2d ed., 2016)

K. Roach, *The Supreme Court on Trial: Judicial Activism or Democratic Dialogue*, (Toronto: Irwin Law, rev'd ed., 2016)

C.L. Rossiter, Constitutional Dictatorship, (1948) (Princeton: Princeton Univ. Press, 1979)

L. Sarna, *The Law of Declaratory Judgments*, 3rd ed. (Toronto: Thompson Carswell, 2007)

A. Sathanapally, *Beyond Disagreement: Open Remedies in Human Rights Adjudication*, (Oxford: Oxford Univ. Press, 2012)

Carl Schmitt, *Political Theology, Four Chapters on the Concept of Sovereignty*, G. Schwab (trans.), (Chicago: Univ. of Chicago Press, 2005)

R.J. Sharpe and K. Roach, *Brian Dickson: A Judge's Journey*, (Toronto: Univ. of Toronto Press, 2003)

R.J. Sharpe and K. Roach, *The Charter of Rights and Freedoms*, (Toronto: Irwin Law, 2013)

E. Steiner, ed., *Comparing the Prospective Effect of Judicial Rulings Across Jurisdictions*, (Switzerland: Springer, 2015)

M. Stelzer, *The Constitution of the Republic of Austria: A Contextual Analysis*, (Oxford and Portland, Oregon: Hart Publishing, 2001)

A. Stone Sweet, *Governing with Judges: Constitutional Politics in Europe*, (Oxford: Oxford Univ. Press, 2000)

B.L. Strayer, *The Canadian Constitution and the Courts*, (Canada: Butterworth, 3rd ed., 1988)

B.L. Strayer, *Canada's Constitutional Revolution*, (Edmonton: Univ. of Alberta Press, 2013)

R. Sullivan, *Statutory Interpretation*, (Toronto: Irwin Law, 2d ed. 2007)

B.Z. Tamanaha, *On the Rule of Law: History, Politics and Theory*, (Cambridge: Cambridge Univ. Press, 2004)

P. Thibault et al., ed's, *Essays in Honour of Gerald-A. Beaudoin: The Challenges of Constitutionalism*, (Cowansville, Que.: Yvon Blais/Societe Thomson, 2002)

H.W.R. Wade, *Administrative Law*, 6th ed. (Oxford: 1988)

H.W.R. Wade and C. Forsyth, *Administrative Law*, 10th ed. (Oxford: 2009)

P.W. Young, *Declaratory Orders*, (Sydney: Butterworth-Heinemann, 2nd ed., 1984)

S.N.M. Young and Y. Ghai, *Hong Kong's Court of Final Appeal*, (Cambridge: Cambridge Univ. Press, 2014)

H.K. Woolf and J. Woolf, *Zamir and Woolf - The Declaratory Judgment*, (London: Sweet & Maxwell, 3d ed., 2002)

THESES

M. Liston, *Honest Counsel: Institutional Dialogue and the Canadian Rule of Law*, PhD Thesis, University of Toronto, 2007

P.Y. Lo, *Judicial Consideration of the Basic Law*, PhD Thesis, University of Hong Kong, 2011

INDEX

ABOUT THE AUTHOR

Arthur Peltomaa is a partner of Bennett Jones LLP, Toronto, where he advises on a broad range of public and private law issues. Called to the bar in 1981, he has served as a law clerk to the Chief Justice of Ontario, a teaching fellow at Osgoode Hall Law School, a lecturer at Brock University, and a consultant to the Law Reform Commission of Canada. He is recognized in Lexpert's Guide to the 100 Most Creative Lawyers in Canada.

95038714R00153

Made in the USA
San Bernardino, CA
14 November 2018